Vodou en Vogue

WHERE RELIGION LIVES

Kristy Nabhan-Warren, editor

Where Religion Lives publishes ethnographies of religious life. The series features the methods of religious studies along with anthropological approaches to lived religion. The religious studies perspective encompasses attention to historical contingency, theory, religious doctrine and texts, and religious practitioners' intimate, personal narratives. The series also highlights the critical realities of migration and transnationalism.

A complete list of books published in Where Religion Lives is available at https://uncpress.org/series/where-religion-lives.

Vodou en Vogue

Fashioning Black Divinities in Haiti and the United States

Eziaku Atuama Nwokocha

The University of North Carolina Press CHAPEL HILL

*This book was published with the assistance of the University of Miami
and the Anniversary Fund of the University of North Carolina Press.*

Set in Merope Basic by Westchester Publishing Services
Manufactured in the United States of America

Library of Congress Cataloging-in-Publication Data
Names: Nwokocha, Eziaku Atuama, author.
Title: Vodou en vogue : fashioning Black divinities in Haiti and the United States /
    Eziaku Atuama Nwokocha.
Other titles: Where religion lives.
Description: Chapel Hill : The University of North Carolina Press, [2023] |
    Series: Where religion lives | Includes bibliographical references and index.
Identifiers: LCCN 2022043912 | ISBN 9781469674001 (cloth ; alkaline paper) |
    ISBN 9781469674018 (paperback ; alkaline paper) | ISBN 9781469674025 (ebook)
Subjects: LCSH: Vodou—Rituals. | Mambos (Vodou)—Massachusetts—Boston. |
    Mambos (Vodou)—Haiti—Jacmel. | Clothing and dress—Religious aspects—Voudou. |
    Material culture—Religious aspects. | Aesthetics—Religious aspects. | Black people—
    Religious life. | LCGFT: Ethnographies.
Classification: LCC BL2490 .N96 2023 | DDC 299.6/75097294—dc23/eng20230111
LC record available at https://lccn.loc.gov/2022043912

Cover photo by author.

To Brianna Eaton, Bashir Hassan,
Laura Tinker, and Jasmine Omorogbe
My dear friends who hold me up with true love.
Where my head always rests.

Contents

Illustrations

Gede possessing both Manbo Maude and a Vodou practitioner (in white) while posing with members of Sosyete Nago—Manbo Gina, Manbo Carmel, Manbo Hugueline, and Manbo Cynthia—in Mattapan, November 2021

Manbo Vante'm Pa Fyem comforts a Vodou practitioner after being confronted by Ogou during a ceremony in Mattapan, March 2022

Simbi possessing Zetwal Ashade Bon Manbo while embracing Manbo Hugueline in Mattapan, March 2022

Gede, possessing Manbo Maude, interacts with participants through Zoom in Mattapan, November 2021

Manbo Cynthia places a cup of water on an altar during a Danbala ceremony in Mattapan, March 2022

Manbo Hugueline and Manbo Carmel fix Manbo Cynthia's head wrap in bedroom before a Danbala ceremony in Mattapan, March 2022

Manbo Maude looking over an assortment of trimmings at Sewfisticated in Cambridge, Massachusetts, March 2018

Houngan Jean Marc praying to Ezili Dantò to commence her ceremony in Jacmel, July 2015

Practitioners resting during a lull in a Gede ceremony in Mattapan, November 2021

Kouzen possessing both Manbo Maude and Houngan Babbas as they playfully negotiate the price of produce with practitioners and audience members in Mattapan, May 2022

Vodou practitioner adjusting Manbo Lunine's head wrap after an intense possession experience in Mattapan, November 2021

Gede possessing Manbo Vante'm Pa Fyem during a ceremony in Mattapan, November 2021

Gede, possessing Manbo Maude, thinks pensively while resting with one hand on his stick and the other on his chin in Mattapan, November 2004

Preface

I have grown weary of arguing for Haiti's wholeness. I have grown weary of arguing about Haiti in the face of the pervasive anti-Black insistence that the country is barren, broken, deficient of resources and culture, and unable to express the decidedly human impulse of stylish adornment. While presenting my work at universities and colleges over several years, I repeatedly faced a question that always caused me to furrow my brows and burn with frustration: What about Haiti's poverty? And then, the inevitable follow-up: Why, if Haiti is so poor, are the participants in the ceremonies I describe so lavish in their dress?

Underlying these inquiries is a larger concern about Black people's relationship to wealth that colors perceptions about Black communities. When Black people accumulate wealth and then choose to show that wealth via dress — a Black woman on the Southside of Chicago in a fur coat, Caribbean men wearing Gucci belts, Black teens sporting Jordans, or wealthy Nigerians leading opulent lifestyles in Lagos — they challenge the dominant White colonial social order on some level. The idea of conspicuous consumption, of lavish spenders who neglect their basic needs in the service of status, is frequently at the heart of anxieties about how Black people spend their money. These issues are complex, and I cannot claim to have explanations for all of them. Yet, when someone raises their hand at a university and asks me why Black practitioners of Vodou spend money to practice their faith when their country is so poor, I hear echoes of these anti-Black themes in their question.

This book is not about Haiti's poverty. If you are seeking a conversation about the country's economic condition or the relative poverty of Haitian people, you will be disappointed by the pages that follow. My aim instead is to challenge our ideas and assumptions about Black practitioners of Vodou. Vodou and wealth are falsely understood as opposites, as mutually exclusive. Haiti and Vodou are represented as poor without any investigation of the geopolitical White supremacist forces that create that poverty in the first place. To define Haiti through poverty is to negate the long-lasting and ongoing impacts of colonization and the continuing postcolonial stripping of wealth from its national coffers by France, the United States, Canada, and, increasingly, China, a country eager to extract resources from Haiti. The insistence on calling out Haiti's poverty in the face of the Global North's wealth ignores how Western Europe and North America gained and maintained their wealth. It also fails to account for the incalculable amount of wealth that Haiti has created for European powers. Simplistic questions about Haiti's poverty are distracting, dismissive, and denigrating and often devoid of rigorous theoretical foundations. Usually, criticisms about Haiti's poverty and the stylish adornment practices in Vodou do not involve political or economic arguments that might animate the concerns of a Marxist, for example. These criticisms do not condemn the way capitalism operates in the Western Hemisphere but merely the perceived material excess of Vodou. The many conversations and lectures about Roman Catholicism I participated in and heard throughout my time in academia never included questions about its lavish ceremonies and vestments in relation to the wealth or poverty of the laity. Yet the ritual adornment in Vodou is often categorized as a showy demonstration of social status and improper spending, rather than an expression of religious beliefs.

Preoccupation with the spending habits of Vodou practitioners reveals an assumption about their ability to meet their own material needs and to make sound judgments about expending money on religious practices. I thought that taking the time to explain the inner economic workings of Manbo Maude in her Vodou temples would illustrate the complexities of her religious practices, yet I continued to hear the same questions. The specter of poverty and poverty's often unacknowledged racialisms haunt perceptions of Haiti, warping its shape in people's minds. This book is an attempt to exorcise these ghosts and name White supremacy as the genesis of the haunting.

Vodou is a Black religion that is wrongly demarcated as a religion solely for the poor. The relentless focus on Haiti's poverty completely misses creative expressions of faith and adornment in service of the spirits. Vodou is about love. Vodou is about self-love. Vodou is revolutionary love. Vodou has created revolutions. Vodou defies gender and sexual boundaries. Vodou is pro-Black. Vodou is anti-White supremacy. It imagines a world beyond the material realities of the anti-Black political present we inhabit, and it venerates the spirits, the people, and the community. When Manbo Maude emphasizes the display of relative material wealth in her ritual clothes, she is met with discomfort and skepticism by people of all colors, Black and White, Haitian and American. Within societies shaped by White supremacy, all Black wealth is perceived as ill gained. Only White people deserve nice things, and Black poverty is the standard. People of all races are affected by these perceptions.

For Manbo Maude, the persistent concern about her wealth or poverty does not result in punishment from a state power, yet people express disdain for her showy religious ceremonies. Over the phone in the summer of 2020, I said jokingly to Manbo Maude, "You've got hella haters, both online and even when people are coming to your temple." She snorted and laughed, "Yes, girl, I have haters. People can hate on me all they want, but I don't care. And this is me on budget. If I had more money . . . ha! They will all see; they will hate on me more."[1]

Manbo Maude has granted readers the permission to hate on her. She is not bothered by her haters. She will not allow outside opinions to dictate how she spends her money. Her spirituality cannot be commodified, even though Westerners try to do so relentlessly. Manbo Maude revels in her celebration of and devotion to the spirits. She thinks about the divine every day and does not deprive herself of stylish adoration practices, no matter her financial means, whatever they may be. I watched how the spirits lovingly move with her and how she affectionately engages with them, even when she is not doing spiritual work. She plays Vodou music in her home and while driving in her car purely for the enjoyment of listening.

This book is an affirmation and a celebration of Black practitioners' relationships with Black divinities and an ongoing conversation with the natural and the supernatural worlds. Manbo Maude respects the spirits because they are real. She argues and negotiates with the spirits because they are real. I do not attempt to challenge the veracity of the spirits' presence; instead, I privilege belief. Ultimately, my book excises Haiti from past narratives defined by deprivation, poverty, and pain. I situate Vodou as a religion in the present with boundaryless futures, unstopped by White supremacist geopolitical practices. Neither poverty nor wealth can define Vodou. Like Haiti, it is whole and fraught with haters.

Acknowledgments

It took many hands in both earthly and supernatural realms to create this book. For more than a decade, *lwa* (spirits) have spoken to me through dreams and through the mouths of possessed practitioners at Vodou ceremonies. They told me I was powerful and that my book would be great—and they even corrected me when I missed a few things that needed to be revised in the text. I welcomed all their notes, whether they were blessings or serious critiques. I am thankful for their grace, their discernment, and their presence in my life. I thank all my ancestors and the spirits for conspiring with me to create this work and for the amazing people they put in my life to support me through this life-changing journey.

I am forever grateful to Manbo Marie Maude Evans and the Vodou community of Sosyete Nago. You all opened your temples to me and welcomed me with open arms. Every time I asked a question, fixed a head wrap, or lit a candle, I learned more about the devotional practices of Vodou. It was a joy and an honor to sit beside each one of you. Thank you for trusting me to tell your story. Special thanks go out to Manbo(s) and Houngan(s) Vante'm Pa Fyem, Portsha Jefferson aka Zetwal Ashade Bon Manbo, Babbas, Patrick Sylvain, Mariline Bernard, Eddie Bernard, Kethely Edouard, Carmel Joseph, Cynthia Joseph, Hugueline Fleurimond, Jean Marc Eugene, Jean Raymond Ridore, Pierre Sito Louis Jean, Gina Jean aka Fok nan pwen bon Manbo, Ramoncite Louis Jean, and Silvanie Nicolas. For the members who chose to maintain their anonymity or for those whom I did not mention, know that you all have my heart. Your presence in this book and in the Vodou community is felt.

I am thankful for the Vodou scholars, practitioners, and aficionados of anything Vodou who sat with me over the years and inspired my work in all its complexities. Your consistent encouragement, your check-ins, your corrections, and your thoughtfulness for my well-being did not go unnoticed. In fact, they are pivotal to my love for Vodou. Claudine Michel, Patrick Bellegarde-Smith, Nadège Clitandre, Jacqueline Epingle, Lorand "Randy" Matory, Lois Wilcken, LeGrace Benson, Gerdès Fleurant, Timothy Landry, Mahsheed Ayoub, and Chryss Yost: I express my sincere appreciation to you all. To my Vodou scholars now turned ancestors—Houngan Max Beauvoir, Karen McCarthy Brown, and Florence Bellande Robertson—thank you for the transformative intellectual conversations. I am fortunate that I had time in the waking world to sit beside you.

Words of appreciation are quite impossible to describe my wonderful friend or, as my mom calls her, the "Editor in Chief," Brianna Eaton, who more than likely has edited her own acknowledgments. Brianna gave me extraordinary support throughout the process. The growth of this book correlates directly with the growth of our friendship. She oversaw the details of the manuscript, making sure I thoroughly explained rituals without underestimating how much a reader needed to know. I called it the "Eaton Effect" when she raked over my work with a fine-tooth comb to make sure the material was sufficient to her standards. I knew that if I survived the level of scrutiny Brianna provided, I had a chance to succeed in other academic spaces. She challenged me to attain better-quality camera equipment to capture fast movements in ceremonies and let me know when I hit the mark with a stunning photo. This book would not be where it is without her sophisticated eye and intellectual generosity. The process of writing this book challenged my emotional, physical, and mental health, but with Brianna, I was never lonely, and the following pages are filled with memories of a beautiful journey with my best friend. Thank you, Brianna. Because of you, I soar.

My heartfelt thanks go to my fabulous research assistants who transcribed and translated interviews and helped with formatting my manuscript in its every stage: Manbo Vante'm Pa Fyem, Mélena Sims-Laudig, Kim Akano, Alejandro "Ale" Campillo, Kelsi Lidge, Oluchi Nwokocha, Eddie Bernard, Ivy Nicole-Jonét, Beulah Osueke, and Lynn Mary Léger. Without your type A personalities, your beautiful work ethic, and strong editing and formatting skills, this manuscript would still be in production. You helped keep me on track and had such keen awareness for the little but extremely important things.

The time that I spent at the Haitian Creole Language and Culture Summer Institute at the University of Massachusetts in Boston was remarkable. My Haitian professors—Marc Prou, Patrick Sylvain, Jean Lesly René, Lunine Pierre-Jerôme, Joel Théodat, and Leslie Rene—made learning Haitian Kreyòl immersive and enjoyable. Thank you for your dedication and support in improving my language skills. Your sophistication in the nuances of Haitian Kreyòl enabled me to thrive in a new country and connect with wonderful people.

I am greatly appreciative of the institutions and foundations that nourished this project from its inception. Funding was supported by the Ronald E. McNair Fellowship; University of Pennsylvania's Department of Africana Studies Research Fellowship, the Center for Africana Studies

Research Fellowship, and the Fontaine Fellowship Travel Grant; the Ford Foundation; Princeton University's Presidential Postdoctoral Fellowship and the Center for Culture Society and Religion; and the University of Miami Department of Religion Faculty Research Fellowship. They provided wonderful resources to enrich my fieldwork experiences. They were also instrumental in enabling me to travel to conferences where I shared earlier incarnations of the stories and theories in this book.

When I was searching for my manuscript home, a forty-five-minute (scheduled for fifteen minutes) conversation with former executive editor Elaine Maisner made it abundantly clear that my work belonged in the Where Religion Lives series with The University of North Carolina Press (UNC). Elaine and the fabulous series editor Kristy Nabhan-Warren were so dedicated to my work and so responsive to my needs. I enjoyed their "tell it like it is," no-nonsense work ethic and took pleasure in the fact that my work would be published in a series centering ethnographies of religious life. When the current executive editor Mark Simpson-Vos came onboard, he did not miss a beat and offered indispensable feedback while overseeing the project and making sure I met my deadlines. Thank you all for your expert critiques and for motivating me to lean into my voice. I also extend my deep gratitude to editor Andreína Fernández and acquisitions assistant Thomas Bedenbaugh for their attention to detail. You all have been a genuine pleasure to work with.

Throughout my journey as an academic, I have been fortunate to call magnificent people, in many institutions, my colleagues and friends. They engaged with my work in every stage, challenging my ideas and elevating the way I think about African Diasporic religions. Mentorship, insight, and learning come in many forms, and I am grateful for how they manifested in each person I mention. Your encouragement and steadfast support were pivotal to my work and my overall well-being.

At the University of California, Santa Barbara, I am grateful to Elizabeth "Lisa" Perez who sharpened my ethnographic skills and encouraged me in all stages of my project. We not only engaged in deep, intellectual conversations but also cared about our physical selves as well. I am grateful for our daily yoga sessions and check-ins that kept my mind and body sharp. I am indebted to your scholastic guidance and holistic care. Additionally, Grace Chang, Roberto Strongman, George Lipsitz, Jeffrey Stewart, Jude Akudinobi, Christopher McAuley, Gaye Theresa Johnson, Mireille Miller-Young, Beth Schneider, Michael D. Young, Stephen Jones, Azure Stewart, and Wenonah Valentine consistently pushed me to be my best self. I benefited greatly from your guidance.

At the University of Pennsylvania, Heather Andrea Williams's attentiveness and mentorship were in a class all their own. Her analytic acuity and encouragement of clarity made every critique she offered extremely valuable. I am so appreciative of her organizational expertise and her ability to sit with disciplines different from hers, as well as her insistence on meeting deadlines. Anthea Butler was instrumental in motivating me to lean into my "Naija-self" and to inquire about finances and economics in Vodou. Her insights in religious studies are powerfully paired with her invaluable guidance in my academic career. The collegiality of Camille Charles, Barbara Savage, David Amponsah, Herman Beavers, Michael Hanchard, John L. Jackson, Grace Sanders Johnson, Jasmine E. Johnson, Margo Crawford, Eve Troutt Powell, Dorothy Roberts, Timothy Rommen, Deborah Thomas, Justin McDaniel, Donovan Schaefer, Steven Weitzman, Tracey Turner, Monica Bradford, Patricia Rea, Audra Rodgers, Venise N. Adjibodou, Brian Jackson, Augusta Atinuke Irele, Carol Davis, Teya Campbell, and Gale Garrison energized my work and prompted conversations that I still hold dear to me. At Harvard University, I am honored by the support of Jacob Olupona who bolstered my explorations of African and African Diasporic religions. I am appreciative of our conversations and your counsel.

At Princeton University, I give special thanks to Judith Weisenfeld whose support is unmatched. Her wit, attention to detail, and overall concern for my well-being have been a great comfort. Her intellectual savviness and grace continue to push my ideas and thoughts forward. I am grateful to the Department of Religion and its Religion in the Americas workshop, the Center for Culture Society and Religion and its Religion and Culture Workshop, and the Princeton Program in African Studies. Wallace Best, Jonathan Gold, Seth Perry, Lauren Kerby, Alphonso F. Saville IV, Aisha M. Beliso-De Jesús, William M. Stell, Caroline Matas, Jessica L. Delgado, Darren J. Saint-Ulysse, Eden G. Consenstein, Heath Carter, Beth Stroud, Jenny W. Legath, Kristine L. Wright, Michael I Baysa, Madeline Gambino, Alyssa Maldonado, KB Dennis Meade, Ahmad Greene-Hayes, Jeffrey Guest, Khytie Brown, Chika O. Okeke-Agulu, Rudo Robin Mudiwa, Timothy Waldron, Onome Daniella Olotu, and Iheanyi Onwuegbucha—thank you for sharpening my ideas.

I am grateful to the Crossroads Project: Black Religious Histories, Communities, and Cultures, and their Black Religious Studies Working Group who read parts of this manuscript. Their feedback was very informed and enhanced my analysis tremendously. Thank you to Judith Casselberry, Nicole Turner, Vaughn A. Booker, N. Fadeke Castor, Matthew J. Cressler, Christina Davidson, Jamil Drake, Ambre Dromgoole, Lerone A. Martin, Alexis

Wells Oghoghomeh, Matthew M. Harris, Elyan Hill, James Howard Jr., Laura McTighe, Timothy Rainey II, Joseph Stuart, Cori Tucker Price, Ashley Coleman Taylor, and Todne Thomas. Special thanks to Ras Micheal Brown who wonderfully assisted me with my chapter subtitles. That was an art and a craft of its own.

My colleagues at the University of Miami have been supportive and generous with their feedback. David Kling, Dexter E. Callender, William Scott Green, Nebil Husayn, Catherine Newell, Justin Ritzinger, Robyn Walsh, Daniel L. Pals, Henry A. Green, Ellen I. Roberts, Kate Ramsey, Marina Magloire, and Jafari Allen are all wonderful folks, and I am grateful to think alongside you.

An exceptional group of scholars assessed my manuscript and offered generous feedback. Sylvester Johnson, Yolanda Covington-Ward, Dianne Stewart, Judith Casselberry, and UNC Press's anonymous reviewers provided instrumental insights into my manuscript that forever changed it. I am grateful for Tistsi Ella Jaji, Marla F. Frederick, Chad Seales, Josef Sorett, Omaris Z. Zamora, Kathryn Lofton, Erica Lorraine Williams, Libby Greene, and Sally M. Promey for their kindness and intellectual generosity.

COVID-19 was hard on many of us, and despite these difficulties, it also brought some of us together. I thank my Academic Therapy homies for engaging my work and, through Zoom laughs and check-ins, pushing my writing forward. I appreciate Natalie Léger, Kellie Carter Jackson, and Mary Phillips. Sincere thanks to the therapists Jeanne Stanford, Batsirai Bvunzawabaya, Pamela Freeman, Yu-Ching Isabelle Hsu, and Latoya Mohammed who kept me sane over the years.

Fitness, for me, went hand in hand with successfully completing this book. Maintaining a balance between physical health and work enhanced my ability to write. Moreover, attending Vodou ceremonies, which often last at least seven hours, can be physically taxing, and I needed all my strength to stay alert and active. Debra Williams at Smart Fitness Studios understood the need to harmoniously blend scholarship and fitness. I am indebted to her drive and dedication to promoting fitness and wellness for women of color in Philadelphia. Special thanks go to Stacia Emeharole, Chantel Thompson, Tymika Henderson, Lynda Shepherd, Megan Gilmartin, LaTanya Myers-Boswell, Joy Ellis, Amanda Christine Bazemore, Lori Ryals (especially the "saucy" drinks she made for me on special occasions), Gabby Ryals, Brittany Salmon, Lauren Williams, Desiree Johnson, Michelle Louvenia, Sharon Irving, Marla Brown, Shaquiyyah Jenkins, Monica Terae', and Ciara V. Lucas. Thank you for consistently caring for my well-being. Every workout was a celebration of what we can accomplish as a collective, and it was a joy to sweat with you all.

I am appreciative of the Black Queendom group in Philadelphia, which was started by the fabulous Jasmine "J'Oprah" Omorogbe. Thank you, Jasmine, for allowing me to fall in love with a new city and for providing the walks, dances, and "sophisti-ratchetness" that I needed to get back to my writing. My deep love goes out to Patrice Farquharson, Kenyetta, Chanae Brown, Deangie Davis, Olivia, Eugénie Elie aka Eve of Strategy, Brianna Reed, Nyikia, Mam Kumba Sosseh, Omua Ahonkhai, Mary Umoh, and Lashowna. You all provided the balance and joy I needed to breathe when I felt burdened by my work.

I am indebted to all the artists, musicians, writers, anime, and media makers who fueled my soul and gave me encouragement to get in the zone to write and focus. Your example inspired me to thrive. Thanks to the late Miriam Makeba, Oprah Winfrey, N. K. Jemisin, Nnedi Okorafor, Viola Davis, Tracee Ellis Ross, Issa Rae, Beyoncé, India Arie, Burna Boy, Tems, Wizkid, Michelle Obama, Lupita Nyong'o, Danai Gurira, Lizzo, Angela Bassett, Ryan Coogler, Ava DuVernay, Gina Yashere, Miguel, Usher, India Arie, Yvonne Orji, Trevor Noah, Tiwa Savage, Cardi B, and the late Chadwick Boseman.

I deeply value my friendships with Bashir Hassan and Laura Tinker. My mom calls Bashir my "Secretary of State" because he has been my righthand partner and is consistently scheming up ways for me to be the very best version of myself. His intellectual prowess and ability to look at any situation from multiple angles are otherworldly. I am forever grateful that we walk together, my friend . . . and you are still not getting your own dragon! Laura's cool, calm, and collected demeanor always keeps me grounded. You provided my introduction to how Black feminism can be embodied. Thank you for your fierceness.

Thank you to my parents, High Chief Syringa Nwokocha and Lola Florence Nwokocha, and my siblings Chimex, Chido, Oluchi, Chibuzo, Chidinma, and Chimobi. The Nwokocha family takes pride in excellence and making a mark on whatever we touch. Together we are stubborn, imaginative, and a beautiful embodiment of light. I thank my family for just being themselves. Because of our love for each other and our constant encouragement of one other, anytime we dream, our possibilities are endless. We are each other's best hypemen.

My deepest gratitude to my Ancestors, Chimeremeze Nwokocha, Clyde Woods, Veronita W. M. Freeman-Nwaoha, Florence Bellande-Robertson, and Chinemeze Chinemeze who walk with me and provided guidance in the living world and beyond.

Vodou en Vogue

Introduction

The Gods Give Looks

A silk, sapphire-colored sheet was pinned to the wall behind the altar, decorated with scarves in varying shades of red and blue in honor of Ezili Dantò, the warrior goddess, protectress of children, and guardian of lesbians and gender-fluid people.[1] Black female ceremonial leaders stood out among the crowd, allowing ruffles, excess layers of cloth, and embroidery to display their status in the room and to the gods. The fabric of their dresses was so voluminous that the skirts extended outward from the waist in a grand bell shape, echoing the aristocratic silhouette of bygone colonizers in a ceremony indebted to West and Central African ancestors in fashion, music, ritual, and spirit.[2] To many, a Vodou ceremony is a feverish movement of bodies and the rhythmic beating of the *yanvalou* drums, but to Manbo Maude, a Vodou priestess in Haiti and the United States, it is also a celebration of ritual fashion.[3] During this ceremony in Jacmel, Haiti, the audience was drawn closer by the lavish dresses, the coral blues and scarlet reds that sashayed through the room as part of the swirling fabric of the female practitioners' outfits. People sucked their teeth in appreciation and shouted in joy.[4] Bright head wraps covered the women's hair. Many women wore makeup and ornate gold jewelry, with rings on every finger. The men, with freshly shaved faces, had ironed their crisp shirts and pants only moments before the start of the ceremony. The colors of their outfits complemented the dresses worn by the women dancing in the ceremony, completing the ritualistic tableau Manbo Maude envisioned for her temple.

In Haitian Vodou, the gods care about how they look. African Diasporic gods are not symbols: they are thinking, feeling, drinking, and talking entities in the lives and ritual practices of devotees.[5] Spirits, or *lwa* in Haitian Kreyòl, shape the lives of practitioners through style, aesthetics, and adornment, investing in the physical presentation of their presence. They are, without doubt, vain. Nowhere was this vanity more evident to me than when interacting with Manbo Marie Maude Evans, a Haitian mental health clinician living in the United States who practices Vodou through numerous avenues, including card readings, possession, visions, and dreams, in both Jacmel, Haiti, and Mattapan, Massachusetts. Her title *Manbo* refers to a

1

female Vodou initiate who has undergone training in ceremonial, spiritual, and ritual work. Through her and the Vodou practitioners who serve the spirits under her guidance, I explore how the spirits provide inspiration for religious dress while intervening in everyday situations in practitioners' lives.

Vodou en Vogue illuminates how the fashion displayed in Vodou ceremonies allows practitioners such as Manbo Maude to connect with the spirits and assert their religious efficacy. She produces clothing to convey her authenticity and power as a religious figure, simultaneously implying her relative wealth and showcasing the spirits during ceremonies. In other words, Manbo Maude fashions outfits inspired by Vodou spirits to satisfy the material demands of deities while also creating unique spiritual practices that shape the experiences of other practitioners and observers in her temple. Throughout my research in Manbo Maude's temples, which I conducted from 2015 to 2022, I kept returning to one central question, which was posed to me by Judith Weisenfeld, a scholar of religion: What do the gods want? My answer is reverence through words, actions, and materials, which most often are beautifully adorned.[6]

Vodou en Vogue focuses on two Vodou temples led by Manbo Maude, one in Jacmel and the other in Mattapan. Manbo Maude's temples — both named Sosyete Nago, Haitian Kreyòl for "Nago Society" — are sites of sartorial innovation where initiates and other participants adorn themselves to demonstrate reverence for the spirits. The religious dress becomes more elaborate as ceremonies continue through the night after practitioners change their clothes during breaks in the proceedings, creating distinctive, spiritually inspired ensembles. I attended several hundred ceremonies in more than a decade of studying Haitian Vodou, traveling to sites and communities in Montreal, Miami, Queens and Brooklyn, Boston, and Port-au-Prince. I center Manbo Maude and her temples in this book because she and her practitioners are particularly innovative in their use of ritual aesthetics. That innovation is the result both of Manbo Maude's experience as a fashion designer and the gods' willingness to speak to her through clothing, shaping her relationship to her faith and her community. *Vodou en Vogue* connects the role of fashion to religious labor, spiritual authority, intimacy, identity, and the power of adornment in facilitating communication between spirits and those who worship them.

The lwa often speak to practitioners through their passions. In 2016, a Vodou practitioner in Brooklyn told me of a *Houngan* — Haitian Kreyòl for a male practitioner who has trained extensively to perform spiritual and ritual work — who worked in construction and used his skills to build a small underground pool in the basement of his house to pay homage to the mermaid spirit Lasirenn. The late Ati Nasyonal Houngan Max Beauvoir, an internationally revered Vodou practitioner, kept a massive garden at his home and temple in Port-au-Prince to honor the divinities.[7] His indoor and outdoor temples featured gardens that contained more than a thousand species of plants, channeling his expertise in biochemistry into a symbol of his devotion to the lwa. Manbo Maude's training as a fashion designer shapes her own expressions of devotion, suggesting the willingness of the spirits to adapt to the abilities and professional and educational backgrounds of the practitioners who worship them. The spirits are cognizant of who practitioners are and what they have to offer. In turn, practitioners open themselves up to the possibility of being molded by the desires of the spirits, surrendering the use of their talents in exchange for guidance, protection, and financial favor.

Vodou en Vogue foregrounds fashion in the religious and social life of Vodou, demonstrating the importance of aesthetics, wellness, and spiritual connection in communal identity formation. The study of dress in Haitian Vodou is often limited to description and the linking of certain colors and objects to the spirits they signify, addressing social interaction and cultural symbolism.[8] Analysis is commonly couched in the history of French colonization and African religious continuities without considering the additional complexities of modern Vodou communities. I expand these explorations by spotlighting the significance of visual and material cultures within contemporary Vodou temples, which have been overlooked and understudied. The dynamic adornment rituals of Manbo Maude's home offer insight into the role that dress plays in the formation of belief and the creation of religious communities. Manbo Maude's careful curation of her own creative narrative facilitates the discovery of those insights. She calls her ritual clothes an "archive" that documents the religious history of her temples and her devotion to the spirits. She stores her dresses in blue plastic shipping barrels in her homes in Mattapan and Jacmel, not only in her bedroom closet but also in other rooms and the hallways. Manbo Maude has an excellent memory. I can point to any of her outfits, and she can tell me what year and what ceremony the garments were featured in, those she loved, and others that still disappoint her. She rarely wears the same dress twice, instead creating new outfits for each occasion. Her dress collection is a material record of religious fashion, inspiring nostalgia and documenting memory.[9]

Before discussing Manbo Maude's ceremonies in detail, let me clarify the use of several words and expressions. The terms "practitioner," "initiate," and "audience" refer to the people in Manbo Maude's temples. A "practitioner" is anyone who practices the religion. An "initiate" is a practitioner who has undergone the formal initiation rituals required to carry out specific religious responsibilities to which non-initiated practitioners are not privy. To be clear, a practitioner does not have to be an initiate, but an initiate is always a practitioner. By "audience," I mean those people who are a part of the ceremonies taking place but are not associated with Manbo Maude's temples. The audience members can be practitioners or initiates in other Vodou temples, but I do not refer to them as such because they are not a part of the cadre of people who organize and facilitate ceremonies and ritual work in Manbo Maude's temples. They seek primary spiritual guidance from other Manbos and Houngans or may be people who are merely interested in the religion. Instead, the members of the audience are witnesses who actively participate in ceremonies through the acts of watching, commenting, dancing, and interacting with possessed practitioners. I use these fashion-related terms— *dress, outfit, clothing, garment, fashion,* and *adornment*—interchangeably because they are aspects of appearance that represent identity in relation to social, ethnic, and cultural markers.[10]

Fashion is a tool through which practitioners create a reciprocal exchange with the spirits in African Diasporic religions—exposing, masking, or adorning the body in the service of rituals and beliefs.[11] When dress becomes a part of religion, it is transformed into a sacred item, connoting beliefs, engaging with power dynamics, acting as a conduit to the spiritual world, and more.[12] Dress includes all decorations worn on the body, any modifications to the body such as tattooing and scarring, the cultural context of dress, and how being dressed makes participants feel.[13] Understanding dress in religion requires investigation of the multisensory experience of religious clothing and adornments—not only their "smell, feel, touch, and even sounds" but also what scholar of religion Sally Promey describes as the "emotional element of memories and impression evoked by dress; the textures, materials, and kinetic element."[14]

Spiritual Vogue: Performing Fashion to Feel/Sense Queer Spirits

The study of Vodou and of other African and African Diasporic religions is often preoccupied on redeeming their cosmologies and rituals, and for good reason. Centuries of denigration have cast these faiths as demonic, evil, and unsophisticated, and generations of scholars have been devoted to correcting those inaccurate, anti-Black constructions. Yet, that necessary work can,

Vodou initiate showcasing her tattoo of Ezili Freda's *vèvè* or "symbol,"
Mattapan, March 2018 (photo by Eziaku Nwokocha).

because of scholars' understandable protectiveness, emphasize the beauty
and positivity of Vodou without fully engaging with its complexities, ambi-
guities, and outright contradictions in practice. By focusing on contemporary
Vodou communities, *Vodou en Vogue* discusses the religion with the assumption that it does not need my protection. I do not battle every anti-Black
perception that has plagued Vodou since its genesis and take its validity as
fact, in large part because scholars who came before me already did exem-
plary work rectifying its reputation. Instead of reiterating their conclusions,

I concentrate on fashion as a gateway into Vodou's intricacies, leaning into as many nuances as I can while knowing that reaching for comprehension of what I heard and witnessed is more important than shielding the faith from attacks others already rebuked.

Vodou en Vogue is concerned with the influence of spiritual traditions in the everyday lives of practitioners like Manbo Maude and her adherents. I use an interdisciplinary methodology that includes history and transnational Black feminist ethnography grounded in Africana studies, religious studies, performance studies, and queer studies. I draw from these fields to think critically about religion and fashion through the senses and their manifestation through visual and material culture.[15] The fraught histories of colonization, enslavement, and modernity have obscured the inherent connection between African and African Diasporic religions and materiality and sensation.[16] In truth, these religions always engaged with material culture and sensation, whether religious studies departments in the United States recognized they did or not.[17] African Diasporic religions are relatively neglected in both religious studies and Africana studies departments, despite the major contributions of scholars of ethnographic historiography and religion throughout the twentieth century.[18] These departments have only recently begun to correct this oversight.

In addition to race, the history of material culture and sensation is also inseparable from conversations about gender and sexuality. For example, the long-running debate between scholars of religion Oyèrónké Oyěwùmí and J. Lorand Matory about the foundations of gender in precolonial Yoruba society in Africa at first glance seems to have only a tangential relationship to my examination of materiality in Manbo Maude's homes.[19] Their argument centers on the role of gender before colonization, and modern Haiti is very obviously postcolonial. However, at the heart of their conversation are the use of sacramental clothing and the role of adornment in connoting visions of gender and identity during religious ceremonies, which influence my descriptions of materiality and gender in *Vodou en Vogue*. Oyěwùmí and Matory's conversation contradicts any notion that African religions and the Diasporic faiths that bloomed outside the African continent are unsophisticated or archaic, and so does this book. *Vodou en Vogue* emphatically asserts the inherent value of Vodou without an interest in comparatively analyzing it to non-African Diasporic traditions, which would ultimately trap discussion inside old and irrelevant binaries. Vodou and other African and African Diasporic religions do not need to be compared to other faiths for their validation, because they already contain expansive ontological and epistemological foundations that deserve exploration.

Manbo Maude's temples are sites of innovation that reflect the dynamic relationship between race, gender, and sexuality in concert with religious ritual, material aesthetics, and spiritual embodiment. I assess Vodou and fashion through the senses because touching, seeing, and listening to fabrics are requirements for the production and use of spiritual clothing in Manbo Maude's home. Over the past twenty years, scholars of religion have turned to the concept of sensory religions to account for the multisensory experience of ritual practices. In "sensational religion," the senses are worthy sites of critical analysis, and religion can be investigated through the experience of the body. When the practitioner's body is the focus of study, material and social contexts can illuminate behaviors, feelings, and beliefs.[20] Just as the body is mutable, growing and aging with time, so too are the materials involved in ritual culture. Materiality contends that objects have meaning and that this meaning is given to them through the context not only of religion but also by the circumstances of devotees' lived experiences.[21] These objects are not passive. They are dynamic because of the messages they convey and the spiritual powers imbued in them by individuals and the gods. Adornment plays an important role in the critical analysis of individuals' self-articulation as practitioners and as members of a religious collectivity, including their direct interaction with the spirits through possession.

African and African Diasporic religions continuously demonstrate the significance of multisensory and material objects and their impacts within the natural and supernatural, the profane and mundane, and the living and the dead. What are seen, felt, and heard in the production and wearing of religious clothing shape how people engage their faith through a sensorial concept I call *spiritual vogue*. I coined this term to address multisensorial ritual practices in Manbo Maude's temples, as defined by the performative use of fashion to unify practitioners and connect with the spirits. Spiritual vogue is an interactive framework centering both the process of being seen through dress and the roles of touch and movement; it focuses on spiritual communication between practitioners and the audience through adornment practices. The spiritual vogue framework underscores fashion as a key example of the aesthetic ritual practices that animate African Diasporic religions like Haitian Vodou, Brazilian Candomblé, and Cuban Lucumí, more widely known as Santería. Through Vodou ceremonies, Manbo Maude's body and those of her practitioners in Sosyete Nago function as ritualistically stylized individuals while simultaneously interacting with one another and the audience, influencing practitioners' actions and the connotations of their performativity in service of the spirits. I argue that spiritual vogue depends on the interactive processes of three crucial groups, which are all necessary for ceremonies to function properly: the practitioners, spirits, and audience. Grasping the concept of spiritual vogue requires understanding that the presence of the lwa in Vodou ceremonies is not symbolic for many participants and devotees but real, and the legitimacy of these spirits has substantive effects on their actions and ritual practice.

The word *vogue* has multiple meanings, some of which are useful to the study of Vodou. Its meaning is derived from a French word for fashion.[22] The term has come to embody sophisticated style in part because of the fashion magazine *Vogue*, which has approximately 1.2 million subscribers across the world and editions in more than twenty countries.[23] "Vogue" is a popular term to describe style in general and is a part of our everyday lexicon in the United States and beyond. Queer Black and Brown people invented the concept of vogue as a dance performance in the transgressive, gender-bending spaces of Ballroom culture, dating back to as early as the 1920s in the United States.[24] Ballroom culture and Vodou are vastly different traditions, yet they share the ability to offer a safe space where Black people can be seen as they want to be seen: both are capable of offering sanctuary.

The primary inspirations of spiritual vogue are the dynamism of Ballroom culture and the invention of vogue by Black and Brown queer people: these provide insights into performance and fashion that shape my perspective on Vodou and Vodou ceremonies. Scholar of gender and sexuality Marlon M. Bailey describes Ballrooms as animated by a fluid "gender system" that articulates gender, sex, and sexuality categories derived from the lived experiences of participants. An integral part of the gender system is the performance of these categories during balls in front of an audience, which, in combination with fashion, makes these categories legible for the community.[25] I am not stating that the gender systems in Manbo Maude's homes are as complex or transgressive as those described by Bailey, although some queer people do play important roles in her temples. To my knowledge, Manbo Maude's homes are largely populated by heterosexual, cisgender people, with a much smaller minority of queer, transgender, and nonbinary people. The sex, gender, and sexuality norms in her temples are clearly more heteronormative and are not formed with queer people at the center. However, Bailey's insights into the importance of the performance of gender provide a meaningful context for Vodou spaces.

As in Ballroom, gender dynamics within Vodou temples grow out of the lived realities of participants and reflect often complex relationships with gender, sex, and sexuality. As Bailey makes clear, identities in Ballroom are not produced in isolation. Instead, they are a product both of individual and communal representation, relying on "performance rituals" to construct expectations in a given community.[26] Performance rituals are also an integral part of Manbo Maude's religious practices, shaping interactions between practitioners, the audience, and the spirits. They are actions and events undertaken in service of communal cultural practices, expressing broadly understood ideals through the bodies of community members.[27] These rituals affirm values and reflect the worldviews of the performers and of the spectators witnessing their display.

In Ballroom and in Vodou, performance rituals are drawn not only from the lived experiences of active participants but also from generations of cultural and religious continuities that stretch back to Western, Central, and Southern Africa: these long histories of enslavement, migration, and innovation show themselves through the intricacies of dance and fashion.[28] The deployment of fashion is a primary link between these two spaces where aesthetic rituals connote ideas of community and power, emphasizing a sense of togetherness that combats the marginalization of the outside world. Ballroom is a unique culture, and yet the performance rituals performed within those spaces and the scholarship generated from its study have meaning for much broader trends in Black cultures. This holds true for the study of Black queer cultures more generally. Centering the insights gained from Black queer people and scholars illuminates previously overlooked parallels between African Diasporic communities, shifting conversations around gender, sexuality, and faith.

Spiritual vogue helps frame the many performance rituals practiced by Vodou practitioners, connecting fashion and performativity in worship. I use the term "vogue" because it connotes not only style but also the body, performance, personality, the audience, and community. Moreover, in Jacmel, Port-au-Prince, Boston, and Mattapan, I saw practitioners who *vogue* during ceremonies to honor the gods, which inspired me to consider the role of performance in Vodou. I combine *vogue* with the word *spiritual* to incorporate the presence of the divine. The spirits play an active part in these religious communities, and I make plain how they mediate in practitioners' lives. The concept of spiritual vogue is useful to the study of religious ritual, performance, and fashion because it gives scholars of African and African Diasporic religion a framework for understanding how practitioners individualize their religious experiences with the lwa.

Although my reading of fashion in Manbo Maude's temple is influenced by vogue's invocation of queer Ballroom culture, I am uneasy about scholarship that imagines Vodou and other African Diasporic religions as queer religions. Vodou, as with all global religions, is not free of the homophobia and misogyny that exist in broader Haitian and U.S. societies.[29] Assigning the term "queer" to religious spaces that still pose dangers to queer people assumes an egalitarianism that is clearly too simplistic. When I use the term "queer" in relation to Vodou, I am investigating how gender, sexuality, and power animate ceremonial spaces. I situate my understanding of queer theory in Black feminist scholar Cathy J. Cohen's definition: "queer theory focuses on and makes central not only the socially constructed nature of sexuality and sexual categories, but also the varying degrees and multiple sites of power distributed with all categories of sexuality, including the normative category of heterosexuality."[30] In other words, "queerness" is a term I use to describe sexual and gender fluidity within Haitian Vodou communities in light of how it disrupts normative power dynamics in religious spaces.

Calling Vodou temples queer without considering the privileges and prejudices that color the interactions among practitioners, audiences, and the spirits reduces the inherent complexities of the religion and the lived experiences of adherents. The ethos of Vodou is open: all people are welcome, and the spirits are capable of speaking to everyone, yet people are shaped by their governing societies, which must not be forgotten. The fact that Manbo Maude does not claim her temples as queer spaces does not diminish the presence of queer people in her homes nor the value of queer studies scholarship in engaging with her religious communities. Queer Black culture is Black culture.

Spiritual vogue invites the unavoidable influence of queerness in Vodou, even if the presence of queer people is complicated by the realities of Manbo Maude's temples and Vodou temples in general. Using vogue as part of my theoretical construct emphasizes the tension between the queerness of the spirits and the societal prejudices that affect perceptions of practitioners. I am not calling the lived experiences in Vodou inherently queer, but I am calling the lwa queer. The spirits are queer because they embrace gender fluidity and accept the myriad of ways in which human beings express gender and identity. They prove their acceptance of diverse sexual and gender identities that have not yet been fully accepted in Haitian and U.S. societies through their interaction with practitioners during possession, spiritual marriage, and *nan dòmi*, Haitian Kreyòl for "in dream."[31] Practitioners shape how they receive the spirits during ceremonies, projecting their beliefs about sexuality and gender onto the divine. Yet the process is a negotiation, and the spirits cannot be fully contained by the worldly perceptions of devotees. What we see in public Vodou ceremonies is the messy result of these negotiations, which vary from practitioner to practitioner, temple to temple, ceremony to ceremony.

The performativity exercised through the body during possession within ceremonies is always defined by a broader historical context.[32] In Vodou ceremonies, the body is a site of religious performance that contests, conforms to, or negotiates with "dominant meaning systems."[33] In these ceremonies, it is not only important to consider how bodies are adorned but also what is happening around them. The "performative reflexivity" of spiritual vogue—the fact that the participants are expecting to be seen by the audience and the spirits—is at the heart of what shapes the concept, allowing devotees to reflect on the "relations, actions, symbols, meanings, codes, roles, statuses, social structures, ethical and legal rules, and other sociocultural components which make up their public [and religious] selves."[34]

Spirit possession or *pran lwa*, Haitian Kreyòl for "take spirit," is central to my discussion of gender fluidity in Vodou. During possession, the body becomes a vessel where the divine and human join as one. In this liminal state, the spirit's voice and behavior take over the initiate, delivering messages (good, bad, or otherwise) to people within the community and the world at large.[35] As possessions occur, gender performances take place: women, for example, take on stereotypically masculine directness and aggression that can be used to confront male community members who engage in poor behavior within their spiritual and personal relationships. Roberto Strongman, a literary scholar of Black studies, calls the gender and ontological dynamics during possession "transcorporeality." In his book *Queering Black Atlantic Religions*, transcorporeality manifests as "the commingling of the human and the divine produc[ing] subjectivities whose gender is not dictated by biological sex."[36] Strongman's assessment of the nature of pran lwa—that the spirits are unconcerned with the gender identity or sex of the practitioner they possess—is consistent with my observations in Vodou temples in general. However, after spending more than a decade as a participant observer in ceremonies, I argue that Strongman underemphasizes the extent to which biological essentialist ideas of the body are still very much present in Vodou.

In Vodou, the gender and sexual fluidity that Strongman describes as *transcorporeality* confronts the social mores of Haitian and U.S. culture that constrain trance possession experiences with the divine for cisgender heterosexual men, while cisgender gay men and cisgender, queer, and transgender women are able to traverse gender lines more fluidly. Many cisgender, heterosexual male practitioners refuse to be possessed by hyperfeminine female spirits because of the cultural expectations of gendered behavior and the potential social consequences of being too feminine within their communities. *Vodou en Vogue* expands the discourse about possession by claiming that the multisensorial performance of gender, which relies on fashion, adornment, and bodily representation, defines how many practitioners and participants in Vodou ceremonies perceive gender. At the same time, the everyday experiences of practitioners and audience members influence how pran lwa functions. Their beliefs affect religious rituals, and religious communities cannot exist outside these societal and cultural perceptions. Patriarchy, homophobia, and misogyny have a clear impact on the ceremonies I witnessed, limiting how heterosexual, cisgender men may interact with female deities and how cisgender, queer, and transgender women and their bodies are perceived.

Spiritual marriages are another central element of my exploration of gender and sexuality in Vodou. During ceremonies and in practitioners' everyday lives, spiritual marriage allows for easier communication between spirits and practitioners. I interviewed Black initiates about their journey toward ritual commitment to the deities and how fashion creates opportunities for multisensorial interactions with the divine. These interactions can take place through possession during marriage ceremonies, as well as nan dòmi, where ongoing communication can facilitate possible sexual encounters between lwa and practitioners. I also delve into the often-unspoken realities of same-gender desire between spirits and practitioners and how they challenge the ritual traditions of spiritual marriage within Manbo Maude's temples. The religious fashion and gender presentation involved in spiritual marriage extend beyond ceremonies into the lives of practitioners.

The practical complexities of gender and sexuality, because they are inexorable aspects of life and therefore of ceremonies, feature prominently in my discussions of spiritual vogue, which hinges on the concept of being seen. Scholar of religion David Morgan expounds on this concept. According to Morgan, the act of looking is a site of knowledge production that affects the senses and draws from assumptions that are part of tradition, have historical context, and are socially and culturally specific.[37] Morgan introduces the phrase "sacred gaze," an embodied sensorial process wherein people understand rituals through looking at images and each other, thereby tying together social, historical, and religious contexts.[38] The sacred gaze is pivotal to the functioning of spiritual vogue, which describes the action of seeing as a religious act integrated into Vodou ceremonies that builds on cultural and historical backgrounds through fashion. Vision within the context of spiritual vogue reinforces beliefs in divinity.

The act of looking and being looked at in Manbo Maude's temples and in Vodou in general involves the triangulation of multiple subjects during ceremonies: the practitioners, the spirits, and the audience. Ceremonial performance rituals, carried out by those interrelated subjects, illustrate the vibrancy of Vodou and its beautification rituals, affirming the communal cohesion of its participants in an environment that is both religious and extremely social. Spiritual vogue, by concentrating on the highly changeable interactions between practitioners, the spirits, and the audience, reveals that the appreciation and exaltation of the spirits foster the co-construction of both spirit identity and practitioner identity.

Vodou Histories: Interlocking Spiritualities across Black Diasporas

For believers in African and African Diasporic religions, Haiti, as well as Cuba, Brazil, Benin, and Nigeria, is at the heart of religiously motivated travel. I approach Haitian Vodou and other African and African Diasporic religions as world religions, firmly situated alongside Christianity, Judaism, Islam, Hinduism, and the like. Each faith has its own place of pilgrimage: for example, Mecca for Islam, Jerusalem for Judaism, Ethiopia and the Vatican for Christianity, and India for Hinduism. For Haitian Vodou, Haiti is that ancestral home, the foundational source of the religion's heritage. Religious tourists from around the globe trek to Haiti to experience the birthplace of their spirituality, a necessary touchstone for many who seek a connection to the spirits. Manbo Maude's temples facilitate global religious tourism, bringing practitioners into Haiti as a part of their religious journey.[39] Travel between countries is an element in the marrow of her religious communities.

The transnational nature of Manbo Maude's spiritual practice is directly tied to the intrinsic transnationality of many African and African Diasporic religions, which are animated by the interactions of vast bodies of knowledge culled from various cultures and locations.[40] Some of these cosmogenic interactions resulted from forced migration.[41] The transatlantic slave trade placed many African peoples and their cultures in the same geographical space in Haiti; what emerged from this contact is a complex system of beliefs that entwined West and Central African religious worldviews, Indigenous Caribbean traditions, and eventually Catholicism.[42] Haitian Vodou is a system of beliefs and rituals that mine the experiences of everyday people for reflection, healing, and inspiration. The religion, intertwined with and responsive to lived experience, is malleable to the needs of its believers; it informs perceptions of individual and collective history and answers to the tribulations of worshippers, providing the potential for valuable healing for a people who have endured historical and ongoing oppression.[43] Interwoven with everyday life, Vodou supplies basic knowledge on how to operate in the world. The sacred and the secular are not mutually exclusive but are entangled, and the divine can be called on for aid and support in moments of celebration or crisis or to address common concerns that confront practitioners in their daily lives.

The origins of Haitian Vodou, although inarguably connected to the belief systems I mentioned, are still subject to debate, particularly in relation to Catholicism. Many scholars claim that the presence of Catholicism in Vodou stems from the French colonial authority that forced Haitians to hide their deities within the images of saints that evoked the same meanings as their spirits; they had to practice a covert religion for fear of deadly consequences. For enslaved Haitians, naming African spirits, owning ritual material, or gathering to practice their religions could result in death. The need for secrecy depended on the region in which Haitian practitioners lived and the degree of influence Catholicism had on each individual or religious community.[44] The vast landholdings of the plantations in Haiti and other Caribbean colonies prevented Europeans from exerting rigid control over the religious beliefs of large numbers of enslaved Africans. The constant influx of Africans to the colonies also increased the sustainability of African religious traditions.[45]

However, historians and ethnolinguists have challenged the primacy of French colonialism in explaining Vodou's involvement with Catholicism. Historian Christina Mobley, for example, uses ethnolinguistic and archival data to chart the movement of Christian people and traditions from Kongo into Haiti in the earliest days of the colony, complicating the cultural and religious foundations of Vodou by centering African contributions.[46] Moreover, scholars like John Thornton, Terry Rey, and Hein Vanhee argue for the importance of Central African and Kongolese Catholic traditions to Vodou's creation; they question typical understandings of devotees' reactions to persecution in Haiti; for example, interrogating narratives about hiding African gods in Catholic symbols.[47] Wherever the roots of Catholicism in Vodou originated from, in the twenty-first century, Catholicism is a force carrying varying degrees of power: some communities embrace its symbols and practices, whereas others focus on the African or Indigenous Caribbean elements of Vodou. Haitians in Haiti and the United States are still creating new significations for their spirits as they continue to adapt their religions to new environments.[48]

The religious rites and ceremonial practices of Vodou are a constant reminder not only of the complexity of the spirits but also of how diverse African Diasporic communities have always been. Haitian religion functions as what scholar of history and African American studies Paul Christopher Johnson describes as a space of memory, tying together African nations, religious beliefs about the divine, the universe, morality, and community and transmitting them across space and time.[49] Vodou traditions pay homage to various West and Central African religious communities. Enslaved Africans in Haiti had to engage in dialogues with people from many religions and ethnic groups, creating an eclectic African Diasporic religious system. In Vodou, the spirits are categorized according to their ancestry and the beliefs they personify. Depending on the temple or region in Haiti, these categories can fluctuate, and different groupings of spirits are prioritized. The dominant nations of spirits are *Rada, Djouba, Nago, Ibo, Kongo, Petwo,* and *Gede.* To simplify, the nations are commonly arranged into three broad groups: *Rada, Petwo,* and *Gede.* The *Rada* section can consist of the *Rada* and the *Nago* nations. The *Petwo* section can hold *Ibo, Kongo, Petwo,* and sometimes *Gede.* The *Djouba* nation is often defined through traits from both *Rada* and *Petwo.*[50] The language used to describe Vodou also reflects the Diasporic nature of the religion. For instance, the word *Vodou* means "spirit" in Fon, a language from Benin. The *Rada* nation is from the Fon people in Dahomey, which is now Benin; the *Nago* nation is from the Yoruba people in Western Nigeria; the *Petwo* nation is from the Congo- Angola; and the *Ibo* nation is from the Igbo people in Eastern Nigeria.

These broad groups are usually defined both by their African origins and the personalities of the spirits they house. The dominant factor differentiating *Rada* spirits from *Petwo* spirits, for instance, is their temperament. Divine dispositions within Vodou pantheons are derived from color designations rooted in Fon and Yoruba traditions.[51] For example, the serpent spirit Danbala, who is tied to the *Rada* nation, is known for wisdom and benevolence and is associated with the colors white and green. These colors connote a cool, calm nature. Ezili Dantò, the *Petwo* warrior goddess, in contrast, wears red and blue to signify her fierce and fiery disposition.

The colors and categories of spirits are just two examples of Vodou's Diasporic foundations. Diaspora, as a framework, demands an understanding of the "claims and practices [of people] rather than [a simple understanding of] biological determination or territory."[52] Pairing the term "religious" with the term "Diaspora" (i.e., religious Diaspora) emphasizes communal ritual practices and beliefs that exist through the intergenerational, transnational transmission of sacred traditions. The movement of people, objects, and ideas across the Atlantic Ocean is an important frame for understanding the religious and cultural continuities and adaptations in African Diasporic communities. Accordingly, the Black Atlantic is a useful transnational concept for thinking about religion, migration, commerce, and material exchanges. Scholar of religion J. Lorand Matory makes use of this frame, in conjunction with historical ethnography, to demonstrate that people of the African Diaspora created transnational "imagined communities," redefining their homelands through individual and collective ingenuity.[53]

Through Afro-Brazilian religion, or Candomblé, Matory illuminates the continuities or "dialogues" within West and Central African linguistic and ritual transformations. Diasporic "dialogues" are an active religious cultural exchange through which Africa and the African Diaspora inform one another and create eclectic ritual practices that are in constant conversation. This exchange contradicts historically anti-Black sentiments that characterized African Diasporic religions as primitive, unproductive, and unchanging. Africa "has never been stagnant," and the ongoing creative agency and strategic choices of its peoples have shaped their transnational lives in their Atlantic realities.[54] Africa has always been a cosmopolitan place through commerce and migration and is at the forefront of transnational cultural formations. The concept of "Diasporic dialogues" is important to my analysis of Manbo Maude, her temples, and her fashion. Manbo Maude is a transnational religious practitioner, taking her goods, services, and culture with her when she travels between the United States and Haiti as she exchanges ideas and religious traditions with her communities. She works with practitioners from multiple countries and is inspired by gods with origins in West and Central Africa and Haiti, all of which shape her sartorial creativity and design. These cultural, social, and material exchanges inform the way she creates and understands religious fashion.

Fashion Trends through the Seasons:
Creating Black Sacred Spaces

In Mattapan, Manbo Maude is employed full-time as a mental health clinician Monday through Friday. Yet practicing Vodou is a 24/7 occupation.

When she is not at work, Manbo Maude is constantly on the phone with other practitioners or giving spiritual readings. Her weekends are filled with labor-intensive spiritual work for clients. She barely rests. Sometimes her professional and spiritual worlds overlap. She incorporates critical listening into her spiritual readings when applicable and uses the language of her faith to connect with patients as a clinician. Her skills as a mental health professional have proven as valuable to the gods as her talent as a fashion designer.

In Mattapan, she holds ceremonies during the months of November, March, and May—each of which aligns with a particular spirit: November is for Gede, the spirit of life, death, and sexuality; March is for Danbala, the serpent spirit of wisdom; and May is for Kouzen Azaka, the spirit of agriculture and the market; or for Ezili Dantò, the protectress mother-warrior spirit; or for both. She also holds spiritual marriages in Mattapan. Her ceremonies in Jacmel take place during the month of July into early August and are much larger than those in Mattapan; in Haiti, she conducts initiations, ceremonies, the feeding of the spirits, and spiritual marriages. The chapters in *Vodou en Vogue* do not flow through these seasons chronologically; instead, they incorporate stories from different time periods that are organized into themes illuminating issues and ideas within Manbo Maude's temples and within Vodou in general.

Manbo Maude resides in Mattapan, a suburb outside Boston, and practices her religion in the temple in her basement for most of the year. The basement is often a neglected space in American homes, relegated to storage, but for practitioners of this often-stigmatized religion, the basement is reappropriated into a sacred space.[55] In Mattapan, Manbo Maude's neighbors are predominantly Black: American, Jamaican, Haitian, or Afro-Latinx. Her block reflects Mattapan in general, which has a large population of Black immigrants.[56] The demographics of the neighborhood and of nearby Boston, which has the third largest Haitian population in the United States, contribute to making Manbo Maude feel comfortable when performing ceremonies. Haitians have been immigrating to Boston and its surrounding areas since the 1950s, beginning with those seeking refuge from the violently repressive regimes of President Francois Duvalier and his son Jean-Claude Duvalier. This first wave of immigration largely comprised elite Haitians from urban spaces. After 1980, middle-class and poorer Haitians from both rural and urban areas began arriving. Political and economic crises, as well as natural disasters such as hurricanes and earthquakes, continue to drive much of the movement from Haiti to the United States. The number of Haitians in the Boston area also increased because of secondary migration from other population hubs like New York and Miami, with many attracted to the region's universities and colleges.[57]

This population growth has created burgeoning and thriving African Diasporic religious communities, not only as a result of Haitian practitioners finding one another in the United States but also because their presence gives Black Americans of other national and ethnic backgrounds the opportunity to explore their potential connection to Vodou. Manbo Maude's neighborhood, coupled with the ceremonies themselves, becomes what critical race theorist Robin D. G. Kelley calls an "alternative" cultural space, where shared religious and cultural knowledge of Vodou creates a potential refuge from the racism and sexism of the world beyond her home.[58] With friendly neighbors and a significant number of Haitians in the area, her religious activities are not viewed as strange or dangerous but as offering a potential sanctuary for her devotees.

In Jacmel, Manbo Maude has more space and is not confined to the converted space of a basement. She owns a house and several apartments that she had constructed on her property, with enough room to accommodate some local workers and visitors attracted by her religious practices. Her Vodou temple, where she conducts her ceremonies, is a separate building five feet away from her home. She pays Haitian ritual workers, both initiated and non-initiated, to aid in initiation rites and religious services in extravagant ceremonies that honor the gods. Having more resources in Jacmel allows Manbo Maude to conduct bigger, more elaborate, and lengthier religious rituals.

Throughout this book, in both locations, I deliberately center the opinions and experiences of members of the African Diaspora to explore the complexities, contradictions, and creativity of Black identities and communities: Haitians, Haitian Americans or *Dyaspora*, Black Americans, and Black people with roots in other Caribbean nations. I examine how participants envision and make use of Vodou, how they imagine the religion's relationship to their own heritage, and how fashion helps them orient themselves in an African Diasporic religious space. For example, head wraps and ritual clothing in Manbo Maude's homes in Mattapan and Jacmel operate as intraracial practices that reinforce ideas of Black sisterhood and identity, which are negotiated through interactions with White practitioners within Manbo Maude's temple. The bedrooms in Manbo Maude's homes also emphasize the informal social interaction between Black women. Her temples become sites of religious innovation reflecting the relationship between gender, sexuality, and race in religious ritual, material aesthetics, and spiritual embodiment. Fashion connects practitioners and initiates within Manbo Maude's homes, yet race, gender, and sexuality threaten the unity she tries to create with her religious garments.

Ethnography on the Runway: Making Knowledge as an Insider/Outsider

My interest in understanding the particularities of materiality in Manbo Maude's temples began in the summer of 2015 over a meal in her kitchen in Mattapan. Manbo Maude was born in Jacmel and raised in Port-au-Prince in a poor working-class family. She will not tell me how old she is, but through context clues and her friends, it is clear that she is middle-aged. She has three children and has lived in the United States for more than thirty years, arriving as a young adult in the 1980s to pursue a college education. She comes from a long line of Vodou practitioners through her maternal lineage and is invested in passing on that legacy to her spiritual and biological children. Transmitting her knowledge to successive generations requires her to continuously organize ceremonies in which practitioners can learn, be initiated, and cultivate community. Traveling to Haiti, where she conducts many ceremonies, is also crucial, so Manbo Maude saves up her sick days and vacation days from her job to be able to take the necessary time off. Living in the United States gives her the opportunity to take a wide selection of textiles to Haiti to be used in her religious practices.

In 2015, I was paying for a room in Manbo Maude's home while I studied Haitian Kreyòl at the University of Massachusetts, Boston.[59] I first learned about her during my master's program at Harvard Divinity School from other scholars who had attended her ceremonies. She speaks publicly about Vodou throughout Boston and is a familiar figure to religious studies, psychology, anthropology, political science, and history students and educators. Her prominence is also a product of her fluency with the English language and her education. She has several graduate degrees and is therefore capable of explaining Vodou and its traditions in a manner that is comprehensible to academics. After a colleague introduced us in spring 2012, I kept in touch with her both because I wanted to practice my language skills with her and because of her obvious expertise about Vodou as a Manbo. Eventually, she encouraged me to visit her temple in Jacmel and participate in the ceremony she was going to conduct in the summertime, "where it really goes down."[60] The ceremony I witnessed three years later in Haiti convinced me that her temples were unique. Without traveling to Jacmel, I could not have fully understood the nature of her faith or the intricacies of her temples.[61] Jacmel, a three-hour drive south from the Haitian capital Port-au-Prince, is a city that lacks the population density of the much larger capital but nevertheless supports a thriving artistic community; it is one of the oldest cities in the Caribbean.[62] It is also the site of thriving Vodou communities.

Researching the temples in Mattapan and Jacmel involved both participant observation in her homes and temples and ethnographic and historical research on Haitian Vodou. I conducted formal and informal interviews with more than sixty Vodou practitioners and attendees at her ceremonies, some of which were conducted using Haitian translators, including Manbo Maude's daughter Vante'm Pa Fyem.[63] As a participant observer, I interacted with members of her communities and aided in ritual and nonritual services. I wrapped headscarves, braided and washed hair, washed clothes, applied makeup, and helped people dress, all while engaging in conversations in both English and Haitian Kreyòl. Most of the people in Manbo Maude's Mattapan temple are working class, middle class, and upper middle class; in Jacmel, most are poor and working class.

During the public ceremonies, I did not try to hide the fact that I was a researcher: I carried around a huge notebook and camera. Initially, I seemed to make people feel uncomfortable, and some came up to ask me what I was writing about. My notetaking and photography became less obtrusive when I began using my cellphone. I blended in because many practitioners and audience members have their cellphones out to record the ceremony, call their friends, or text others to figure out where the next party or Vodou scene would be. I recorded and surreptitiously took notes on my phone instead of solely relying on my memory, adapting my ethnographic strategies to better fit Manbo Maude's community.

The participant observations and interviews that made this book possible occurred through trial and error. Early on I worried about the language barrier, particularly between Haitian practitioners in Jacmel and myself, because my Haitian Kreyòl was still a work in progress. Our social and cultural expectations, especially in relation to gender and sexuality, also differed. At the start of my research, my approach was extremely blunt. I asked practitioners direct questions about their sexual and gender identities and how these identities affected their relationship with Vodou. Often my questions were met with eye rolls or blank stares, or people simply walked away from me. In Mattapan, many practitioners were open to speaking about potentially sensitive topics, but the same questions were nonstarters in Jacmel. I learned quickly that in Haiti, sex and sexuality were taboo subjects reserved for private settings and were completely inappropriate for religious spaces. The issues were not forbidden, yet they required a level of tact I was not displaying. This was made clear to me in 2015 during an afternoon ceremony honoring the spirit Ezili Dantò. Dantò possessed Manbo Maude and three other Haitian women, delivering messages to practitioners and the audience. She admired the rings Haitian men wore to represent their commitment to her and offered advice. I expected similar treatment.

In the past, Dantò had shown me favor. Not. This. Time. She glared at me and pulled out her dagger, aiming it at my chest.[64] The dagger represents Dantò's status as a warrior during the Haitian Revolution and is a symbol of her protectiveness of her followers, though in that moment it seemed more like a threat. Three things went through my mind: (1) *Fuck!*, (2) the dagger was real, and it hurt when she pressed the sharpened point against my skin, dispelling my suspicions that some ritual items used during ceremonies were fake, and (3) I had messed up. She lingered for several long seconds, staring at me, and then ran the dagger across my lips in the shape of a cross. "*Pa pale*," she said, Haitian Kreyòl for "don't speak." The demand made me anxious about my work, and I sought clarification from other practitioners and scholars, who told me I needed to be careful about the way I spoke to members of Manbo Maude's temple and to consider how to tailor my ethnographic strategies to suit the specific communities I engaged.[65] The message *be careful* helped me fundamentally reshape my approach to studying Manbo Maude's temples. I did not need to ask such frank questions when the issues that concerned me — race, gender, and sexuality — permeated every aspect of the religious rituals I witnessed. This research required me to be flexible and creative.

Vodou en Vogue takes seriously the use of Black feminist ethnography in religion and therefore privileges belief.[66] In Manbo Maude's temples and African Diasporic religions generally, the divine is not a metaphorical presence.[67] When practitioners say the spirits speak to them, I take them at their word. A number of scholars have become initiates in the religions they study, some from a genuine belief and others to gain access to secrets. Zora Neale Hurston, Katherine Dunham, Karen McCarthy Brown, and Elizabeth McAlister are some of the scholars who have been initiated in Haitian Vodou. In religions like Vodou, secrecy is part of the faith. As a non-initiate, the border between outsider and insider is a boundary to interrogate and respect.

I vehemently reject the idea that to meaningfully study African and African Diasporic religions I have to become initiated in the faith. To become initiated purely for the sake of my work would be disingenuous and disrespectful to the communities I engage with. When presenting my research, I am often asked whether I am initiated in Haitian Vodou. This question comes from anthropologists and religion scholars, including those who study African and African Diasporic religions. I want to complicate the impulse to ask and answer this question. I rarely hear this inquiry directed at scholars of other religions. No questions are asked about whether a scholar is a born-again Christian or has converted to Islam or Judaism or Hinduism. Why should initiation in Vodou be any more necessary for scholars than baptism in Christianity and Catholicism? Why is initiation judged as required for the study of African Diasporic religions? I believe it is because of the connection between magic, Blackness, the occult, and Vodou in the public imagination. Vodou is "othered" and cloaked in mystery because of its perceived differentness from other faith traditions.

To avoid the potentially voyeuristic connotations of becoming initiated solely for the pursuit of sacred knowledge, let me state clearly that I am not an initiate in Manbo Maude's temples or in any other temple in Haitian Vodou. Unquestionably, this restricted the information that Manbo Maude and other initiates were willing to share with me. The strength of my conclusions does not rely on spilling secrets but on the length of time spent as a participant observer. The more time I spent with Manbo Maude and her community, the more ceremonies I visited over the course of numerous years, the more intellectual and theoretical clarity I gained. I had to become comfortable with not knowing and recognizing that my work relied on the valuable insights gained through public performances of Vodou ceremonies and conversations with practitioners. The relationship between religious rituals and community identity is the most salient in public-facing ceremonies, as are the ethics of care on display: fixing head wraps, handing people water when they come out of possession, setting up altar displays, providing food for the spirits, and feeding the audience/community after the ceremony has ended.

Though I am not initiated, my race, my cisgender queer-femme identity, my relative youth, my Nigerian Igbo heritage, and my gradual familiarity with the people in Manbo Maude's temples occasionally afforded me access typically denied to other non-initiated individuals. For example, I was allowed to touch Manbo Maude's head to tie head wraps, tie *moushwa* on possessed initiates, and salute spirits during ceremonies. My identity and the cultural capital that came with it shaped my ethnography by affecting how the community responded to me, as well as my own interpretations of experiences in the field.[68] I was rarely allowed to sit idle in her temples. The labor I performed and observed others undertaking led me to analyze gendered religious labor through categories established by historian of religion

Judith Casselberry: emotional, intimate, and aesthetic. These categories are useful in exploring the religious and economic work that is required to maintain Manbo Maude's temples and her spiritual community. Considering what I call *negotiatory labor*, the ritual work required by the deities and by practitioners in her temple, illustrates that Manbo Maude's spiritual efficacy is demonstrated through her ability to delegate responsibilities and resources.

Although I was put to work, there was plenty of time for socializing, drinking, and laughing. After all, Vodou ceremonies are a *fete*, Haitian Kreyòl for "feast." Celebrating was expected. Gradually, Manbo Maude and her practitioners became more comfortable with me. When they started including me in their jokes, I garnered the moniker *se gwo Blan nwa* or *se gwo Afrikenn*, which in Haitian Kreyòl means the "big Black foreigner" or the "big African," distinguishing me from the other Black American visitors in her temple. I immediately understood that the nicknames were usually used affectionately, although I periodically scolded people for their unnecessary rudeness. Growing up in a Nigerian American household where my size was frequently referenced equipped me to understand that such comments were not meant as insults but as harsh, factual identifiers. By socializing with Manbo Maude and the other participants in her temples, I employed reflexive "up-close ethnography" during ceremonies, in Manbo Maude's kitchen, and while doing makeup and changing into ritual clothes with participants, exploring how Vodou is engrained into their everyday lives.[69] Accordingly, this book is a part of a queer Black feminist ethnographic tradition that privileges the knowledge produced by all Black women.

Up-close ethnography brought me nearer to demonstrating what the gods want from practitioners and ceremonies. Manbo Maude and the people and lwa she has built her temples with have shown me that material adornment is crucial in discerning the needs and desires of the divine. This answer is clear to me yet interpreting the spirits largely through the material demands they place on devotees is not a uniformly accepted perspective. Years ago, Houngan Max Beauvoir told me I placed too much emphasis on the human interpretation of the divine. He was highly respected, and his opinion was important. He told me that the gods existed on a plane that was beyond us; therefore, their wants were in many ways impossible for me or anyone else to determine. I still take his words seriously. And yet the interactions that Vodou practitioners and I had with the gods were often mediated through other people. The spiritual cannot be divorced from the human, at least not on earth. I cannot truly know the inner workings of the divine, but I believe practitioners when they tell me the gods speak to them and that the performance rituals of a ceremony have the capacity to reveal some sliver of the deities' intentions.

The fashion on display in Manbo Maude's temples tells the story of an adaptable faith wedded more to the needs and experiences of practitioners than to any orthodox interpretation of rituals. The divinities, too, are dynamic entities that defy simple conclusions about how they inspire dedication in practitioners. The following chapters showcase why Black creativity in religious fashion matters. Manbo Maude is a trendsetter, affecting the sartorial choices of other Vodou homes beyond Boston and Jacmel. Her influence has spread further through her online presence and the in-person impact of her fashion, galvanizing spectators to carry ideas from her ceremonies into their own rituals elsewhere. The future of African and African Diasporic religions is built by Black practitioners and Black audiences who continually define their faith through their lived experiences, using adornment to articulate their creative personal connections to Black spirits.

CHAPTER ONE

Ad(dress)ing the Spirits
Color and Cloth to Show off as Lwa

When I arranged to see Manbo Maude in Mattapan in January 2018, I did not know the Boston area would then be experiencing an exceptionally harsh cold spell. Eighteen inches of snow fell two days before I was to fly there, and it was questionable whether my plane in Philadelphia would ever make it off the ground. Manbo Maude and I discussed the difficult travel conditions over Facebook, and she assured me that she would be willing to go fabric shopping with me another time if this trip were not possible. My flight was delayed for more than two hours, but I was able to travel to Boston and have the outing we had planned. It was bitterly cold from my very first steps outside Logan Airport. My jacket, warm enough for Philadelphia winters, was no defense against the Boston wind chill.

The taxi dropped me in front of Manbo Maude's house that I had visited numerous times, although it was nearly unrecognizable with the snow piled high in her front yard. Hers was a three-story house built sometime before World War II, with an attic that had been converted into a bedroom and a basement she used as her ceremonial space. The railing next to the stairs leading to her porch was wobbly from use and rust, and wind chimes rang out along the front entrance. The red paint was peeling from the paneled, wooden exterior of the home, revealing the ruddy brown color underneath. For many people in North America, Europe, and the Caribbean, this place was their Vodou home. Practitioners and clients visited almost every day for readings and spiritual work. I rang the doorbell, and even before the door opened, I could smell the food being prepared in her kitchen. I thought it was *diri ak pwa*, a Haitian dish of rice and beans. When the door opened, my expectations were confirmed, and Manbo Maude ushered me out of the cold. She was smiling and had a broom in her hand, which she used to clear her floor of the detritus brought in on the bottom of people's shoes. Manbo Maude was about five feet, six inches tall, with brown skin and shoulder-length pressed hair she had pinned up and covered with a head wrap. She was thin but not skinny. Although she was middle-aged, her face did not carry all those years, and she appeared a decade younger. When she was not

Manbo Maude at Sewfisticated shopping for fabric in Cambridge, Massachusetts, March 2018 (photo by Eziaku Nwokocha).

performing a ceremony, her glasses were perpetually perched on the brim of her nose, and she peered at people over the top of the frames.

"Welcome, Eziaku," she said, "Are you hungry?"

That question was frequently posed to guests entering Caribbean and African households, and it warmed me to hear it, not only because I was hungry but also because of its familiarity. I dropped my belongings in her daughter's room and returned downstairs to eat and talk with Manbo Maude. We started planning our next day, when I would accompany her as she shopped for fabric for the religious dress she was producing for a Vodou ceremony in honor of the serpent spirit Danbala in March. The *fete* was three months away and would fall on St. Patrick's Day, the holiday celebrating the Catholic saint that was a counterpart to Danbala.

The fabric store opened the next morning at 10 A.M. But Manbo Maude told me, "I'm not trying to get there that early." I then suggested, "We can leave by noon."

Manbo Maude seemed uncommitted to the timeline and looked away, rather than agreeing with me: it would happen when it happened. We ended up leaving her home to go to the store at 2:30 P.M. the following afternoon after a Black American neighbor helped us dig her car out of the snow. We drove twenty minutes to Sewfisticated: Discount Designer Fabrics in Cambridge. The owners of the store traveled widely in search of the fabrics they sold, which could come from anywhere in the world. Manbo Maude said the store in Cambridge had better fabric choices than other locations and she had a good relationship with its staff. "I feel like a queen," she said, and when we entered the store, I understood what she meant.[1] The staff greeted her by name in a chorus of friendly hellos and warm smiles. One staff member immediately went to the back of the store and returned with sixteen reams of fabric, which included pink and blue denim with white lace and stitched flowers. Manbo Maude had already given a down payment on this fabric to be used to serve Azaka or Kouzen Zaka, the Haitian *lwa* of agriculture, in the summertime, and was going to ship it to Haiti soon. She shipped fabric and other materials to Haiti throughout the year in preparation for her ceremonies.

Manbo Maude frequented the store with enough regularity that she was able to pay for her materials in installments, and the owners had full confidence that she would honor this payment arrangement. When we arrived, one of the owners was attending to another client but came to greet Manbo Maude as soon as she was finished. She asked after her mother; Manbo Maude replied that her mother was doing better after having suffered a stroke. The owner seemed interested in her answer: they appeared to have developed a friendly rapport during Manbo Maude's countless visits to her store during the past fifteen years. Because of this long-term business relationship, the store owner often kept Manbo Maude's preferences in mind when she traveled in search of new materials to sell in her store.

Manbo Maude spent the rest of our time at Sewfisticated browsing through their selection of fabrics, not only for the Danbala ceremony she was anticipating but also for anything that struck her as suitable for the many spirits she served and for the ceremonies she would be performing throughout the year. The store was meticulously organized by color and texture, with sections dedicated to trims and to styles, such as African cotton prints, lace, and sequins. The walls were lined with shelves packed with fabrics of every color and pattern, ranging from light shades to dark hues.

The spirits often ask for lace, cotton, and denim, which symbolize aspects of Haitian agriculture, nature, luxury, West and Central African ancestry, and colonial history. Manbo Maude's choices are dictated both by functionality and glamour. Cotton is breathable and affordable, lace is glamorous, and denim represents peasant culture and agriculture.[2] Manbo Maude wanted green and white fabrics for Danbala and yellow for Papa Loko, a Haitian lwa who presides over initiation rites and gives ritual powers to Manbos and Houngans, because she sometimes celebrated them simultaneously. White is a color that pleases all the spirits in the Vodou pantheon.

The colors Manbo Maude used to identify the spirits are widely understood designations in Vodou and stem from traditions in Yoruba, Dahomean, and Kongo cultures. In Yoruba tradition, there are three color-coded groupings: *funfun*—white, silver, and gray—signifies coolness, age, peace, reconciliation, and wisdom; the *pupa* group, which includes warm or hot colors such as red, orange, deep yellow, and pink, is understood to connote heat, passion, and aggression; and the *dudu* group, which connects the cool and hot, includes darker colors like black, blue, purple, and green.[3] The *Kongo* spirits are often depicted through ritual items like dolls that incorporate a rainbow of color.[4] When I asked Manbo Maude how she decided on the fabrics for the spirits, she said, "I'm open. I'm listening to them."

She stopped by an island of cloth labeled "designer fabrics" and ran her hand over a red, lace textile. She pressed her forehead against it and stood there pensively. It seemed that she might be praying, but perhaps she was only carefully thinking about the prospect of buying it. Eventually, she moved on from the fabric. She was not satisfied. We went to the section of the store that had many green and yellow materials. I asked her whether she had found anything of interest for the fete dedicated to Danbala and Loko and how she would know what was appropriate when she saw it. "If I come and I see fabric just for Loko I'm like, okay, you're talking to me," she answered. "Or, if I'm really seeing all white that I like, I'm like, okay, let's do it." Manbo Maude did not find the fabric she wanted for Danbala and Loko, but she found material that might suffice for the spirit Ezili Freda and she also paid for the fabric she had selected for Azaka. The owner assured her that she would be traveling soon to find more fabric for the store and that she would keep in mind Manbo Maude's preferences. My experience shopping with Manbo Maude revealed how her access to a plentiful fabric store, where she can look through materials from around the country and even the world, contributes to her ability to innovate in her production of religious dress.

At the start of her tenure as a Vodou priestess decades ago, fashion was an integral part of her ritual practices, and over time, she discovered that the production of fashion presented a unique opportunity to elevate her religious ceremonies. Growing up in poor, working-class households in Jacmel and Port-au-Prince, Manbo Maude learned early on that her physical presentation affected how she was received by others. Her older sister made her dresses and skirts for school, ensuring she was neat and proper. Manbo Maude believed that her appearing presentable gained her more favorable treatment from her teachers, which helped her maintain a good standing in school. Education was one of the few opportunities she had to improve her chances in life, and she was determined not to squander it. Her belief in education carried her into college, where she earned a bachelor's degree in economics from the Institut des Hautes Etudes Commerciales et Economiques in Haiti, a fashion degree at the Academie de Haute Couture et de Beaux Arts Verona also in Haiti, and a master's degree in counseling psychology at Lesley University in Boston. The skills she gained in school, particularly in relation to fashion and money management, directly contribute to her effectiveness as a Manbo and inform her connections to the spirits.[5]

Manbo Maude's childhood concern with appearing presentable and her subsequent education in fashion have blossomed into methods to distinguish herself and her Vodou homes, suggest her relative wealth, and showcase the spirits. She does not make a significant profit from her creation of religious dress. Rather, she uses fashion to construct a signature style for her Vodou ceremonies. Living in the United States gives her the opportunity to ship a wide selection of textiles to Haiti for her ceremonies. She gains inspiration not only from the spirits, her communities, and her own creative thinking as a fashion designer but also from the resources available to her. Manbo Maude's work with the store owner and the seamstresses she hires in Haiti and Mattapan creates an informal, small-scale production network that intersects culture, transnationalism, and religion.

These religious and sartorial innovations bear distinctions born of her personal influence, but this capacity for change and adaptation is not unique to her temples and ceremonies. Manbo Maude represents a point on a spectrum of evolution that runs through Vodou stylistics; she is one in the long line of contributors to Black Atlantic religions and Haitian Vodou in particular.[6] The aesthetics of rituals in Vodou are constantly being reworked and remade, drawing from an endless array of cultural and religious inspirations and dynamically shifting to suit the needs of diverse communities throughout the African Diaspora. Manbo Maude's creative, religious perspective is continuously growing through her interaction with the spirits and her religious communities. Her connection to the divine is an integral part of her everyday life. Deities are a tangible presence in Manbo Maude's homes and communities that make their presence known through dreams, fashion, ritual, and possession. The aesthetics of religious fashion provide a way for practitioners to co-construct religious experiences while responding to and interacting with spirits. Clothing is collectively imagined, with the spirits asking for specific colors and materials that practitioners then fashion for themselves.

The ritual purposes of the clothing used in Manbo Maude's ceremonies and in Vodou in general, as well as the complex communal process of creating and giving meaning to this fashion, is articulated through *spiritual vogue*. In Manbo Maude's temples, spiritual vogue operates as a multisensorial experience that incorporates the presence of the spirits, movement, and touch within the context of her ceremonies and her fashion. The ceremonies I observed in Mattapan and Jacmel depend on the interactive process of looking between the practitioners, the spirits, and the audience. Considering spiritual vogue requires understanding that the presence of the spirits in Vodou ceremonies is not symbolic but real for many participants and devotees and that the legitimacy of these spirits has substantive effects on their actions and ritual practice. Spiritual messages received in dreams and the effortful preparations for rituals develop into public-facing Vodou ceremonies where the aggregated work of practitioners coalesces into a religious event for the broader community. Without the waiting eyes of the audience, Manbo Maude and her temple would be unable to fully comprehend the success of their garments and to judge the worthiness of their exaltation of the spirits. Spiritual vogue captures the layers of communication that animate these ceremonies and give meaning to the religious fashion on display in service of the spirits.

Visit from the Goddess: A Vodou Designer Emerges

In the early 1990s in Mattapan, Manbo Maude was not yet a Vodou initiate. She was referred to as a *Manbo Makoute*, a person who visits temples, communicates with the spirits, and performs some religious rituals and ceremonies without being officially initiated. Even though she was uninitiated, the title *Manbo* was given to her because of her spiritual power and the training she received from her grandmother. She has been communicating with the spirits since she was three years old. In the 1990s, she did not have a temple of her own and so attended ceremonies in the local Haitian community she was familiar with through her friends and family. While we were discussing her clothing's connection to the lwa after shopping at Sewfisticated in 2018, she described her formative years as a Manbo Makoute. She used to wear outfits she defined as "simple": plain clothes in basic white lacking any personal touch or flare, which she purchased from stores anyone might frequent. Often, she wore pleated white skirts with a collared, buttoned-down shirt; they lacked the voluminous amounts of fabric she incorporated later into flowy designs. "You could dress a little kid with it," she told me.

The initial inspiration for wearing white in her ceremonies came from her spiritual mother and what she witnessed in Haitian ceremonies in Jacmel. She explained, "After I did my initiation, my spiritual mother, I saw her at her *peristil* (a Vodou temple); I saw people wearing white. You know, when I do *kanzo* (a type of Vodou initiation ritual) in Haiti, people are wearing white. So, my spiritual mother [and] her people were wearing white. I thought it was the most beautiful thing in the world. So, when I was doing my thing, not thinking that I kept that in my mind, I was thinking, you know, people should be coming to a fete in white." Her spiritual mother required the practitioners who participated in her ceremonies to wear white, which Manbo Maude emulated. The connection between white and spiritual rituals emphasized by Manbo Maude and her mentor stretches back to Yoruba and Fon cultural traditions in Nigeria and Benin, transported through the Atlantic slave trade, where the color connoted wisdom and purity.[7] This tradition and her experiences with her spiritual mother guided Manbo Maude's early forays into religious fashion, but eventually the spirits demanded more from her.

On one occasion, a spirit appeared to Manbo Maude in a dream the day before she was to attend a friend's fete, at which she intended to wear her typical white outfit. Receiving a visit from a deity in her dreams is not an unusual occurrence for Manbo Maude. In Vodou, dreams are realms through which the gods can relay direct or indirect messages to devotees, sometimes through visceral, tactile visions.[8] Dreams, or *nan dòmi*, which is Haitian Kreyòl for "in dream," represent an in-between state: in between the conscious and the unconscious and in between the physical world and the spiritual one. Nan dòmi is a state of lucid dreaming that Vodou initiate and Haitian musician Mimerose P. Beaubrun described as "profoundly asleep and fully conscious."[9] For Beaubrun, nan dòmi is a space where mysteries are revealed and a person is allowed "to see abstract things unknown until then."[10] Her definition emphasizes that what happens in the dream world affects the waking world. It follows that communication between spirits and humans is very common in this space: dreams are a conduit to the spiritual plane.[11] However, they do not remain segregated in the unconscious; it is important for practitioners to interpret spiritual messages for practical use in their everyday lives.[12] For Manbo Maude, dreams affect not only how she negotiates problems in her life and in her communities but also how she designs religious dress. Her dreams are sites of reflection, where the spirits inspire her and where she can envision her own potential as a Manbo and as a religious fashion designer.

The message she received in this particular dream concerned her clothing choices. A dark-skinned, middle-aged woman with "salt and pepper hair" appeared somewhere in the distance, singing a Vodou song. Based on the woman's age, Manbo Maude recognized her as Ezili Je Wouj, who is part of the Ezili family of spirits in the *Petwo* nation. Manbo Maude makes a distinction between the Ezili deities based on age rather than on personality: "Ezili Dantò is young. She is mature and has a child. She's not that old. She's around her twenties and thirties. Je Wouj is a powerful woman with a lot of maturity, and she is in her late forties, going on fifties. For Gran Ezili, she is the wise older woman. She is a very old woman who could be around her mid-sixties to early eighties." Often, Ezili Je Wouj is contrasted with the rest of the Ezili pantheon as the evil or vengeful manifestation of the spirit. Ezili Freda is generally described as a light-brown–skinned woman who embodies love, luxury, and desire; Gran Ezili is an old, stooped woman; and Ezili Dantò is a dark-skinned, independent single mother who raises children, as well as being depicted as a protectress and warrior. Ezili Je Wouj is often a footnote or merely one more name in a list of deities in the scholarship surrounding the Ezili family.[13]

Ezili Freda and Ezili Dantò are frequently the focus, with special attention paid to their contrasting skin tones and the complicated issues involving colorism evoked by that contrast. Scholar of religion and anthropology Karen McCarthy Brown writes, "These female spirits are both mirrors and maps, making the present comprehensible and offering direction for the future. In the caricature like clarity possession-performances, the Ezili sort out, by acting out, the conflicting feelings and values in any given life situation. By interacting with the faithful as individuals and groups, all the Vodou spirits clarify options in people's lives; and the Ezili do this especially well for women."[14] Ezili Freda, then, is not merely a shallow stereotype of female vanity but a "mirror" capable of showing to her followers the characteristics and strengths they may possess in their own hearts and minds. Moreover, there is power in Ezili Freda's shameless, proud embrace of her overtly feminine qualities. They do not simply connote weakness or catty superficiality but are parts of the female experience that practitioners can reflect on and gain wisdom from in their own life experiences.

Another Ezili to consider in relation to Dantò and Freda is Lasirenn, a mermaid lwa. Unlike Dantò and Freda, Lasirenn does not have a fixed skin color: sometimes she has dark skin, and other times she is described as light-skinned, a consequence of living under the water away from the sunlight. The fluidity of Lasirenn's color is a result of the same "mirror" offered by the Ezilis. The water not only refracts and obscures Lasirenn's appearance but also provides a mirror of reflection for the practitioners attempting to catch a glimpse of her visage. If Dantò is dark and Freda is light, Lasirenn is both: a shifting representation of the politics of skin color, changing to fit the needs and assumptions of the practitioners calling on her, challenging or reinforcing their own perceptions of color and femininity. Thus, the Ezili constitute a "map" offering paths of reflection that value femininity while also acknowledging some pitfalls of gender as a constructed idea: vanity, the elevation of light skin over dark, jealousy, the vying for male attention, and female competition.[15] The Ezili are not lwa that can be easily quantified or simplified, and this is where their value lies.

Despite not receiving much attention in the Ezili pantheon, Ezili Je Wouj is a familiar figure in Manbo Maude's life. The deity has been appearing to her since she was six years old, frequently encouraging her to become a Vodou initiate, but her parents and extended family insisted that she was too young. Decades later in the 1990s, Je Wouj returned to make the same demands. In the dream, Manbo Maude listened to the beautiful melody and asked the deity who taught her how to sing. Ezili Je Wouj responded, "You can sing just like me. You can sing like this as well." Singing is a typical feature of Vodou ceremonies, and Je Wouj's insistence that Manbo Maude possessed a voice worthy of this ritual was a suggestion that she take on more responsibility as a practitioner. In the dream, Manbo Maude was carrying a bell in her hand, which is used during ceremonies by practitioners who are non-initiates. She described the encounter: "She was like, [she] looked at me and sized me up and down and she's like, 'You know what, it's about time you put the bell on the side. I want the *ason* [the sacred rattle]. I want to show off, I want to show off! I want people to know who I am. I want you to put the bell away. You know what they are saying about you. . . . They are calling you *Manbo TiKolet* because of the way you dress.'" I asked her what the phrase meant, knowing the term *kolet* could be translated as "no money." Manbo Maude called on her daughter Vante'm Pa Fyem to help with the translation. She regularly asked her daughter to translate and provide clarification when she speaks in Haitian Kreyòl. Vante'm Pa Fyem answered, "It means little Manbo with no means, or Manbo with little means." Manbo Maude agreed with the interpretation.

While I sat at the table in her kitchen eating *diri ak pwa*, she shared Je Wouj's demands in more detail. She demonstrated the way Je Wouj spoke to her in the dream. "I want to show off," Manbo Maude imitated, sticking her chest out and swaying her hips like Je Wouj. "I want to show off! I want people to know who I am. . . . I want big dresses; I want beautiful dresses." Although she respects the spirits and their wishes, Manbo Maude's immediate response was not to follow the lwa's instructions. At first, she told me, "I smiled. I'm like *hmm*, this lwa has some nerve to talk to me like that." She then contacted her cousin to tell her about the encounter. The cousin confided that what she had been told was true: people in their community had been calling her Manbo TiKolet and said her style was not in fashion. Ultimately, the discussion surrounding her clothing was not only about its specific style but also about class and social status, which were conveyed through her fashion choices. Manbo Maude cared about the opinion of her community and showing proper respect for the spirits, and she needed to answer to both. She could not merely meet the bare minimum for ceremonial fashion; she was required by her community and the spirits to show her status through her clothing and emphasize her religious potency. Vodou spirits are not only concerned with morality and holistic worldviews but also with their own vanity. What a Manbo, initiated or not, wears during a ceremony reflects on the deities they serve. Showing off is an aspect of spiritual vogue, illustrating the urgent need of the spirits, in this case Je Wouj, to be seen by an audience and represented by practitioners through fashion and material culture.

For Je Wouj, it was essential that Manbo Maude understand the importance of presentation and that she adopt a mode of display that emphasized the ritual potency of sartorial expression. Moreover, Manbo Maude could not expect to inspire fellow practitioners or have new initiates follow her to her own temple if her fashion did not connote her ability to provide for herself and for others. A Manbo who represents wealth conveys the message that her religious community will also prosper and that her ceremonies will be materially plentiful enough to please the spirits, feed the community, and properly complete ritual work. Wearing white was a perfectly acceptable and traditional way to honor the spirits, yet for Manbo Maude it did not communicate her own vision of religious fashion. By incorporating bigger, more colorful ensembles into her ceremonies, she crafted a religious fashion that was inspired by her personal connection to the spirits. The need to "show off" as Ezili Je Wouj demanded was a way not only for the spirit to be represented through Manbo Maude's material display but also for Manbo Maude to stand out as a prominent religious figure in her community.

After her dream, Manbo Maude attended the next ceremony in her plain clothes simply because she did not have the time to create a new outfit. However, she told me she "felt embarrassed" by what she was wearing. "I felt like I wasn't representing the culture, and I was putting the culture down." The importance of personal presentation had surfaced again, decades after Manbo Maude first reckoned with it as a schoolgirl in Port-au-Prince. She was no longer responding to the preferences of schoolteachers but answering to the direct demands of spirits. Still uncomfortable but obligated to fulfill her duties as a Manbo Makoute, she took her bell to the ceremony and, at the end of the night, forgot to take it home. A week later, the person who had overseen that ceremony called Manbo Maude and told her she found the bell in her home. I asked her how she could have forgotten her sacred bell. She responded, "Exactly. It's not like me to forget a bell. But I think that Je Wouj made me forget the bell because she didn't want me to have the bell. She wanted an ason."

Manbo Maude understood her seemingly uncharacteristic forgetfulness as a spiritual intervention and confirmation that she was no longer supposed to use the bell but should graduate to an *ason*, the sacred rattle used by initiates instead. Having the ason meant she would have more responsibility and become a full Manbo, a distinguished leader in her community. Manbo Maude described the dream and the messages conveyed by Ezili Je Wouj as very impactful on her practice of Vodou: "Since then, I have been thinking about how to improve my clothes. I would ask the spirits, 'How do you want me to dress?' And they will tell me. I will get inspired by style, and it will come to me by design." Accepting the ason meant accepting the responsibilities of becoming a full Manbo, which included representing herself well in front of the spirits and her community. To answer Je Wouj's call, she needed to elevate her religious fashion. She needed to "show off."

"Look at Me!": Dressing Gede to the Nines

When Manbo Maude began hosting her own ceremonies in the early 1990s, branching out from her spiritual mother's guidance and creating her own Vodou temple, she decided to honor Gede. She was no longer a Manbo Makoute and was establishing herself as a Manbo with her own home and her own traditions. She would hold the ceremony in the basement of her home in Mattapan. The basement is usually an overlooked space in the house, consigned to storage. Yet, for those who practice Vodou, it is turned into a sacred space.[16] Gede was one of the spirits for which Manbo Maude had a special affinity and that provided guidance in her life. The *Gede* nation, composed of many familial lwa, is possibly one of the most-studied spirits in the Vodou

Manbo Maude possessed by Gede in Mattapan, November 1990
(photo by Patrick Sylvain).

pantheon. This is perhaps because Gede reigns over the cemetery, life,
death, and sensuality—universally important elements that affect
people's everyday lives. Gede also occupies the border between life
and death, which makes him especially important in healing rituals.[17]
Moreover, the ceremonies that celebrate Gede can be some of the most
elaborate and expressive—from the religious dress, the vibrant ritual
dances, the pale chalk smeared across the practitioners' faces, to the sexu-

ally suggestive performances of the devotees and the audience.[18] The unconventional decision of some female practitioners, like Manbo Maude, to wear pants during a ceremony bends the norms of gender in Vodou, but when honoring Gede, flouting these kinds of norms is allowed.

The *Gede* nation was "born in Haiti."[19] *Gede* perfectly illustrates spiritual innovation in the African Diaspora, because *Gede* is conjured from various spirits (including West African and Indigenous Caribbean) that speak to the unique lived realities of the New World.[20] In particular, this nation expresses the history of colonization. The *Gede* deities emerged in response to the harsh, unforgiving labor required on Haitian sugar plantations, the horrific number of enslaved Africans who joined the land of the dead as a result, and the ancestors who were lost in the Middle Passage.[21] Members of the Vodou tradition who embody *Gede* wear religious and ritual materials that often include a black top hat, sunglasses, pipes and cigars, and a black suit and tie.[22] Additionally, they may cover their faces with white chalk to signify that they are from the land of the dead, not the living. The white chalk can also evoke the image of a skull.[23] Sometimes one lens of Gede's sunglasses is removed, leaving one eye visible and the other shaded. The absent lens represents his natural sight into the land of the dead, whereas the intact lens offers him a view into the land of the living.[24] The stylistic signifiers used to suggest the image of Gede draw from Haiti's colonial past: wearing a suit and tie mocks the type of aristocratic respectability associated with French colonial powers as practitioners dance sexually and use profanity.[25] Gede's appearance is not only mimicry but also an interpretation of fraught images connected to colonization and all they have meant in Haitian history and society: it reinvents the style into the form of a deity who negotiates the roles of life, death, and sex in practitioners' lived realities, with all the complexities, contradictions, and ambivalences inherent to such broad and complicated experiences.[26] Gede, like all lwa, has many incarnations, including Bawon Samedi, a guardian of the cemetery; Gran Brijit, an old woman, keeper of the cemetery, and Gede's partner; and Gede Nimbo, a male spirit who is often honored by queer people and who appears as an effeminate dandy.[27]

A few weeks before the first fete in Mattapan began, Gede appeared to Manbo Maude nan dòmi. He looked sharp, wearing a tailored black suit with a white buttoned-down shirt and a wide purple tie. He told her, "This is me, Gede. This is how I want to be dressed." Gede modeled for her. Stretching out his arms into a T-shape, he slowly rotated clockwise so that Manbo Maude could capture every detail of his garments. His visit was corrective. By this time, in response to her earlier encounters with Je Wouj and the spirit's insistence that wearing all white was too simplistic, she usually wore African fabrics featuring shades of purple and black that would not have been considered improper for many Vodou ceremonies in Haiti or the Haitian Diaspora. But in this case, Gede did not approve.

A few days later, with her reverie still in mind, she went to the Men's Warehouse store in East Cambridge, Massachusetts, and told the tailor she wanted to be sized for a custom suit. In confusion, he told her he made suits for men. They went back and forth on the subject, playfully arguing, until finally she said, "Today, I am a man; size me up." Still a bit incredulous, he asked her if she wanted to rent a suit, and she again said she wanted to buy one. He told her it was expensive, but she did not care. Gede demanded a suit, so she was going to buy him a suit. As they discussed the fitting of the clothes, the tailor was intrigued that Manbo Maude wanted to wear a tailored suit. Content to keep her mysteries, she smiled and laughed mischievously, saying, "You don't know. You really don't want to know."

Gede's appearance in her dream, modeling his outfit for her, was essentially a dynamic invitation for Manbo Maude to use her skills and capacity for innovation to interpret the vision in the real world. In this dream, the gods spoke to her in a way that was legible in the context of her experiences and her talents. Manbo Maude had been educated in fashion design, and so this was the avenue through which Gede spoke to her about devotion and worship. Gede pushed her religious fashion even further than did Je Wouj by demanding a specific suit, an outfit designed to please him in every detail. Like Je Wouj, Gede's spiritual message had real consequences for Manbo Maude's life and altered the way she glorified the spirits in her ceremonies, enabling her to begin distinguishing herself from other practitioners through her religious dress and adornment.

After the instructive dream and the costly visit to the tailor, Manbo Maude was ready to honor Gede. At the beginning of the ceremony, she wore a white dress to honor all the spirits. Then, it was time to summon Gede. During a lull in the service while the drummers, singers, and dancers rested, she disappeared into her bedroom to change and put on her ritual outfit. Changing clothes in the middle of a fete is unusual. Typically, Manbos and Houngans start and end their ceremonies in the same outfit, wearing clothes in the colors that honor specific spirits. Gede, for example, is honored through the colors white, black, and purple. Manbo Maude was attempting to shift this tradition to align with her own sensibilities.

In her bedroom, Manbo Maude buttoned up her tailored, black dinner jacket and slipped on her pleated black pants. A male friend helped fix her purple tie. She stuck a pipe in her mouth and placed a pair of black sunglasses on the ridge of her nose. She emerged from her room transformed. As she recalls it, when she walked down the stairs into the basement, her carefully, professionally crafted suit won her audible appreciation among the other participants in exclamatory *oh ooh*'s and *eh eh*'s. The ceremony began anew, and Manbo Maude was mounted by Gede. An initiate's body / head is a vessel that lwa can "mount" or "ride." While mounted, the spirit's personality and speech are animated through the initiate.[28] This ceremony allowed Manbo Maude to transgress gender boundaries, at least within the walls of her own basement, where the clothes that she was wearing signal to her audience that the spirit Gede is inhabiting her body. The lived experiences of Manbo Maude and those in her home shape the performance. By donning men's clothes and embodying a male spirit, she performs a version of masculine power that is legible to her audience: a virile, authoritative masculinity dressed up in the trappings of an aristocratic past. During the ceremony, Gede is handed a wooden stick, a traditional ritual object offered to those mounted by the spirit. The stick, too, is a sign of Gede's masculine persona. It is a phallic symbol that he invites practitioners and audience members, male and female, to kiss, often holding it erect at his waistline during his confident, nearly braggadocious performance of maleness. "My dick is bigger than yours," he tells male practitioners and audience members in the basement, before claiming they are incapable of matching his sexual prowess. Often Gede's interactions with men walk the line between flirtatious and dominating. Playfully, he asks women if they are sexually satisfied and invites them to sleep with him instead, blowing them kisses and winking.

Gede's potentially dominating overtures toward men during ceremonies indicate the queerness of the spirit, yet that queerness is not centered; it is not the aspect of his persona that is emphasized in Manbo Maude's ceremonies. The focus is trained on his masculinity and his predilection for sexual contact, particularly with women. Frequently, there is an outward embrace of cisgender heterosexual constructions of gender and sexuality that is simultaneously contradicted by the spirits and the practicalities of performing religious rituals. This duality is inherent to Manbo Maude's ceremonies: it is a feature, not a bug, and it expresses the possibilities of gender fluidity present in Vodou practices.

Gede's delighted embrace of sexuality is an undeniable display of male desires. The spirit manifests in multiple genders, like his female counterpart Gran Brijit, but only the male versions are so explicitly sexual. No female deity in the Vodou pantheon expresses sexual desire so emphatically or bluntly in a ceremony. There are female spirits who are coy, mysterious, vengeful, or wise, but not one proudly proclaims her sexual desires. Gede remains the primary sexual outlet for both men and women practitioners and audience members during ceremonies.

The ceremonial absence of female spirits with explicit sexual desire reflects the lived experiences of practitioners and is tied to the history of gender, sexuality, and race in Haiti. During the centuries of enslavement in Hispaniola, enslaved Black women were subject to routine sexual abuse from White enslavers and others with the power to dominate them. To justify this commonplace brutality, Black women were constructed as hypersexual temptresses and prostitutes who were always available for sexual conquest. The end of enslavement did not destroy that construction. In reaction to this history of sexual trauma, Black institutions in independent Haiti—churches, schools, and political organizations—recoiled from openly discussing Black female sexual desire. This response was protective, but it was also reactionary and controlling, curtailing women's autonomy over their own bodies and desires. To combat the construction of Black women as hypersexual, their sexual desires were ignored entirely, characterized by reductive binaries that placed whores on one side and good, chaste Christian women on the other: there was no room for the actual desires of real women.[29] Gede's appearances during ceremonies are influenced by this history, as are those of the rest of the Vodou pantheon. The vivid remnants of enslavement manifest in the freedom of Gede and in the relative restrictions on the Ezilis, for example, who despite their power and importance rarely flaunt their sexual desires in the same way Gede does. Lived religion is always at the mercy of the experiences and histories of the people who bring it to life.

Gede's over-the-top performance is playful and sometimes satirical. He is celebrating sexuality and inviting practitioners to contemplate its role in their own lives while, at the same time, offering the potential for critique, particularly when channeled through a female body. In that basement ceremony, Gede is speaking, and yet it is still Manbo Maude's female body channeling that power; it is her mouth telling men they are sexually inferior, her hands wrapped around the phallic stick. The performance is at once amusing and mocking, reinforcing the virility of men while also showcasing the absurdity of masculinity in excess. It is not Gede alone who tells men of their shortcomings but his female mouthpiece as well. Gede does not require a female host to mock men, yet his boisterous performance seems particularly critical when enacted through Manbo Maude's body. An understanding of "identity as malleable and mutable" illuminates the dynamics of performative possession rituals that occur during ceremonies.[30] The identities of practitioners are mutable, capable of being overtaken or changed by the gods and by the accompanying clothing and adornment. By shifting their own consciousness to accommodate the gods, practitioners also create the potential for challenging the power dynamics that dictate their lives outside the ceremony. Women especially are given an authority that they might not enjoy if not possessed by the spirits.

Manbo Maude, as Gede, gave messages, danced, and blew smoke from her pipe and cigarettes; these actions were documented by several female and male practitioners and observers present at the ceremony who later showed her photos of the event. There are different stages in *pran lwa* with varying degrees of recall. Often, people who experience possession rely on others to inform them of their actions during the ceremonies or spiritual readings. In this instance, Manbo Maude was fully possessed and had no recollection of what she said or did while mounted by Gede. She was dependent on the stories others told her and the photos they showed her for knowledge of her actions during this length of time. Moreover, the fact that she had not suffered any injuries being mounted told her that Gede was happy and satisfied by her and the ceremony.[31] Thus, pran lwa is an intra- and interpersonal process in which the intensely personal experience of possession becomes a community experience. The witnesses at the ceremony are the only people who can explain to the previously possessed what the spirits did during the time they spent mounted. The retelling of the ceremonial possession is a visual and oral experience made possible by stories and photos and videos. The recollections of her community were what confirmed for Manbo Maude that Gede was pleased by her outfit. "He would go around and talk," she explained, "Like, he would go to [practitioners and observers] and say, 'Look at my outfit.'" She pulled on her shirt and extended her arms, "Look at how I am handsome. Look at my outfit. I am not just anyone; I am a general. I am Gede. Look at me!"

Gede's satisfaction with Manbo Maude's stylistic choices was gratifying because of the effort she expended in producing the outfit; more than that, it was confirmation that she had prepared properly for his arrival at the ceremony. In Vodou ceremonies, fashion becomes another invitation to the spirits, along with altars, songs, drumming, and food. "If they can be comfortable, they can be happy," Manbo Maude said when I asked her about Gede's manifestation at her ceremony. She continued, "You have to have the outfit for the spirit. The color associated with that spirit and then a style that they are comfortable with. And you have other items like the liquor, or if they take like a machete or a knife, or whatever they want on the altar. If you have all that ready for them, you are serving the spirits. So, they know, 'Oh I have my clothes right there and this is my dollar, this is my perfume, I have everything, I feel comfortable. I am needed there.'" Manbo Maude wore Gede's ritual outfit to please her audience and to invite the presence of the deity. Clothing in Vodou ceremonies is not exclusively about fashion but is a functional aspect of religious ritual meant to attract the presence of the gods by pleasing them. Her body was prepared not only spiritually but also sartorially for the experience of pran lwa. The material culture of Gede's ceremony welcomed the spirits into a space where they knew they were appreciated and needed, thereby preserving the relationship between the spirits and practitioners. The use of symbolic material items signifies the ongoing exchange between religious communities and the spirits they honor.

As the fete continued in her basement in Mattapan, Gede also possessed several other female and male practitioners. When these Gedes caught sight of the possessed Manbo Maude in her new suit, they were overjoyed. They pulled on her clothes admiringly, brushing away imaginary dust to show how clean and classy she looked. Her fashion was thus validated by the gods. Encouraged by the twin approvals of Gede and her community, Manbo Maude continued to create new clothing for different rituals. She was developing the format for the ceremonies she would perform well into the future, changing into specific outfits during events in a flair of deliberately planned pageantry. Practitioners who were initiated under her tutelage and remained a part of her temple joined in her fashionable innovations. Her reputation as a Manbo grew. I asked her how she felt after establishing a model for the use of clothing in her ceremonies. She said, "I'm happy . . . comfortable. I feel confident going into the ceremony. I am not worried about what people are going to say about me." Manbo TiKolet was no more.

Understood through the context of Manbo Maude's dream and subsequent display in honor of Gede, spiritual vogue reveals how the spiritual becomes tactile during religious rituals. Manbo Maude's purposeful stride is intended to serve herself, the audience, and the spirits. As she walks down into her basement in Mattapan in the outfit inspired by Gede's message, the stairs become a site with added spiritual validity: they are transmuted into a runway where she models spiritually blessed religious dress, highlighting the religious fashion that represents her spiritual home. The runway is constituted by the moment of the reveal, the initial walk down the stairs in religious dress that emphasizes the clothes she is wearing. When she saunters back into the ceremony, posing in her suit, Manbo Maude attracts the attention of the audience, thereby showcasing the divine, herself, and her home simultaneously. Other moments in the ceremony may focus on different ritual elements, such as prayer or spirit possession, but while Manbo Maude is descending the staircase and entering the basement, there is little else for the audience to do but watch her. In his analysis of Ballroom culture, scholar of gender and sexuality Marlon M. Bailey emphasizes the connection between fashion and communal recognition.[32] In the basement, animated by Vodou culture, this nexus is evident in Manbo Maude's walk down the stairs, where her outfit and behavior articulate her community's religious expectations. It is a moment deliberately built around recognition. She draws attention to herself not only to highlight her own fashionable presentation but also to reinforce practitioners' and audience members' belief in the spirit she is meant to embody. See the outfit, and through her body, see the god.

Moreover, her presence signals the end to the break in the ceremony. In most Vodou ceremonies, the drumming and singing of the worshippers dictate the starts and stops in the event. By leaving the room to change her clothes and then walking down her staircase in religious dress, Manbo Maude changes this rhythm and recenters the role of fashion. Her presentation of spiritual garments begins the ceremony once more. Manbo Maude's movement represents a multilayered experience, wherein she is blessed by the gods and invites the audience to take part in the event, to witness this spectacular display. Her religious exhibition situates her as different from many of her peers, distinguishing her from the other practitioners in the basement through style and procedure: her suit was created through her personal collaboration with Gede, and the break in the ceremony, followed by the walk down the stairs, highlights her role as a religious leader. The display illuminates her devotion to the spirits in a way that captures the historical and social context of the *Gede* nation. The gods, Gede in particular, inspire her fashion as a practitioner, which then affects not only how she speaks to the spirits in her ceremonies but also the audience's involvement and response at these religious events. That her use of religious dress led to the increase in the number of her practitioners and the size of her audience is, for Manbo Maude, proof that the gods were pleased with how she honored them. The connection between the spirits, the practitioners, and the audience dictates the ways spiritual vogue is articulated in a religious space.

In the years since she descended the staircase in her basement, Manbo Maude has developed an online presence. Googling "Haitian Vodou" brings up her photo instantaneously. Her spiritual children contribute to this online presence by sharing photos and videos through social media on Facebook,

Manbo Maude possessed by Gede in Mattapan, November 2021
(photo by Eziaku Nwokocha).

Instagram, and YouTube. She no longer relies solely on word of mouth to find new practitioners and clients. Yet her expanded online presence brings both negative and positive attention. Some online commenters praise her for hosting "beautiful" and "authentic" ceremonies, whereas others lambast her for "excessive" and "lavish" material displays.[33] Often, religiously conservative Haitians leave comments under her videos condemning her to hell for practicing Vodou. Conversely, she also receives messages from Haitians telling her she has revealed a beauty in Vodou that had been unknown to them. Others watch her videos to learn more about the faith. Manbo Maude is aware of this and views herself as a public figure representing her religion and Haiti to a broad audience. Tens of thousands of people view her videos; some have as much as a hundred thousand views. "It is not just that I am serving my spirits," Manbo Maude told me. "I am extending the benefits to the public." The online attention garnered by her ceremonies, in large part because of her unique fashion, affords her the opportunity to expand her religious home and educate others about Vodou.

Manbo Maude's use of fashion in her religious and social life in both Jacmel and Mattapan reflects practices followed in the African Diaspora for centuries. The combination of fashion and exhibition in the creation and expression of identity and community has been explored by many scholars in relation to fashion shows, parades, drag balls, and strolling in the context of Black America.[34] Historians, for example, describe strolling as a prominent tradition in the early twentieth century, especially in Harlem and Chicago. Many Black residents of those areas left their homes in their best clothes and walked the streets of their neighborhoods, interacting with their neighbors, friends, and complete strangers as they went. The point of this stroll was to be seen. Strolling celebrated Black style and identity in public, allowing Black people to announce their status, their fashion sense, and their creativity to their communities.[35]

The necessity of being seen, and the use of fashion to connote social and cultural identity to a larger community, is exemplified by the history of strolling, demonstrating how collective exhibition is not unique to Haitian religion or to any single community in the African Diaspora.[36] Scholar of religion Monica Miller investigated an earlier facet of African Diasporic identity creation in the mid-nineteenth century in the United States. Throughout southern and northern regions of the country, Africans and American-born Black people threw extravagant parades showcasing their eclectic fashion shaped by African and European influences; in these parades, they formulated community and identity in a society ruled by a system of enslavement.[37] Through such flamboyant public events, they forged new community ties in the United States and wore the transnational nature of their identities on their bodies by mixing style influences and designs.

These parades announced the presence of Black American communities and asserted their dynamic, evolving sense of shared identity to a broader society that denied everything about their humanity. Like strolling and the church fashion shows in Chicago and New York, these parades reflected the enduring link between fashion, identity, and community within the African Diaspora in the United States, as well as the continuing role of seeing and being seen. When Manbo Maude saunters down the steps of her basement in Mattapan wearing the tailor-made suit she purchased for the occasion, she and the other attendees at the ceremony are conjuring elements of a tradition that has a long history in African Diasporic communities. Her ceremonies present another avenue through which to explore the performance of Black style and identity.

Manbo Maude's use of fashion in religious spaces echoes these African Diasporic cultural formations because her elaborate displays showcase her relative wealth and distinguish her from other Vodou practitioners by emphasizing her religious potency. As is true in Manbo Maude's ceremonies, the sartorial presentations in strolling and parades were concerned with more than distinguishing social and economic difference: instead, they bound together participants and onlookers as partners in identity creation and community formation.[38] I link Manbo Maude's use of fashion to the traditions of Black Americans because of her location in Mattapan, where she lives among, worships with, and is influenced by Black Americans. She travels back and forth between Haiti and the United States, and the use of fashion in the ceremonies she performs resonates with the histories of both places. The ceremonies Manbo Maude and her fellow practitioners perform are a continuation of these African Diasporic traditions, reimagining and reinforcing community by drawing on the past and on diverse cultural influences to craft religious identities that express their contemporary realities.

"I Nailed It!": Fashioning the Sights, Smells, and Sounds of Spiritual Community

Manbo Maude's commitment to religious fashion is not a preoccupation she can satisfy alone. She used to design her own dresses, but after she became so busy with her spiritual work and her full-time job as a mental health clinician, she decided to employ a Salvadorian seamstress, her "secret weapon," to help her produce the clothing. This seamstress lives in Mattapan, only a ten-minute drive from Manbo Maude's home, and they have been working together for more than fifteen years. They often communicate through texts, with Manbo Maude sending the seamstress images of her sketches of dresses; at other times she drives to her house to describe in person the dress style she wants created. She has never told her Salvadorian seamstress that she is making the dresses for Vodou ceremonies. I asked her why, after working with the same person for more than fifteen years, she would still keep the purpose of the clothes a secret. Why keep a secret from her own *secret weapon?* She answered, "Not everyone has to be in my business. I give her a job to make my clothes. She tells me she can do it, and that's it. I keep it separate." Manbo Maude is careful about whom she allows into her religious space, wary of those who do not fully understand Vodou. She is selective about sharing information with people outside her community, divulging only what is necessary for the work to be achieved. Her inclination toward secrecy is consistently part of her production of religious fashion. It is partly motivated by protectiveness: she believes many people are frightened by the idea of Vodou; keeping her religion relatively private is a strategy to avoid negative reactions to her religious work.

This proclivity toward religious privacy does not extend to Haiti. Manbo Maude has two seamstresses in Haiti who make her clothes, and they are fully aware of the intended use of the garments.[39] Moreover, they openly display Vodou dresses in their homes to showcase their work and to point to as examples for other clients. In preparation for a ceremony in Jacmel, Manbo Maude invited me to meet one of the seamstresses so I could commission a dress that would allow me to participate in a fete honoring Dantò. Because I was a student, the seamstress said the cost of the dress would be $50, though I did not know whether this price was indeed lower than usual. At the time, I was too nervous to ask her for the specifics of her pricing, so I was uncertain whether the cost enabled her to still make a profit or would require her to take money from her own ritual funds.

In July 2015, in Jacmel in Manbo Maude's dining room, two Haitian women, along with Vante'm Pa Fyem who filled the role of translator, took my measurements for my dress. Despite the sweltering heat of the Haitian summer, I knew from observing other women and attending other ceremonies that it was not appropriate to request a sleeveless dress. I had seen many women with lacy, voluminous sleeves, but I could not imagine tolerating the extra fabric in hot weather. I compromised and asked for short sleeves with elastic at the ends, so that they would stay in place well above my elbow. I chose a V-neckline because I judged it to be more flattering for my full figure.

Bailey's insights continue to resonate with my experiences in Manbo Maude's homes. He describes the competitive categories showcased in Ballroom as celebrating and defining specific visions of gender, sex, and sexuality. In Manbo Maude's home, there is only one category, and it is that of a dutiful, sexually modest worshipper. Any of my suggestions for altering my garment would have been rejected because such changes would negate its purpose; I would no longer be defining, for myself and for the community, the correct idea of a Vodou practitioner in the temple. Because I was not an initiate, I was not obligated to display the more elaborate decorations and designs in my dress and so opted for a simple style that prioritized comfort. For this ceremony, the designated colors chosen by Manbo Maude were crimson red, emerald green, and royal blue. I decided to use all three colors in my dress.

Later that day, I hopped on the back of a motorcycle and rode to another section of Jacmel to undergo a second fitting, this time by the seamstress. The seamstress, whom I call Astride, lived in a concrete one-story house with light-blue walls and a peach-colored door. Initiates in Manbo Maude's home frequented her business. A gutter ran along the street in front of the home with free-flowing sewage. A slab of wood lay over the gutter, leading to her door. There was no sign designating her home as a business, but there were clear signals: clothing was piled outside her door, decorated her walls, and was nailed into the concrete walls or dangled from hangers. The house was small; it would only take a few steps to walk the length of the front room, which was crowded with fabric. Her sewing machine was the first thing to greet me as I walked through the door. She sized me again for my dress to confirm the correct measurements. I was cautious about speaking. I was worried that the sound of my American accent would inspire her to raise the price of my dress. My wariness stemmed from the time spent with my extended family in Abia State, Nigeria, where my cousins warned me not to speak while we were shopping in the markets because my obvious foreignness would incentivize the sellers to state a price higher than what they demanded from those native to Nigeria. It might have been obvious from the moment I stepped into her home that I was not a Haitian: my body size and my demeanor were probably telling. Even if she assumed I was a part of the Haitian *Dyaspora*—Haitian Kreyòl slang used to describe Haitian Americans born in the United States or Haitians who have immigrated to the

United States—it was clear I was not a native. I received my measurements and took the motorcycle ride back to Manbo Maude's home.

The next day, Manbo Maude said that I needed to pay Astride twenty dollars more for the dress than originally agreed on. Because the dress was a larger size, Astride had to use more fabric for its production. I was suspicious and irritated. I felt that Astride raised the price because she knew I was a foreigner and could bilk more money out of me. I shared my frustrations with Manbo Maude. We had already agreed on the price, and my budget did not cover more money for the dress. I was not asking for the complicated designs and embellishments that other women were demanding, which I thought required more labor and therefore justified a higher price. Manbo Maude was sympathetic. "You know, I think you're right," she said, "I see why you're frustrated. I'm going to talk to her and see what I can do. Don't worry, I will use my own money to pay for it. You know this, Eziaku, some people feel money grows on trees for Americans."[40] We negotiated, and I gave Manbo Maude ten dollars extra for Astride instead of the full twenty. I had seen and participated in enough haggling in Haiti and Nigeria to understand that I did not have to pay the full price she demanded. The deal was accepted, and I gladly received the dress before the start of the ceremony.

The following day, hundreds of people gathered at Manbo Maude's temple, which was built adjacent to her house, for the ceremony in honor of Ezili Dantò. For the first four hours, the participants celebrated *Rada* spirits such as Legba, Danbala, and Ezili Freda by drumming and singing Vodou songs dedicated to them. It is traditional in Vodou ceremonies to honor the *Rada* spirits, the "cool" spirits whose origins reach back to Benin, before transitioning into serving the *Nago* nation, personified by the spirit Ogou, and then the *Petwo/Kongo* spirits, such as Ezili Dantò.[41]

Though I was not a Vodou practitioner or a member of Manbo Maude's home, she allowed me to participate in the ceremonial event. The practitioners changing into their ritual clothes were mostly members of her temple. She also included Manbos and Houngans from nearby temples who aided in ritual work and donned the spiritual clothes designed for Manbo Maude's ceremony. Because they helped Manbo Maude with her spiritual and ceremonial services, she provided their clothes free of cost. Including them helped cultivate the idea of a broader Vodou collective, and the additional bodies added a sense of grandeur to the proceedings.

During the planned lull in the ceremony, while observers drank alcohol and socialized, I went with Manbo Maude and a group of practitioners to change into our ritual outfits in the dining room, kitchen, and several bedrooms of her home. This break had become a standard feature in her ceremonies ever since she established the practice two decades prior when serving Gede in her basement in Mattapan. It had become her signature. In Jacmel, the runway is not contained to a basement but is the path around her property and into her temple. The duration and route of the runway shift depending on the ceremony.

Men changed their clothes in the kitchen, and women took over the bedrooms and the dining room. Women who had to take off their underwear changed in the bedrooms; other practitioners kept their undergarments on and swiftly slipped into their new outfits in the dining room. Manbo Maude's dining room, kitchen, and bedrooms were thus transformed into changing rooms. They smelled like perfume and hair grease, and devotees took photos of themselves while helping each other put the final touches on their outfits. They looked good, and they were proud of it. After every dress was zipped up, every scarf tied, and every shirt buttoned, we marched down the stairs into Manbo Maude's yard, singing songs and holding candles in our hands, careful of the melting wax sliding toward our unprotected fingers. Manbo Maude led the procession down her pious runway. It was dark outside. Most of the light was from the candles we held and from a lone, bright streetlight that towered over the event. People poured out of the nearby temple to take pictures and gawk at those who dressed up for the ritual. As we walked by, some people shouted *bel rad*, which is Haitian Kreyòl for beautiful garments. Members of her home were wearing the elaborate, carefully constructed blue, red, and green clothes that were prepared for the ceremony to honor Ezili Dantò. The fabric of the women's cotton skirts swished around audibly as we moved; some women kicked the hems of their skirts away from their feet, and others waved the material back and forth to cool themselves. Though not dressed as elaborately, the men were also adorned for the occasion and doused with overpowering amounts of cologne. They wore collared shirts with blue pants, all made from the same fabrics as the women's dresses. The men also had cut intricate patterns into their fresh fades with small razors. The shirt colors and patterns varied from person to person, with differing combinations of red, blue, and green. The faces of the practitioners were solemn. They were focused on the ritual.

Manbo Maude and other Manbos in her inner circle wore lace, which was considered more elegant and luxurious. The distinctions in fabric differentiated participants based on status, which was determined not only by their religious positions but also by their social proximity to Manbo Maude. Three other Manbos, who were her confidantes in either Mattapan, Jacmel, or both locations wore lace, as did her daughter. Typically, Manbo Maude separated herself from others in the ceremony through fashion to emphasize her role as a Manbo and as a leader in her religious community. Her blouse was blue silk, with red lace sewn over it to provide a vivid contrast of color. Her sleeves featured trims of green and red lace that accentuated them with flair. She is especially fond of using trim to add detail to her outfits, layering the colors to make the dresses even more extravagant and to incorporate movement into her garments: this trim provides the finishing touches that distinguish her designs.

Her skirt was the reverse of her blouse: red silk with blue lace on top. When she reached down to grab her skirt and pull it outward, the fabric was plentiful enough to stretch the full length of her arm span. The large amount of fabric was a literal signifier of wealth: Manbo Maude had the funds to pay for lots of fabric, which she incorporated into her dresses. She tied a green lace sash around her waist; her head wrap was made of the same fabric. She adorned herself with a gold necklace and gold rings, which represented her commitment to Vodou spirits. An embellished red bra strap peeked out from under her collar and curved around to her back to reveal a lace pattern. Her daughter had encouraged her to add this detail, a U.S.-inspired innovation in her layered lace aesthetic. When I asked her what aspect of her ritual outfits made her feel the most satisfied, she replied, "When I put this dress on, and I look in the mirror and I see myself as being beautiful, and this dress, I can't see it anywhere, it's just my creation, and you know this dress suits me. That's when I say, 'You know what, I nailed it.'"[42] Glorifying the spirits through fashion was important, but so was her own comfort and gratification.

Some people in the procession made the walk through the yard barefoot over the rocks and dirt; some held onto each other for balance. After watching other practitioners start the trek without shoes, I imagined braving the rocks on my bare feet to enhance my perceived holiness; I abandoned the idea because I could not bear the pain of the rocks. We cupped our hands around the small flames of the candles to protect them and keep them lit. The wind carried the scent of burning candle wax, dirt, and manure from nearby farms. Roosters crowed, and the attentive silence of the marchers was periodically punctured by the participants' quiet chatter. The procession passed the temple and walked past a large field to a massive sacred Mapou tree[43] covered in vines with exposed, timeworn roots that plunged deep into the earth.[44] The tree trunk had been wrapped in red and blue cloth.[45] The remnants of past spiritual work—melted wax, gourds, small clay pots, and herbs—littered the ground near the trunk to be used again and to serve as a reminder of previous rituals. The long line of practitioners looped around the tree and passed the temple again, making our way along the field. We paused to give a prayer at the crossroads between the cluster of buildings on Manbo Maude's property, paying respect to Legba, guardian of the crossroads. Finally, marching through the crowd of onlookers who parted at our approach, we entered the temple, still singing. Inside the temple, we circled the *potomitan,* or sacred center pole, and set the candles down at its base, ready for the ceremony to begin again.

The path I walked with Manbo Maude and her practitioners in Jacmel was long, ritualistically rich, and visually compelling. In Manbo Maude's ceremonies, illuminated through spiritual vogue specifically, the spirits and the people who serve them co-create a religious space through fashion and adornment, engaging in a spectacular display of African Diasporic religious traditions. By drawing from symbolic resources—extra fabric to accentuate the arms and length of the dress, pleated pants, elaborate head wraps, makeup, and sashes that are tied across the neck or diagonally across the chest—practitioners in Manbo Maude's temple use cultural practices and traditions from Haiti and the United States, all of which have material symbolism.[46] Manbo Maude's ceremony in Jacmel illustrates the multisensorial experience of religious ritual and is instructive in exploring the act of looking and being seen in relationship to Vodou ceremonies and through spiritual vogue. The ritualistic walk that Manbo Maude and her practitioners took was immersed in the senses: the touch of other participants, the smell of the land and the candles, the sound of the singing, and the sight of the religious garments.

Throughout this walk, onlookers witnessed the devotees' demonstration of faith. Their presence as spectators was not incidental to the ritual but rather an integral part of it. The audience members' physical proximity and their act of witnessing the event reinforced the practitioners' own beliefs and sense of community, affecting their actions and sartorial displays in the procession. The visual spectacle—the long procession of worshippers with candles and elaborate outfits—shaped the way Vodou was experienced and viewed by the audience, and the practitioners were aware of this fact. The participants were engaged in a reciprocal relationship with their audience of seeing and being seen. Therefore, the ceremony in Jacmel, as well as those in Mattapan, was a multisensorial experience that affected the practitioners, the audience, and the spirits. The devotees knew they were being watched by the onlookers and the gods and collectively understood that their purpose was to create a religious moment that relied on fashion for the expression of reverence and belief.

The anticipation of being watched by a crowd of onlookers inspired the careful preparation in Manbo Maude's home before the start of the ritual. Wearing makeup, grooming facial hair, pressing the wrinkles out of garments, and donning lavish outfits were critical elements in the creation of this religious production. By joining the procession, the practitioners created the sense of a larger religious community and a larger religious commitment. The walk was made sacred because the gods were present, and the participants were engaging in ritual for the purpose of serving them. This trifecta—the participants, the audience, and the spirits—depend on one another; without any one element, the other two would be rendered incomplete. Manbo Maude was not initially aware of this confluence of influences, but once she realized the impact her fashion had on the audience and her fellow practitioners, she capitalized on this element of her ceremonies. Perhaps this was the reason the spirits had been persistently and consistently pushing her toward ritual fashion, not only to satisfy their own vanity but also to facilitate Manbo Maude's creation of a religious community. The spirits' desire to show off channeled Manbo Maude's skills and life experience into her unique ceremonial adornment practices. By listening to the spirits in her dreams, she not only gained insight into pleasing them but also found new traditions that showed off her own religious authority and increased the visibility of her temples at the same time. Increased exposure brings with it more worshippers, grander ceremonies, and ultimately a broader collection of spiritual and economic responsibilities that Manbo Maude would need to negotiate to maintain the growing collective around her.

CHAPTER TWO

Kouzen's *Makout*

Labor and Money in the Economy of Vodou

Practicing Vodou is intimately tied to economics—the financial capacities of individuals, of temples, and of whole communities. Indeed, that observation could be made about all world religions throughout the entirety of their histories.[1] Examining the exchange of goods and money in religious communities is revelatory both of what is required to maintain religious practice and of the values and beliefs that animate faith traditions. Every purchased ritual object, ceremonial meal, or spiritual garment provides insights into the broader cosmologies they are meant to serve.[2] In her efforts to build a religious community in Jacmel, Manbo Maude must concern herself not only with maintaining the financial viability of her practice but also visibly portraying that economic stability. Building up her property—adding apartments, updating the infrastructure of her temple, fencing off the property—is an investment that helps sustain the long-term sustainability of her religious community. To continue attracting practitioners and initiates, whose presence generates work for locals in Jacmel, requires maintaining her property and offering religious services on an ongoing basis. As always, there are the spirits to consider. Manbo Maude believes there is a common misperception that Vodou spirits are poor but rejects it wholeheartedly. "They are not poor," she said, "They are kings and queens. They are African royalty, and they deserve to be treated as such."[3] Dressing well is integral to her perception of how to honor the *lwa*. All of this, to state the obvious, requires money. The survival of her temples depends on it. The work she does in Jacmel is replicated in Mattapan, but there are fewer people and less ritual resources at her command in the United States. I focus this chapter on Jacmel because, of her two temples, the labor relations there are more intricate, and the scale of those relations is much larger.

Over time, Manbo Maude has learned how to negotiate the economics of her spiritual work with members of her community and the spirits. In Haiti, practitioners pay for dresses and services not only with money but also through doing manual and ritual labor in her home and temple in Jacmel; in contrast, practitioners pay for their dresses solely with money in Mattapan.

Kouzen negotiating with a Vodou initiate while possessing Manbo Vante'm Pa Fyem, Jacmel, July 2018 (photo by Eziaku Nwokocha).

Yet both temples are sites of religious innovation that reflect the dynamic relationship between gender and sexuality in relation to religious ritual labor, material aesthetics, and spiritual embodiment. I assess the work that occurs in her temples via a practice I describe as *negotiatory labor*: the negotiations around money and resources that are necessary for the performance of ritual work and serving the spirits. This term is used in the field of economics to describe a contract between employees and employers, but it has unexplored potential in religious studies.[4] My definition of this concept draws inspiration from the work of Judith Casselberry, a scholar of religion and feminist studies. Manbo Maude engages in work that connects her to Casselberry's descriptive analysis of Black women's "labor of faith." Although I explore both men and women in her temples,[5] Black women are at the forefront of religious self-fashioning: I make plain the centrality of Black female authority figures to the work of fashioning the spirit.[6] Yet, serving all genders is crucially important for Manbo Maude to be able to demonstrate and solidify her spiritual efficacy; these gender roles, although evident, can be flexible.

A common refrain among Vodou practitioners is *yo sèvi lwa*, or "I serve the spirits."[7] The sentiment not only connotes belief in the divine but also suggests that faith requires action. Serving the spirits takes intention. It takes work. The ceremonies Manbo Maude and her communities throw are the results of ongoing labor by her and a collection of other practitioners and workers in the United States and Haiti. She maintains her spiritual homes through endless effort, attempting to balance the faith labor necessary for the lwa, her practitioners, and her own financial stability. Through fashion and her negotiation of spiritual labor and payment, Manbo Maude is able to "produce, navigate, claim, and sustain spiritual authority."[8]

Manbo Maude is the primary authority figure in her temples, and Black women's labor is essential to maintaining the religious polity. Casselberry defines the labor of faith by distinguishing three categories—aesthetic labor, emotional labor, and intimate labor[9]—which are useful in the analysis of the religious and economic work occurring in Manbo Maude's temples; more broadly, they are helpful in investigating labor and economic negotiations in African Diasporic religious communities. In Manbo Maude's temples, *aesthetic labor* defines the importance of self-presentation and the connection between personal presentation and the values of the laborer's religious institution.[10] It describes Manbo Maude's presentation of herself and the members of her temple through fashion and how fashion articulates the religious values important to her community, thereby reinforcing her religious efficacy. Self-presentation and community are conflated: her personal presentation as a Manbo affects the reputation of her religious communities, and the reputation of those communities then influences how she is perceived as a Manbo. *Emotional labor* refers to interpersonal relationships, both public and private, that are defined by the face-to-face effort exerted in negotiating social and religious spaces.[11] This concept helps explain how Manbo Maude speaks with initiates, observers, lwa, and other practitioners to mediate problems in the community and resolve tensions between members of her temples, herself, and the spirits. The community connections that Manbo Maude emphasizes through fashion cannot be maintained solely through the quality of the garments. Undergirding the highly visual ceremonies is an endless amount of emotional labor undertaken by Manbo Maude and other practitioners in her temples.

The final category of Casselberry's taxonomy of labor, *intimate labor*, describes the embodied personal interactions defined by the act of caring.[12] It explains the labor done during religious services, when Manbo Maude and her practitioners perform work that is spiritual and physical, tending to other attendees and especially meeting the needs of possessed devotees. Intimate labor also describes the ceremonial care work done for the spirits through the reverence of touch, ritual offerings, and adornment. These categories of labor explore the nuances of the religious work done in Manbo Maude's temples, as they overlap constantly. The operation of emotional labor, intimate labor, and aesthetic labor in Manbo Maude's religious practices in Jacmel and Mattapan illuminates the economic realities of Haitian Vodou. The performance rituals and fashion in Manbo Maude's temples are ultimately a product of all three labors. This work is accomplished by Manbo Maude, the lwa, other practitioners, workers, and even the audience. There is an inextricable link between appearance and power: how practitioners fashion themselves brings them closer to the divine and facilitates communication with the spirits to obtain resources for spiritual work and thrive in their daily life.[13]

By focusing on Manbo Maude's temples, I unearth the earlier mentioned negotiatory labor—another aspect of faith labor within Vodou that is defined by everyday practices of bartering and redistributing funds required to maintain the religious community. The work Manbo Maude does in service of her community and her faith, in part consisting of conversational and material exchanges between practitioners or between practitioners and the spirits, aids in the execution of ritual labor. Negotiatory labor describes the financial negotiations done in direct service of maintaining the temple and religious community and of serving the spirits. This concept illuminates how the spirits facilitate economic exchanges and expands the types of labor performed in service of faith. Negotiatory labor's foundation is the financial, spiritual, personal, and professional negotiations practitioners engage in to facilitate spiritual work. It also describes the necessary labor of providing spiritual guidance in response to the everyday tribulations of individuals and of their faith communities. Negotiatory labor is not exclusive to Manbo Maude's temples but is present in other African Diasporic religions such as Candomblé and Santería.[14]

Without negotiatory and faith labor, public ceremonies like those thrown in Jacmel would cease to exist, and without ceremonies, *spiritual vogue* cannot occur. Labor is foundational to spiritual vogue; gathering materials, corralling crowds of people, constructing garments, and carefully conducting performance rituals all demand work, and all are necessary for the success of a ceremony. The machinations of performance rituals involve aesthetic, intimate, emotional, and negotiatory labor within the space of the *fete* between practitioners, audience members, and the gods.

The economics of Manbo Maude's temples and community extend beyond fashion alone. As the leader of her temples, Manbo Maude is in control of the finances of her religious communities and is meticulously aware of where her money is coming from and what she is spending it on. The practitioners who execute ritual work are paid monetarily for their religious service, and she negotiates compensation for the religious services and rituals she provides to clients. In June 2015, I asked Manbo Maude how much money I would need to bring with me for my first trip to Jacmel the following month. She told me $500 would be sufficient for the week I intended to stay there, and I took her advice. I planned to pay her around $200 for allowing me to stay in her home during my time in Jacmel, leaving me with $300 to spend on the island. From the time I disembarked from the plane, I was dismayed at how quickly my funds dwindled. I had to pay to get into the country; I had to pay to eat; I had to pay the driver to drive me from Port-au-Prince to Jacmel; I had to pay for my ritual dress. By the time I reached Manbo Maude's home, I only had $150 left and could not pay her the money I promised for room and board. Manbo Maude was frustrated, expressing her dismay to me; she explained that the money I had told her I would bring was earmarked to pay for food and the ritual items needed for the upcoming ceremony. Manbo Maude was constantly calculating how much money she had and how she would spend it and so naturally had already budgeted my room-and-board money into her plans. I was very apologetic and also frustrated that following her instructions had resulted in conflict. The next day, I hurriedly went to the nearest Western Union office and asked my partner at the time to send me money. Western Union outlets are easy to find in Jacmel and throughout Latin America and the Caribbean where they enable the flow of billions of dollars from the Diaspora every year.[15] These remittances are an integral source of funds for Manbo Maude's temples. She and other practitioners, Haitian and non-Haitian, continuously send money to members of the temple in Jacmel.

When the money from my partner arrived, I was able to pay Manbo Maude what I owed her. It was the first of several lessons I learned about the economics of Manbo Maude's temples and how carefully she budgeted for the religious services she provided and for the funds she redistributed to Haitians in her community. That same week, I was confronted by another unexpected financial obligation that revealed both the broader economic realities for non-Haitian members of Manbo Maude's religious communities and the emotional labor necessary for navigating the social life of these same communities in Jacmel. One day, in the time between ceremonies, a Black American woman named Shori, an audience member who was close to Manbo Maude's family, and I decided to go to the beach with other members of the community; a few other Americans from Manbo Maude's temple tagged along. Local Haitian vendors set up tables on the beach for people to sit, eat, and drink. We sat down and people began ordering drinks. Our group began to grow, as people arriving on the backs of motorcycles joined us: I had no idea who they were. Based on the playful reception they received from the members of Manbo Maude's home, I assumed they were friends. They ordered refreshments as well. We had fun and spent hours in the water. When the bill arrived, I thought most of the people present would contribute to paying it. However, the only ones reaching for their wallets were the Americans. I assumed the Haitians who had spent the day with us drinking and eating would pay some portion of the bill — smaller than the amount the Americans paid but at least a few *gourdes*. Most of the people on the beach trip were Black, and I had assumed a solidarity that was now deteriorating along the lines of national identity. I thought our shared Blackness and the communal religious space we had been inhabiting would influence everything, including our leisure time. Yet, it became clear that the Americans were expected to pay the full amount, which immediately irritated me.

Paying for that food and drinks was another expense I had not accounted for when planning for the trip, and I had not carried a great deal of cash to the beach. I had to rely on Shori to cover some of my part of the bill. She noticed my annoyance with the situation and told me it was only a small amount of money to feed a large amount of people. "It's appreciation," she explained, "For all the help they've given us: cooking our food, washing our clothes. If we need supplies, they run to the store and get it for us."

"But we pay them for that," I said. None of the tasks she mentioned were done for free.

"You know, Eziaku, this is what you do," she responded, a little exasperated. "We have it; they don't. This is where we can help."[16]

Ultimately, I did not mind paying for community members to enjoy a day at the beach, but the presence of so many strangers was aggravating, especially because I had not budgeted for their attendance. Nor did I appreciate owing Shori money. I felt annoyed for the rest of the day, though I stopped arguing about it. Indeed, I remained annoyed with the arrangement for the remainder of my stay and made sure I was never the only American in any group heading for the beach. By the following year, I had incorporated such expenditures into my budget, despite my reservations. The day at the beach was a learning experience that taught me I needed to account for a host of unexpected costs when traveling to Haiti. I let go of my assumption that, as a Black person, I would not be held to the same generalizations about money and wealth that pertained to White Americans. My specific circumstances were irrelevant: it did not matter that I was a student without a full-time job or that I was sending money to my younger siblings and parents. I came to realize that Shori was right. Even without a salaried job, even as a graduate student, I was an American who had the money. The median income in the United States is higher than most European countries, and just the fact that I had the funds to travel to Haiti was evidence enough of the gap in wealth between myself and the Haitians at the beach.[17] I learned to bring extra funds with me to Haiti. Negotiating the financial obligations of visiting the beach and my minor squabble over money with Manbo Maude were part of the emotional labor necessary for my time at the temple and in Jacmel. My social interactions not only had financial implications but also affected my engagement with the religious community.

Negotiations over money would always be a part of travel to Jacmel, so the next time I visited I calculated my expenses and then added three to four hundred dollars to the total. If I wanted to spend my leisure time with Haitians in the Vodou community, I had to account for the fact that I would be expected to pay for their food and transportation. In any event, I had friends, partners, and family I knew I could call on if I needed money wired to me in an emergency. Manbo Maude factors this disparity between the resources available to Americans and to Haitians into the ritual dress and services she offers in her temple. There is a practical difference between what she can charge Americans and what she can charge Haitians. Haitians alone do not have the money she needs to maintain her temples, but Americans and members of the Haitian *Dyaspora* do.

For some Manbos and Houngans, the ritual work in Vodou is their full-time job.[18] Manbo Maude, however, works full-time as a mental health clinician, because she does not want to rely solely on Vodou for her economic stability. The money she receives from these services fluctuates, and the fees collected from practitioners and others who request ritual work go to pay for the lavish ritual services provided in her temples. Often she has to use her salary to cover the temples' expenses, including initiations, ceremonies, and the workers needed in Jacmel and Mattapan. A community of people also contribute labor to ensure the effective functioning of her temples and the continuing success of her religious practices. To organize and properly compensate this community of aides, Manbo Maude created a system of payments for the tasks required in rituals and services: sewing the dresses, cooking, retrieving purified water, constructing the altars, purchasing ritual objects and animals, obtaining fuel for generators, cleaning, laundering ritual clothes, and assisting in initiation services. She is pulled in so many different directions by her commitments to her religious communities that she entrusts certain individuals, often family members, with buying her supplies in Jacmel in a timely manner. In Mattapan, she delegates tasks to only a few members for major tasks. For example, the cooking is usually done by one Haitian woman, but every initiate helps decorate the altars and the basement.

The money that Manbo Maude saves throughout the year from her salary as a mental health clinician is used not only for ceremonial work but also for stipends that she offers to members of her community in Haiti. These stipends support them as they maintain her temple throughout the year and compensate them for performing the necessary ritual services during the month of July when Manbo Maude resides in Jacmel. The money she gives to members of her temple helps them survive throughout the year, supplementing whatever wages they earn from other work. She also provides money to send at least a dozen children to school. She ships clothing, school supplies, makeup, and over-the-counter medicine to Haiti, thus providing materials not only for ritual work but also for everyday life. When I visited Manbo Maude in June 2016 in Mattapan in the weeks before she left for Haiti, her dining room was piled high with boxes and suitcases filled with supplies she was preparing to ship to Jacmel. Overwhelmed by the volume of material she accrued, she eventually learned to send supplies throughout the year, rather than only in the weeks before her annual July visit.

Her commitment to financially and emotionally supporting her community is another link to the social formations of Ballroom culture. The houses or temples in Vodou often operate similarly to houses in Ballroom culture, with Manbos or Houngans acting in ways that are comparable to house "mothers and fathers."[19] They often provide shelter, food, guidance, and a system of support for people who are both biologically and nonbiologically related to them.[20] Manbo Maude, in addition to regularly shipping supplies to Jacmel, also had a small number of apartments built on her property to house members of her temple. She cultivates a relationship with hotels in Jacmel so that when the number of guests at her ceremonies swells beyond her capacity to shelter them herself, she can ensure that their housing in the city is still affordable. A few local families have given up guardianship of their children to Manbo Maude, entrusting her with that responsibility so their children can go to school or learn a trade while being sheltered and fed. Every year Manbo Maude improves her home and temple: the tarp tent outside her house became a concrete temple in 2014, a generator for the lights of the temple and a gate encircling her property that stood ten feet tall were added in 2017, and additional guest apartments were built in 2018. The gate is not only a physical marker of the borders of her property but also provides protection. As the leader of a Vodou temple, she is always aware that her faith may garner negative attention that may even lead to violence. Sometimes Vodou temples are raided and robbed of their resources; during political or ecological crises, Vodou temples and practitioners can be scapegoated as the source of the pain being suffered by Haiti.[21] Manbo Maude is conscious of the fact that, for her home and temple to operate as a supportive community, it must be safe.

In Jacmel, ceremonies are not spread out over the course of months as they are in Mattapan but are packed into the month of July and the beginning of August. During those few weeks, she honors lwa, performs spiritual marriages, initiates practitioners, and teaches practitioners how to correctly execute rituals. Manbo Maude can rely on many laborers for help in organizing and throwing Vodou ceremonies. For example, her cousin Fabienne operates as her assistant. Fabienne is in charge of the money Manbo Maude saves and then sends through Western Union during the year and assures that all ritual items are purchased and ritual needs met.[22] She makes any nec-

Two Houngans constructing a niche for Bat Gè, a three-day ceremony for
new initiates in Jacmel, July 2018 (photo by Eziaku Nwokocha).

essary trips to Jacmel or Port-au-Prince for supplies. Fabienne's compensation for her assistance is sent via Western Union or delivered by hand once
Manbo Maude arrives in Haiti. Manbo Maude is also able to trust five to seven
cooks to prepare food during her ceremonies. They cook not only for the
gods and the participants but also for the many guests who frequent her
ceremonies.

In preparation for ceremonies, Manbo Maude relies on dozens of Haitian laborers—mostly from Jacmel and Port-au-Prince but even from the
Dominican Republic—for cooking, cleaning, laundering, butchering, driving, and construction. They have regular or sporadic jobs outside Vodou
and work with her seasonally in July and August when she performs rituals
in Jacmel. Some of these workers rely on the money Manbo Maude pays
them before, during, and after her ceremonies for the entirety of the year.
A week or two before the ceremonies in Haiti begin, Fabienne seeks out potential workers for hire, weeding out undesirable recruits. Manbo Maude

often speaks to them over the phone and then again in person when she arrives in Jacmel. She wants to understand their personalities before hiring them, thereby reducing the potential for interpersonal and professional conflict.

Engaging in this emotional labor before the ceremonies begin not only ensures Manbo Maude reliable workers but also aids in the facilitation of intimate labor when the ceremonies and rituals begin. She needs people she can trust to perform the care work that occurs during ceremonies, where practitioners rely on the help of others for successful ritual work and communion with the spirits. Over the decade she has spent growing her temple in Jacmel, Manbo Maude has amassed a community of dependable workers. Through their trusted recommendations, she finds new workers. If they implore her to hire a relative or friend, she is inclined to listen because of the relationships they have built. Employing local people she trusts also reduces the labor Manbo Maude must personally perform at her temples. If there is little conflict, she will not need to intervene: the right people will be capable of resolving any conflicts on their own, engaging in their own forms of emotional labor while working at the temple. The proactive emotional labor that Manbo Maude and Fabienne perform effectively smooths relationships among the personalities and persons who temporarily join their community.

The number of people involved and the ample space on her property in Jacmel increase the types of ritual work she can engage in and the frequency with which she can perform these rituals. In contrast to the basement in Mattapan, her temple—a *djèvo*, which is Haitian Kreyòl for "initiation room"; a literal crossroads on the long dirt road that leads to her house, a grassy field, a Mapou tree, and nearby wildlife—in Jacmel provides generous room for ritual work. She holds ceremonies in the daytime, usually from 11:00 A.M. until two or three in the afternoon, and in the nighttime, when the ceremonies can last on average from 9:00 P.M. until the next morning or early afternoon. The number of available workers directly affects her abilities as a Manbo: more laborers means more and longer ceremonies. Because Manbo Maude interacts with a large number of laborers, her time in Jacmel is defined by constant negotiations to adjust ritual work to suit the needs of individual participants and workers. The length of laborers' employment with Manbo Maude, the working hours, and the price of their compensation are always points of negotiation. She mediates conflict between the people she employs and accommodates guests from multiple countries, which also requires arbitrating cultural and linguistic clashes.

Fé Pris ak Kouzen: Negotiating the Price for Spiritual Labor

Manbo Maude's need to balance her emotional, intimate, and aesthetic labor with her salaried work defines the negotiatory labor she engages in with her faith and the spirits. Every year, Manbo Maude saves the money she makes from spiritual work and full-time employment to fund the summers she spends in Haiti, but she often spends more money than she has. When she returns to Mattapan and to her job as a mental health clinician, the cyclical process of earning to pay off her debts and saving for the next summer in Haiti begins anew. One spirit was especially helpful in her quest to obtain what she owed: Kouzen Zaka or Azaka—the spirit of the market, labor, and agriculture who often appears in ceremonies to speak on money and debt. He is often the spirit called on to mediate financial disputes. The name "Kouzen," which translates to "cousin" or another common moniker Papa Zaka, reflects a link to the idea of family; Manbo Maude, for instance, uses Kouzen and Papa Zaka interchangeably. The origins of the name are mysterious, but according to scholar of religion Leslie Desmangles, it may have been a derivation of the Taino Indian words *zada* or *maza*, which mean corn.[23]

Kouzen is a part of the *Djouba* nation and is commonly defined by a mix of hot and cold temperaments. In Manbo Maude's home, Kouzen is predominantly characterized by his *Rada* traits. His general persona in Vodou suggests ties to the Fon spirit of agriculture called *Yalode*.[24] Kouzen often appears to devotees as an illiterate peasant, wearing a straw hat and blue denim, and sometimes smoking a pipe. He also dons a straw satchel, called a *makout*,[25] slung across his shoulders, in which he keeps Barbancourt rum, sacred herbs, and his money. The presence of money in his bag is not a given, because Kouzen sometimes arrives penniless to ceremonies, reflecting the economic conditions of many of the practitioners attending the fete and warning others of an economic status that is fearfully possible. His appearance and demeanor connote the importance of connection among family, ancestry, and the spirits.[26]

Most Haitians are intimately connected to the land and the labor their ancestors spent farming that land for sustenance and profit—profit for themselves or for the French colonialists who enslaved countless Haitians several generations ago. Kouzen is tied to Haiti's colonial past, where sugar and tobacco plantations defined the largest and most profitable portions of its economy.[27] Kouzen negotiates financial situations. When he materializes in ceremonies, Kouzen is known to negotiate with guests about the prices of the sacred foods on display. He also celebrates the long history of bartering over goods in peasant culture: he is a barterer, another indicator of his connection to Haiti's agrarian roots.[28] Access to food is a symbol of wealth and prosperity, so his preoccupation with bartering is directly aligned with his role as the spirit of the market and his association with money. He evokes the abundance of resources—not only food but also ancestral knowledge that can be derived from the land and agriculture. Serving Kouzen helps practitioners in the labors of life and faith and prepares them for the economic negotiations that inevitably define the contours of their everyday experiences. Negotiatory labor is a necessity inside Manbo Maude's temples, and Kouzen's presence is a reminder that the economic realities of life may always require compromise.

When Manbo Maude was becoming a Manbo in the 1990s, she performed negotiatory labor under the guidance of Kouzen, who helped her demand compensation for her spiritual work. In the early days of her career as a Manbo, she had to figure out through trial and error how to price these services and how to ensure she was paid what she was owed. It took her years and many economic misfortunes to figure out the correct procedures. She used to be flexible with her rates, but because she was taken advantage of in the past, she was no longer as willing to negotiate with most potential clients. She realized that she was using a great deal of her own money to deliver spiritual services, often because people refused to pay despite previous promises to do so. These losses began to negatively affect the lives of her children, as she sacrificed their needs to the requirements of her religious services. Thus, her inability or unwillingness to engage in negotiatory labor jeopardized both her personal and professional financial situation. Therefore, Manbo Maude instituted the use of contracts for initiations and ritual services to avoid being cheated out of payment for her services.

While living in Mattapan, Manbo Maude had a cousin who became ill. She sought help through the gods, and the spirit Kouzen informed her of a grim prognosis: this cousin was being spiritually and physically drained by three zombies.[29] Scholar of French and comparative literature, Carrol F. Coates, defines a zombie as "a person whose soul has been captured by a sorcerer, leaving the individual without a will of their own." Zombies can affect people emotionally, physically, and mentally. In this case, Manbo Maude's cousin became gravely ill. Thankfully, Kouzen told Manbo Maude how to cure this fearful affliction. Only initiates are privy to the details of dispelling zombies. Manbo Maude was required to make a small offering for her cousin, and she gladly purchased the necessary items.

The healing process took several grueling days. On the first day, Manbo Maude rid her cousin of two zombies. The final zombie was defeated on the third day. After the services were complete and her cousin was on the mend,

Kouzen again came to Manbo Maude *nan dòmi* and told her to collect the money he was owed, even asking for a specific amount. Manbo Maude refused. This was family: she would not request money for curing her cousin of her sickness. Kouzen was unmoved by her reasoning. "You have family," he said, "I don't. I need to be paid for the services I provided." Still, Manbo Maude was uncomfortable. Kouzen stubbornly maintained his position. They argued, until finally she told the spirit that if he was so determined to receive payment, he would have to speak to her cousin himself. Kouzen agreed. A few days after the contentious dream, Manbo Maude's cousin called her and asked how much she owed for the services. Manbo Maude insisted she owed nothing. The cousin replied, "I don't owe you; I owe your spirit." Kouzen had demanded from her the exact amount he had told Manbo Maude. The cousin gave her the money, and Kouzen was finally satisfied that his needs had been met.[30] Within her dreams, Manbo Maude engaged in negotiatory labor with Kouzen, gaining vital spiritual knowledge to help her cousin while still maintaining a respectful relationship with the deity.

Manbo Maude's efforts to rid her cousin of the zombies that were harming her health exemplified intimate labor: she provided a religious service defined by her ability to care for and heal her cousin, physically attending to her needs for several days. These services would normally be offered for a price, but because of the familial connection, Manbo Maude was initially willing to forgo payment. It was Kouzen who demanded payment be rendered for the services provided. For Manbo Maude and her cousin, Kouzen was a real entity with as much right to negotiate for compensation as they had, which is why Manbo Maude engaged in the negotiatory labor necessary to please him. Kouzen provided spiritual knowledge to Manbo Maude, negotiated face-to-face in the space of her dreams, and expected to be paid for that labor. By receiving compensation, Kouzen's worth and his contributions to Manbo Maude's ritual work could be rewarded, reinforcing the connections between the spirits and the people who serve them. Though Kouzen had a symbolic connection to the idea of family, it was a nuanced perspective that interacted with economic concerns. To have family and to take care of family also involved being compensated for the emotional and intimate labor that one offered. That Manbo Maude was related to the woman she treated did not negate the economic demands of religious labor, and her cousin acknowledged this truth by paying for the services despite Manbo Maude's protests.

The negotiatory labor involved in this incident was twofold: Manbo Maude was engaging both in an interpersonal interaction with her cousin about ritual work and payment and in direct negotiations with Kouzen for the purposes of spiritual guidance and compensation. She had to satisfy both parties, resolving the issue without displeasing her family or the spirits. Kouzen provided a way for Manbo Maude to negotiate a potentially sensitive financial situation with a family member. Whether Kouzen truly demanded the same price of Manbo Maude and her cousin in separate dreams was irrelevant; his presence facilitated negotiatory labor between the two women, enabling them to discuss payment for the services rendered without compromising any social mores. Manbo Maude was able to obtain payment from a family member while maintaining the nicety of claiming it was unnecessary. The cousin was able to give her this supposedly unnecessary payment without traversing that same awkward boundary and without depriving her relative of her fee. Kouzen was a mediator between them, smoothing the interaction. With Kouzen as a mediator, Manbo Maude was able to receive payment for the emotional and intimate labor she provided to her cousin. Manbo Maude could not continue her ritual work without proper compensation, even from her own family. Kouzen illuminated this fact, and through him, she was able to articulate the economic value of her religious labor. His knowledge as a healer was crucial to Manbo Maude in aiding her cousin, and his insistence on negotiating for monetary compensation exemplifies the continuing importance of negotiatory labor to the economic feasibility of Manbo Maude's religious services, reinforcing her faith in the spirits' ability to shape her life.

Kouzen's connection to negotiatory labor is also apparent during ceremonies, where his image is largely defined by his interaction with money. On July 25, 2018, Manbo Maude threw a fete for Kouzen at her temple in Jacmel. Earlier in the day, Haitian practitioners had slaughtered and cooked a cow, several goats, and chickens to feed the spirits and the community. The ritual feeding of the spirits lasted for several hours in the afternoon, followed by a break of a few hours more. The ceremony for Kouzen began later than the typical starting times of nine to eleven at night because the dresses were not ready: it did not begin until about 2 A.M. One seamstress usually made the dresses for the forty-five practitioners in Manbo Maude's home. The detailed aesthetic labor she performed for the temple was specific not only to a given practitioner but also to the lwa. Kouzen's dresses are some of the most complicated because of their elaborate patchwork, requiring many different fabrics to be sewn together to form the garment. The careful eye and artistry of the seamstress contribute to the success of the ceremony; Manbo

Maude relies on her precise hand to execute the particularities of her overall sartorial vision.

In the temple, I overheard the seamstress speak to Shori about how she had been working all night to complete the dresses and as a result did not have the time to prepare her own dress for the ceremony. Yet she still wanted to attend to see what her finished products looked like. The inability to complete the dresses was not the only reason for the late start of the ceremony. Manbo Maude and her initiates had also taken longer than usual to prepare, and a last-minute dash into town was needed to purchase some necessary items for the rituals. Audience members and other practitioners idled outside, buying snacks and drinks from the local vendors who showed up whenever the temple was organizing a ceremony, knowing there would be people willing to buy their products. Attendees were also socializing, reconnecting with friends, and making romantic connections. Occasionally, the sociality of the ceremony generates trouble—a love connection goes awry, or tensions arise, caused by the close press of bodies—necessitating the face-to-face conflict resolution characterized as emotional labor. Fights between and among audience members and practitioners happen, and when they do, other audience members or practitioners rush in to resolve the conflict before an argument erupts into physical violence. The interpersonal relationships during a ceremony are in constant need of management. The practitioners of the temple spend time squashing arguments, looking after more vulnerable members, and maintaining the overall peace for the sake not only of the people present but also for the religious ceremonies they have come to be a part of.

New initiates are often showcased during ceremonies honoring Kouzen. The eight new initiates into Manbo Maude's Vodou home were already outside the djèvo when I arrived. Because I was not an initiate, I was not privy to everything that happens in the djèvo or to all the intricacies of the initiation process. The djèvo contains a great deal of ritual materials used for ceremonial and ritual work, which are moved in and out of the broader public ceremony by the initiates and Manbo Maude's practitioners. The initiates were all Haitian and Haitian Dyaspora women, the third time Manbo Maude was guiding a group of initiates who all had a Haitian heritage and all lived in the United States. They wore different outfits than did the broader community to signify their status as initiates: their dresses were a patchwork of different patterns and colors made from denim and cotton fabrics. The fabrics had plaid and floral designs, as well as solid colors in blue, green, and pink, with white cotton connecting the square or triangle patches. The initiates wore straw hats that they had to keep on for several days after leaving the djèvo. They wore *koulie* beads wrapped around their chests to signal their recent initiation. The night before, the initiates had received their Manbo names and were baptized by a Haitian man who regularly performed Catholic rituals; he sprinkled holy water on them and burned frankincense in a thurible, which is a type of container that carries incense and is burned during Catholic religious rituals.

Kouzen's legibility to audience members and practitioners during ceremonies depends on the sartorial or aesthetic labor done by Manbo Maude and the members of her temple. His presence is signified through several specific items of adornment that make up a recognizable aesthetic. Possessed practitioners don these items and then interact with the audience, asking for money and offering advice. After the initiates emerged from the djèvo, Kouzen mounted eight initiates and practitioners. To signify his presence, the initiates and practitioners were adorned with a blue or red *moushwa*, or scarves, on their arms, a straw hat, and a makout, or straw satchel, decorated with multicolored bandanas tied at various points on it. Some carried a cane to represent an older version of Kouzen. Others clutched a machete and a rake to symbolize Kouzen's role as an agricultural worker. They began asking people in the audience for money, holding out their hats, their makout, or their hands. The money they collected went to Manbo Maude's temple at the end of the ceremony to support the spirits and the ritual work. The varied Kouzens sometimes asked for ridiculous sums of money and ran from person to person, or they would collect the goats offered as gifts and jealously guard them from other Kouzens for the rest of the ceremony. They also attempted to steal money from one another. People who offered them money usually asked for favors in return, such as help in their love life, financial situation, or for overall protection. The Kouzens took the money offered and tucked it inside their shirts and blouses. Kouzen would sometimes listen very intently to what he was being told or would fixate on the money and listen distractedly. It was a playful, often humorous display.

The ceremony celebrating Kouzen exemplifies the process of spiritual vogue because of the interaction between the spirits, audience, and practitioners involving Kouzen's use of ritual accessories. Kouzen is honored through performance rituals and offerings, and the audience receives advice, blessings, and food in return. The practitioners, by interacting with Kouzen, facilitate communication between the spirit and the audience, and in turn they receive money, which is used to maintain the temple where the ceremony takes place. Spiritual vogue demonstrates the symbolic importance of money in Kouzen's presence: the possessed practitioner acts as a vessel for Kouzen, who holds out his makout to receive offerings from audience members and other practitioners; this in turn enables their negotiatory communication with one another. His accessories not only visually signify his spiritual connection to the marketplace and agriculture but also are ritual items that indicate his interest in financial matters and facilitate discussion of economic issues with devotees.

While Kouzen meandered through the fete, practitioners who were not possessed were also weaving their way through the crowd, offering people water, soda, rum, and snacks. If they noticed that Kouzen seemed tired or hot, they offered him water or rum as well. Ceremonies, especially once possessions start, demand care work that is inherent to intimate labor. As previously noted, Vodou ceremonies last many hours, and it is incumbent on Manbo Maude and her temple to protect each other and their guests from the dangers of exhaustion or overexertion by offering food and water for energy or a chair for rest. The spirits can be exuberant when they mount people, and other practitioners are constantly trying to maintain the safety and dignity of the possessed. They pull skirts and dresses back down to keep women covered; they wipe the dirt from peoples' faces after they have writhed on the ground; they fan them if they become too heated. When a lwa vacates a vessel, practitioners may faint. They are caught before they can injure themselves, lowered to the ground or into a chair by the caring arms of their fellow practitioners. Intimate labor is a necessity, integrated into every facet of possession rituals, as essential to the ensemble as Kouzen's makout.

I had already met Kouzen in Mattapan and Jacmel in previous ceremonies and was familiar with the process, so I saved money for the event and knew to spread my money out evenly among the Kouzens, which I accomplished by using small bills of twenty-five, fifty, and one hundred *gourdes*. However, I did not account for the length of the ceremony nor how many times Kouzen would rotate through the room asking for money. I had given him everything I brought with me early in the ceremony and had to tell him I had nothing left several times. "*Mwe pa gen lajan*," I said, Haitian Kreyòl for "I don't have any money." I held out my empty hands, shrugged my shoulders, and put my head down. Kouzen looked sad, asked why I had nothing to give him, or told me it was okay and still offered his blessing, before moving onto the next person. It was a frustratingly repeated experience, and I was not pleased I had run out of money. But I had to remember that the repetition was part of the process of the ceremony and that the discomfort I felt was ultimately a reflection of my own relationship to money. Kouzen's presence, and the ritual processes prompted by his manifestation, encouraged thoughtfulness about personal finances and emphasized the fact that money was not always available: sometimes I had it, and sometimes I did not, but either way my relationship with it would always need to be negotiated. Kouzen's presence during ceremonies is a dramatization of negotiatory labor and how this type of labor is often necessitated by the precariousness of people's financial situations. When practitioners do not have money to give Kouzen, they often make promises to give him labor in exchange for his favor and advice.

During ceremonies, Kouzen exhibits the same willingness to negotiate as Manbo Maude, reaching deals with practitioners and audience members even if they have no money to offer. In Jacmel, Kouzen mounted Manbo Maude's daughter Vante'm Pa Fyem during the ceremony. While possessing Vante'm Pa Fyem, Kouzen interacted with a young male Haitian initiate who had no money to offer the deity in exchange for his help. But the young man tried to negotiate, promising that if Kouzen would bless him with a better job, he would bring money with him to the next ceremony. Kouzen was sad. He looked disappointed, though he still listened carefully to what the initiate said. Kouzen was ultimately satisfied and promised to aid the young man in his search for employment. After this part of the ceremony, the Kouzens went into the djèvo and emerged with food that they carried in half of a calabash shell which also contained a lit candle. The food included rice, corn, plantains, goat, chicken, and pork. They drank Couronne, a type of orange soda, as well as beer and other soft drinks. The Kouzens sat in chairs, on the floor, or on the base of the potomitan, a sacred center pole in a Vodou temple, and ate their fill of the food. When they finished, they offered the rest of the food to other practitioners and initiates who had been blessed by their touch. Offering Kouzen food and drink is an expression of intimate labor: practitioners show their care for the deity by honoring him with his preferred meal, and in return Kouzen shows them care by giving practitioners the food that was prepared in his name. One of the female initiates handed me a large piece of goat meat, which I gleefully ate, famished by the long ceremony. Slowly, the mounted initiates began to faint as they were released from their possession. Other initiates and I cared for them by offering chairs for rest and water for recovery, another example of the intimate labor necessary during ceremonies.

Earlier in the evening, Vante'm Pa Fyem had changed out of her initiation outfit into an outfit that was the same as her mother's. It was a mix of denim and cotton fabric. The top was plain blue denim, and the sleeves were ruffled in five tiered, multicolored, plaid layers. Each layer of cotton featured different colors and designs. The fabric choices signified an agricultural lifestyle and the type of clothing worn by farmers. Manbo Maude used these traditional elements but beautified them by creating an elaborate ceremonial dress with many layers and ruffles. The bottom part of Manbo Maude and Vante'm Pa Fyem's dresses was an open skirt, which revealed denim pants underneath. They were the only two practitioners whose dresses featured this design because Manbo Maude wanted to distinguish her status from the rest and to signify her connection with her daughter. Wearing denim jeans was another gesture to the agricultural roots of Kouzen. Manbo Maude was never taught by her spiritual mother nor learned from experiences in other ceremonies to wear pants as a female practitioner. This addition reflects her desire to innovate by incorporating nontraditional fashion into her ceremonies for all spirits, male and female. Participants understand the colors and fabrics associated with spirits; they form a shorthand they can follow to figure out which lwa is present based on how they are adorned. Manbo Maude has expanded these traditions, broadening the aesthetic expressions possible during ceremonies.

As discussed in chapter 1, the sartorial choices of pants or a suit and tie aided in the masculine perception of the spirits during Manbo Maude's ceremonies for Gede. Given that they donned a skirt, as well as pants, in this ceremony for Kouzen, Vante'm Pa Fyem and Manbo Maude were not offering the same conventional masculine signifiers as for Gede. They welcomed Kouzen even while dressed in feminine attire. This is typical of Voudou ceremonies. Female practitioners, queer and straight, traditionally wear dresses and skirts when honoring and being possessed by male or female spirits. Cisgender heterosexual Houngans do wear dresses while performing spiritual work in service of certain spirits and for ritual work and treatment for their clients, but only rarely during ceremonies.[31] Manbo Maude has seen gay men don dresses for ceremonies, although that is not the norm and does not occur in her temples.

In the space of the ceremony, denim and patchwork patterns represent Kouzen, and this incarnation of Kouzen is male. Therefore, the skirt does not erase the masculinity of the spirit. Manbo Maude, Vante'm Pa Fyem, the practitioners, and audience members understand this because they understand the norms of performance rituals and clothing during ceremonies. The presence of the spirit does not untether practitioners from their earthly existence, and gender expectations are foundational to Vodou traditions. This is why I describe women's presence as liminal: simultaneously, the female body is read through clothing and physical presence, while the fabric and color of their outfit mark the presence of or invitation to a male spirit. Women practitioners' gender is reinforced and negated at the same time. It also reflects the spirits' apparent indifference to the style of clothing on display and their seeming preference for certain sartorial signifiers. Manbo Maude, by channeling her devotion into her spiritual garments, is offering as enthusiastic an invitation as she can imagine. The invitation does not rely on a specific garment but on the effort and creativity expounded on that garment and the surrounding ceremony.

An obvious question emerges in relation to the presence of the spirits and ritual garments during this ceremony: Is Kouzen wearing a dress? The answer, in Manbo Maude's estimation, is a hesitant yes. She admitted to me that Kouzen is wearing the dress, though she made that point with far less surety than she did when discussing Gede while wearing the suit she had made for him. "I don't think you should get caught up in that," she cautioned me, before emphasizing the gender fluidity of Kouzen, suggesting that he ultimately does not care about clothing.[32] "Kouzen is fluid," she explained. "He can do whatever he wants."[33] Manbo Maude broadened her analysis to include the rest of the Vodou pantheon, stating that all the spirits are fluid, and that people are the ones who impose gendered meaning on spiritual garments, saying, "I don't think it matters for any of the spirits. We as humans, we get caught up on that, but not the spirits."[34]

Manbo Maude and other practitioners returned to the fluidity of the spirits, as a concept, numerous times over the course of my research. Later chapters engage with the idea in more detail. For now, what Manbo Maude's words reflect is the persistent theme of negotiation. Not even the spirits can appear in a fete without negotiating. They, as Manbo Maude implied, are made to contend with the gendered realities of the practitioners who call on them, and those realities shape how the lwa are served. Manbo Maude pushes at the boundaries of these social conventions, but she too contends with the expectations her community is unwilling to abandon, no matter how appealing the style.

H.B.I.C: Managing Labor to Sustain the Temple

After Kouzen and the other spirits leave the earthly realm and after her guests return to their homes, Manbo Maude and her practitioners still have more work to do. A constant stream of tasks is necessary not only in the immediate run-up to a ceremony but also afterward to make the next one possible. Much of this labor is centered around maintaining her temple and managing the people who work on her property. Manbo Maude engages in emotional and intimate labor, negotiating interpersonal relationships in an effort to maintain not only her spiritual efficacy but also the structure of her religious community in Jacmel and Mattapan as well. This labor requires her to get involved in the day-to-day interactions and arguments of workers and practitioners at her religious sites. The religious community also engages in these labor categories in their professional and personal relationships with each other. The community members are as essential to the functioning of the temple as is Manbo Maude: the routine tasks of managing the temple are shared across many people.

The work in Manbo Maude's temple is often divided by gender, with men largely attending to tasks that involve more strenuous physical labor and construction, and women concentrating on household cleaning and cooking. Yet both women and men retrieve supplies, like chickens, small goats, flour, alcohol, fruits, vegetable, gasoline, and bags of water, and are responsible for building altars and doing ritual work, including initiation rites. As an observer, I noted that men have more leisure time during the run-up to ceremonies. After they move the power generators or repair parts of the temple's infrastructure, the men are free to play soccer, go to the bar, or generally lounge around with their friends. The women, in contrast, are in constant motion. They are prepping food, cleaning, cooking, and taking care of children. Women socialize too, talking and laughing with each other, yet the labor never stops until hours after the ceremony is done.

In Manbo Maude's temple, child-rearing is most often women's work, no matter a woman's sexual identity or gendered expression. Sometimes, cisgender gay men move between these delineations and participate in cooking. However, I have not seen any men, of any sexual orientation, wash ritual clothing, and in a home so dedicated to sartorial presentation, washing ritual clothes, a form of aesthetic labor, is an essential task. Laundry is consistently situated as women's work. In Jacmel, for example, a member of Manbo Maude's spiritual home, whom I call Nikol, washed ritual and everyday clothing for guests of the temple and had earned a reputation as a difficult person.[35] Many of the people who gathered at Manbo Maude's temple in the summertime viewed her as strange. Haitian practitioners and workers were not fond of her and considered her dishonest, prone to fabricating wild and implausible stories. She was given to staring at people long enough to make them uncomfortable and frequently interrupted other people's conversations. As a result, Nikol had a hard time making friends with the other women.

Manbo Maude has scolded people for not washing ritual clothes correctly, because clothing is an integral part of her spiritual home and her reputation as a Manbo. Nikol was skilled at her job, and Manbo Maude valued her thorough work. As a laundress, she helped practitioners maintain their personal presentation, buoying the sartorial reputation of the temple as a result. In the summer of 2014, Nikol grew uneasy with the workplace because many women openly gossiped about her. Perhaps exacerbating some women's poor relationships with Nikol was her ability to speak English and communicate with many foreign visitors, which opened up opportunities for material and financial benefit.[36] She was able to travel with Americans during their time in Haiti and translate for them, for which she received a fee.

Unwilling to endure the ongoing alienation from the other women, Nikol left Manbo Maude's compound and did not return for a year. The emotional labor she expended working with the other laundresses proved too taxing, especially because she also did paid jobs for the temple. The following summer in 2015, at a marketplace near her home in Jacmel, Manbo Maude saw Nikol and asked her why she no longer attended her temple. Nikol explained that she felt uncomfortable working around the other women because she did not feel welcome. Frustrated by the situation, Manbo Maude told her to return and promised to resolve the problem. Several days later, Nikol came back to the temple, and when she arrived Manbo Maude took her by the hand and brought her to the laundry area. She told the women in the room that Nikol deserved to be a part of the community and that no one should be bothering her or speaking ill of her. To secure Nikol's place in her temple, Manbo Maude relied on emotional labor, convincing Nikol it was safe to return and laying out the options for the other laundresses: they could work farther away from Nikol or leave, but they could not continue to treat her poorly. This was not a negotiation: it was an ultimatum. As a result of Manbo Maude's intervention, Nikol resumed her work at the temple.[37] Wanting to keep earning the money that Manbo Maude provided, the laundresses distanced themselves from Nikol as they worked or avoided her as much as possible.

The emotional labor involved in resolving this conflict was clear: Manbo Maude had to listen to Nikol's concerns and respond to them by negotiating the interpersonal conflicts between the laundry workers. The drama between the laundresses was a microcosm of conflicts found in the larger community: Manbo Maude could not maintain the integrity of her religious space without attending to the social experiences of the people who occupied it. Manbo Maude's skills in negotiating conflict have been strengthened by her educational and occupational experiences as a mental health clinician. She knows how to listen, and she understands how trauma, for example, can shape people's behavior. She uses this knowledge to search for the roots of the problems in her temple and to find solutions. Moreover, the emotional labor inherent in her position as a Manbo extends to the economic elements of this interpersonal issue.

In this case, one of her workers, Nikol, was no longer able to provide aesthetic labor because of the interpersonal relationships in her workplace on Manbo Maude's property, which affected the economic system that allowed her to stage the ceremonies performed in Jacmel. Manbo Maude had to show that she cared or at least act as though she did, because the problem affected the production of her religious fashion and services. This aspect of emotional labor can be performative, in that the affective qualities of caring can be used to solve an interpersonal problem. Her position as an authority figure is reinforced when she successfully resolves these types of issues. This authority was also secured by an economic arrangement: Manbo Maude controls the money that these women earned from their work in her laundry area, so it was beneficial to their financial situation to heed her commands. Whether they completely ceased gossiping about Nikol or not, they understood the hierarchy of the temple well enough to know that openly engaging in this behavior was unacceptable and could jeopardize their employment. Resolving the conflict and other similar conflicts is an integral part of maintaining Manbo Maude's religious community and an unavoidable responsibility as a Manbo.

The laundresses were not the only community members who provided aesthetic labor. Laurel, a young Haitian woman initiated under Manbo Maude, also worked at the temple in Jacmel.[38] Laurel had known Manbo Maude for more than eighteen years and watched her spiritual home grow from a tent into the temple it was now. Despite her long acquaintance with Manbo Maude, Laurel was only initiated in 2017 after deciding to prioritize being initiated by a woman. She was worried that, in a temple led by a man, she would be pressured into exchanging sexual favors for religious services when and if she was unable to find the money to pay for those services. Manbos and Houngans in Haiti and the United States hold great spiritual authority over initiates seeking spiritual guidance and ritual help. Sometimes, this authority results in sexual, economic, and ritual abuse. Laurel is one of several practitioners who shared with me that Manbo Maude offers a refuge from these potential abuses. Laurel trusts Manbo Maude to perform the intimate labor necessary for ceremonies and ritual work without abusing her religious authority. *Pran lwa* and some rituals require spiritual, emotional, and physical vulnerability in relation to the divine and other practitioners. Intimate labor maintains trust in these vulnerable spaces, illustrated by the care shown to the recently possessed during ceremonies, or in changing rooms where practitioners help each other dress, or during the exhausting initiation rituals in the djèvo. In Manbo Maude's temple, Laurel felt safe, and when she could not afford to pay for the dresses for ceremonies or the religious services she needed, Manbo Maude allowed her to work in the temple in exchange for the ritual services. Thus, Laurel and Manbo Maude engaged in negotiatory labor, working in the temple to pay for her religious dresses. What could not be provided in *gourdes* was supplied in ritual work. Because of their arrangement, Laurel is able to participate in the sartorial displays during the ceremonies, donning new styles along with the rest of temple. Laurel takes her work for Manbo Maude seriously, and her commitments to the temple even affect her personal life. She explained, "My services are what I can give, and Mami Maude did not take money from me for me to *kanzo* and I can't give her money. But what I can give her is my services because even if I had a husband, because you know there shouldn't be sexual contact in the moment that you're serving the spirits. So even if I had a husband, I would send him away because Mami only comes once a year, so I need to devote that time to her."[39] In service to Manbo Maude and her religious home, Laurel cleaned the temple and the home, laundered and ironed clothes, and helped set up altars. She emphasized her dedication to Manbo Maude by stating that even a husband could not compromise the work she was committed to doing for her religious home. For some members, sexual contact while preparing for ceremonies and serving the spirits could be a distraction and detract from the religious nature of the work. In fact, some rituals require celibacy. So, Laurel decided to eliminate it during the time Manbo Maude spent in Jacmel. Laurel was one of the people to whom Manbo Maude sent a stipend for her work maintaining her home and temple throughout the year. Felipe, a Haitian male Houngan in his mid-twenties who is also a member of Manbo Maude's temple, elaborated on these stipends, saying, "So, throughout the year I work in construction to get work. But Manbo Maude still provides in terms of food and everything. She still sends money, but I don't wait around until she sends [me] money. So, like I work in the meantime until she gives us some."[40] Felipe prides himself on his skills in construction work, often using them to maintain the infrastructure of Manbo Maude's home and temple in Jacmel. During the summer when she is in town, he is called on almost constantly to help with constructing the altars, carry large loads of supplies, or fix the generator that often breaks down. In fact, it is difficult to speak with Felipe without being interrupted by someone looking for his assistance.

Felipe and Laurel use part of the stipend that Manbo Maude sent to pay for the clothes they wear in Manbo Maude's ceremonies, as well as other ceremonies they attend in Jacmel. They, like many others, often attend ceremonies outside their spiritual home, not only for religious fulfillment but also to socialize with friends, judge the quality and spiritual effectiveness of other temples, and pay respect to other temples by being physically present at their ceremonies. It is also common for people to leave one temple and join another. That Laurel, Felipe, and members of Manbo Maude's temple frequent other ceremonies is one reason for the stipends she sends to Haiti: they are essentially advertisements for her temple. Laurel and Felipe are walking fashion models for the ritual efficacy of Manbo Maude's home. If they appear well taken care of, then their appearance may convince other people to join Manbo Maude's temple. They are proof that Manbo Maude has the resources to sustain her temple and its members. When I asked Laurel why the fashion in Manbo Maude's ceremonies is so important to her, she explained, "I like to be beautiful, whenever I go to ceremonies or places like that, I like to be beautiful. I love when people come up to me and tell me, 'Oh, you look so good; the dress looks so good on you.' I live for that."[41]

Vodou Hopping: Fashioning Presence as Spiritual Currency in the Vodou Community

When I visited Manbo Maude's temple in Jacmel in the summer of 2018, other participants and I would Vodou hop with Manbo Maude, traveling from one ceremony to another when she was not throwing one herself. I invented the term "Vodou hop" to describe the movement of practitioners and audience members between different Vodou ceremonies to compare temples, represent their own spiritual home in the broader Vodou community, or simply enjoy multiple ceremonies. The term also applies to the movement of practitioners from one home to another because they are dissatisfied and are searching for a Manbo, Houngan, or temple that better serves their needs or are seeking refuge from an abusive situation. Vodou hopping occasionally frustrates me because attending these additional ceremonies took the place of resting after preparing for and participating in Manbo Maude's events. However, attending other ceremonies is part of Manbo Maude's routine, and as a participant in her temple it is important for me and for the members of her home to show our faces throughout Jacmel. The exchange of people, ideas, and traditions is an integral part of the sociality of Vodou: socializing with other practitioners creates community and reinforces beliefs, as well as helping construct the reputations of respective temples.

Just as houses in Ballroom culture represent themselves as units during balls, Vodou homes commonly portray themselves as cohesive in public ceremonies.[42] As we traveled from ceremony to ceremony as "children" of her home, our appearances and fashion reflected on Manbo Maude.[43] The moniker "child" is given to members of houses in Ballroom culture; in Vodou, initiates in a home are referred to as *ti fèy*, loosely translated as "little leaf" or "child of the house" in Haitian Kreyòl.[44] In both instances, the identifier implies familial connection, although not necessarily biological. Our self-presentation was indicative of how Manbo Maude managed her temple. Manbo Maude uses these visits to showcase her fashion and the material wealth it implies by wearing elaborate dresses that were created for events in previous years. She also makes dresses for the specific purpose of attending ceremonies in other spiritual homes, and she does not compromise the surprise and glamour of her own ceremonies by previewing the fashion that will be on display in other temples. That is why she never wears the dresses created for the ceremonies that she will be leading in her own temple that same summer. Presenting herself well is a necessary exercise in aesthetic labor; dressing beautifully reinforces the reputation she has built for her temple. Usually, she wears white dresses to other ceremonies, occasionally accessorized with a colorful head scarf. As a *Gwo Manbo*, or head Manbo, Manbo Maude must pay respect to other people's temples by appearing in their homes, just as they have done for her. As members of a Vodou home, we could expect to be treated with even more courtesy than other people in the audience; Manbo Maude and her practitioners show the same courtesy when members of different Vodou homes appear at her temple. The practitioners at the temples we visited pulled out extra chairs to make sure we had seats and offered us drinks. If seats were not available, the practitioners found room for us in the front of the ceremony to ensure we could see the proceedings.

When Manbo Maude visits ceremonies in other temples, she is both an audience member and a participant: sometimes she aids in spiritual work, and in other instances she only makes an appearance. Yet Manbo Maude's sartorial choices are always being viewed by the larger community in Jacmel. She is part of a broader Vodou ideology that emphasizes the idea of community, not only within her own home but also with other Vodou temples. She expresses this by making dresses and pants for initiates in other people's homes to emphasize her material wealth and so they can fully participate in the ceremonies. These initiates pay for her labor just as any of her own practitioners would, but her willingness to lend her skills to creating clothes for members of other temples helps construct an image of benevolence and generosity. It both underscores the idea that she is an unselfish Manbo and encourages participants to continue frequenting her ceremonies or consider becoming a part of her home. This strategy has worked; she has gained new members in her home because they believed she was equipped to take care of them. If I had allowed my fatigue and annoyance at the continual travel to prevent me from following Manbo Maude and her initiates into these ceremonies, I would have missed the opportunity to observe the importance of her presence and her spiritual clothing outside her home. She is making statements with her fashion throughout the entirety of her time in Jacmel.

My attention to fashion in Vodou led me to modify my own behavior, and by doing so, I gained invaluable insight into the meaning of fashion in Manbo Maude's home and how fashion changed my ability to participate in the ceremony. After visiting Jacmel and Manbo Maude's temple for the third time, I changed my own approach to fashion and my engagement with the community. I realized that if I wanted to continue to do research on the fashion of Manbo Maude's temples, I should put more effort into my own appearance. I could not always afford the dresses she created, but I could change the way I dressed, wrapped my hair, and wore makeup and accessories so I could participate in her religious community in a deeper way. Throughout the year preceding my next visit to Jacmel, I practiced my skills at head wrapping, learning more elaborate styles, and I purchased more colorful fabrics. I packed colorful dresses and skirts suited for the different deities to be honored instead of the white clothes I had worn in the past. The results were worth the effort. In preparation for the ceremony honoring Kouzen, I wore bright colors: a baby-blue linen skirt, a blue blouse, and a red sequined head wrap. I sported a necklace and a big bracelet that was attached to a ring by a small chain. I opted to wear contact lenses as opposed to my usual glasses to highlight my eyeliner and green and brown eye shadow. I also wore dark purple lipstick. When I arrived at the ceremony, people were shocked. The next day, Manbo Maude told me she had not even recognized me. She shared that people told her they knew I was pretty, but that night I looked like a goddess, and they thought that I should be a Manbo.

That evening, when I approached the ceremonial circle, Laurel and two other women said, "Eziaku, *ou bel!*"[45] They told me I was beautiful again and again that night. During the ceremony, people in the circle came up to me and dabbed my face with the washcloths they kept tucked into the waists of their skirts, wiping the sweat from my forehead while taking care not to smudge my makeup. Women often performed this intimate labor for others during ceremonies, but they had never done so for me. People also playfully pulled me toward the drummers to dance. When they passed around a bottle of rum, I was included. Usually, I brought my own rum to the ceremony and saw other people sharing, but I had never been invited to share before. I recognized that by putting more effort into my appearance, I was also putting more effort into the ceremony itself. By dressing up and wearing makeup, by engaging in aesthetic labor, I was signaling to the other participants in the room that I was a part of their community and that the ceremony taking place was important to me: it was worth my labor.

I felt more absorbed in the process of dressing for the religious ceremony. In the past, I did the bare minimum, and it took me very little time to put on my plain white clothes. The other women would spend hours preparing their outfits, hair, and makeup, while I was ready in fifteen to twenty minutes. Even the men would take at least thirty to forty-five minutes, asking other men to comb their hair and cut designs into their fades and dousing themselves with excessive cologne. They also took the time to iron their clothes or asked women to iron their clothes for them. Because I was doing very little preparation, I was not participating in the same way that they were, though I did help others get dressed.

Vodou ceremonies are a social space, and by presenting myself well and in accordance with others' aesthetic expectations, I became more integrated into that space. Ceremonies are also where people try to make romantic connections, and my appearance attracted more attention than usual. Dressing up and applying makeup allowed me to participate in the ceremony as not only a researcher but also as a welcomed guest and an immersed participant observer. My clothing allowed me more access to the temple and signified the respect I had not only for the community but also for the preparation process involved in religious ritual and the spirits themselves. Showing off and wearing makeup affected my role as a participant and in spiritual vogue by affecting the way I interacted with other participants and the audience. I garnered more attention and praise as a participant, which ultimately increased my worthiness to honor the spirits.

During the fete, I was invited to dance in front of the drummers, an act that honors the spirits. As dancers, our movements were determined by the speed and rhythm of the drums, which dictated the swivel in our hips and the swiftness of our footwork. Usually, I was not afforded this opportunity. By participating in forms of beauty and glamour that projected a traditional type of femininity, I was able to shift the way I was perceived and received in Manbo Maude's temple. I successfully made my femininity legible by appealing to broadly acceptable ideas of beauty through my makeup and clothes.[46] I dressed up for six additional ceremonies during this trip to Haiti, and during my visit, I had a drink with a member of Manbo Maude's temple in a hotel bar in Jacmel. In the middle of our conversation, he told me, "I like you better this year. You seem more comfortable, and you seem more connected. You have a presence."[47] Whatever change manifested in my "presence" was in large part produced through the aesthetic labor I performed for the ceremony. He emphasized the idea that self-presentation is inextricably bound to the perceptions of the broader community and even to the ability to serve the spirits. The connection between aesthetics, community, and the divine is an inextricable element of Manbo Maude's spiritual homes.

Considering faith work through the lens of aesthetic, emotional, intimate, and negotiatory labor provides avenues through which to explore Manbo Maude's religious innovations, her use of fashion, and the economic negotiation that defines her religious efficacy and distinguishes her Vodou temples from other houses of worship. The four labor categories illuminate how religious communities' function: how they care for their members, how they prepare for ceremonies, how they interact with the divine, and how they maintain their temples and larger communities. Without these labors, spiritual vogue cannot occur. In Manbo Maude's homes, labor is inflected by the prevalence of fashion. The aesthetic labor required of Manbo Maude and her practitioners in her ceremonies is all encompassing. Manbo Maude's self-presentation is primarily about her dress, involving all aspects of how she prepares and presents her temple during her ceremonies. Negotiatory labor is at the forefront of her religious practices.

Succeeding in her professional and aesthetic aspirations necessitates negotiating about money and resources with the lwa and practitioners. Manbo Maude offers her practitioners and guests a spectacle that honors the spirits and emphasizes the unique experience of her home and the services she offers. The people who work to make Manbo Maude's ceremonies possible, and the guests who fill the ritual spaces they have dutifully prepared, are a diverse group from various countries, economic backgrounds, and gender, race, and sexual identities. Fashion, even in the name of the spirits, cannot resolve every conflict in the community, and neither can Manbo Maude herself. Fashion and faith can offer common cause to those who gather under the roofs of her temples, yet tension is an inescapable result of attempting to forge spiritual unity in the midst of difference. I pull at the seams of this tension in the next chapter.

CHAPTER THREE

How Tight Is Your Wrap?

Tensions of Race and Sexuality in Vodou Identity

Manbo Maude sat at the edge of her four-poster, oak bed in her home in Mattapan in March 2016. Her room smelled of shea butter lotion, jojoba oil, and Chanel perfume. The wooden floors were creaky, and the walls were painted matte violet. Two pictures, both prints of painted flowers, hung on opposite walls in wooden frames. There was an inactive silver radiator next to the window that Haitian women were resting their clothes on before changing. Four green plastic bins stood tall next to the radiator, overflowing with clothes that Manbo Maude had created for other ceremonies. There was not enough space in her closet or her bedroom for all her ritual outfits plus her everyday work clothes, and so they spread outside her room, stashed in containers in the hallway.

It was 10 P.M., and she was dressed in her ritual outfit. She faced the large mirror attached to the mahogany dresser and stared at her reflection, as she adjusted her green and white clothes. The mirror enabled her to visually affirm that her makeup and clothing were in place. Perfume and photographs of her friends and family rested on top of the dresser, along with ritual beads and necklaces, hair care products, and combs. Sometimes this dresser served as an altar when she wanted to pray or perform small rituals in a space that was more comfortable than her basement, but in that moment, it served as a haphazard resting place for her belongings.

Manbo Maude yelled across the hall for one of her Black female *ti feỳ*, a Haitian Kreyòl phrase that describes a Vodou initiate or a "child of the house," to help tie her head wrap before the start of the ceremony honoring Danbala.[1] I was changing into my ritual outfit alongside Shori in Manbo Maude's daughter's room and overheard her entreaty. When Manbo Maude called, Shori and I followed a ti feỳ into Manbo Maude's bedroom, which was across the hall. We were allowed to help the ti feỳ manipulate the head wrap. I could tell by the way Shori started to wrap the fabric around Manbo Maude's head, with a repetitive wringing motion, that it would not be stable: the twist was too loose. I had never helped Manbo Maude with her head wraps, but I spent years watching and assisting my aunt as she created head wraps for women in the Igbo community I was raised in outside Sacramento. Aunt Rose was

Manbo Maude praying during a Danbala ceremony in Mattapan, March 2017 (photo by Eziaku Nwokocha).

well known for her elaborate head wraps. Community members came to her requesting specific head wrappings, and they also deferred to her opinions on what suited them for different occasions. I remembered my aunt explaining her process: why she folded the cloth one way or the other or why she stuck a pin in a particular place in the wrap. I had always seen it as a collaborative process, as it was in Manbo Maude's bedroom.

"I don't think it's gonna last," I said, eyeing the head wrap warily.

"What do you think about this?"[2] Shori asked, shifting the wrap closer to the center of Manbo Maude's head.

I did not think shifting the wrap would make it more stable. And so, I requested that Shori hand me the two ends of the fabric already tied around Manbo Maude's head so that I could show her what I thought would work better. I tied the base of the wrap tighter and coiled the fabric securely. Shori made suggestions as did I, and in the end, we found a design that suited Manbo Maude, who had been patient with the process, especially because we had not asked her for her opinion. She seemed pleased with the result. In Manbo Maude's temple, every female initiate is expected to wrap her hair for the ceremony to conceal their hair and cover their head. Some members of the audience also want to respect this tradition and wrap their hair as well, though that is not a requirement. The whims of each woman and her knowledge of wrapping techniques determine the elaborateness of the head wraps. Eventually, helping Manbo Maude and other Black women wrap their hair became a common task for me in preparation for ceremonies.

The experiences we shared in Manbo Maude's room—adorning ourselves by wrapping our hair and collectively configuring the aesthetics and techniques necessary to properly dress for the night's activities—were intimately connected to the ritual work ahead of us. Even in her bedroom where this informal social interaction among Black women took place, Manbo Maude's home is a site of religious innovation that reflects the dynamic relationship between gender, sexuality, and race in relation to religious ritual, material aesthetics, and spiritual embodiment within African Diasporic religions. In Manbo Maude's temple, head wrapping is a part of African Diasporic identity creation and evokes a vision of a common African past that participants draw on for their own sense of community. These head wraps claim a generalized African heritage and, in turn, a Black religious subjectivity grounded in the ideological space of Blackness. There are certainly cultural tensions between Black people from different countries and backgrounds, but in Manbo Maude's temples they do not interrupt performance rituals or the necessary work before, during, and after ceremonies.

Manbo Maude believes that all Black people have access to Vodou because of their shared African heritage.

Community formation takes work, and it is constantly shifting depending on who enters and who claims membership. Thinking alongside scholar of gender and sexuality Marlon M. Bailey's work on Ballroom culture is integral to my understanding of how community is created, maintained, and contested in Haitian Vodou and in Manbo Maude's temples. The Black performance and sociality Bailey describes in Ballroom help explain what I observe in Vodou ceremonies, where fashion and performance not only facilitate the connection to spirits but also reflect a religious culture that emphasizes seeing others and being seen by them in turn. Fashion and adornment, like ritual head wrapping, are powerful signifiers of belonging, connoting connection to other practitioners and the divine. Manbo Maude welcomes people from across the African Diaspora and non-Black people as well into her home. Building a sense of connection between them is difficult. Inevitably, tensions across race, gender, and sexuality arise among this collection of disparate people.

The real-world issues that permeate the temples rupture the attempts at sartorial solidarity, affecting not only the cohesion of Manbo Maude's communities but also the shape of people's beliefs. These communal fissures continuously raise questions about who Vodou belongs to, who has a true connection to the spirits, and what types of worship best serve the divine. Earlier I explored the role of fashion in Manbo Maude's home as an expression of religious community and an attempt to forge unity among the practitioners in Manbo Maude's temples. I introduced *spiritual vogue* as a framework for analyzing the multisensorial experience of fashion in Vodou. In this chapter, I explore how spiritual vogue and the triangulation between the audience, the practitioners, and the spirits are complicated by the social constructions that animate the identities of the participants. During ceremonies in Mattapan and Jacmel, for example, there is often an element of spectacle as White people are being possessed; seeing this occur evokes an underlying sense of suspicion or curiosity or anger. *Why are they here*, some Black practitioners ask, and *why are they interested in Vodou?*

Further complicating the cultural and social worlds of Manbo Maude's temples is the centrality of Haitian heritage to the religion. Differences in language and culture within the African Diaspora also affect the attempt to build and strengthen a religious community. Vante'm Pa Fyem, Manbo Maude's daughter, illuminated these differences by explaining how the Haitian Kreyòl word *Blan* is used: "You can be Black, you can be American, but if you are someone who wasn't born in Haiti you are called a *Blan*. You could be African American, Haitian American, if you were not born on this land, you are called a Blan. Blan means white but also means foreign[er]."[3]

Use of the word *Blan* as a catchall for non-Haitians reveals the complexities of attempting to foster solidarity in Black religious spaces, where perceptions of authenticity involve more than adherence to the faith. Even Vante'm Pa Fyem, who is a part of the Haitian *Dyaspora*, frequently travels back and forth between Haiti and the United States, and is the daughter of a Manbo, must contend with being called Blan by Haitians who were born on the island. Donning Manbo Maude's fashion designs cannot change where practitioners were born or the color of their skin. This emphasis on Haitian nationality is magnified in Jacmel. Many Blan, who might have authority in Mattapan, largely recede into the background as guests while Haitian initiates who live in Haiti put on ceremonies in Jacmel. Their authority is especially curtailed if they do not speak Haitian Kreyòl. The cultural and language barriers are significant, but they are not fixed. There are Black Americans who try to learn Haitian Kreyòl and Haitians who try to learn English, increasing their abilities to connect with one another and creating the possibility of navigating both Manbo Maude's temples.

Throughout the discussion of race, gender, and sexuality in Manbo Maude's temples, I focus on the perceptions and experiences of Black people within Haitian Vodou. For some Black folks, Vodou functions as a space of healing and community with other Black people. The inclusion of White people in a space that many view as a refuge from the anti-Black racism of the world beyond the temple is a contentious issue. Often, the Black practitioners I interviewed asked me not to include the opinions and stories they shared about White practitioners, worried about the potential interpersonal conflicts that publication of those stories might cause. For better or for worse, these White practitioners are now their spiritual siblings. As a participant observer who has the luxury of moving in and out of Manbo Maude's temples as I please, I am obligated to respect their boundaries.

The tension between Black and White practitioners is an issue Manbo Maude has had to think about carefully, and she sometimes consults the *lwa* for guidance. The number of White people she allows into her temples sometimes provokes criticism, online and in person, from Haitians and from those in the Haitian Dyaspora. Critics accuse her of welcoming White people so she can benefit from them financially.[4] However, their sense of religious insularity challenges her own beliefs about the role of Vodou. She explained,

If a White person has a cut, and a Black person has a cut, you cannot distinguish which one is the Black one or the White one. I think about it a lot. I'm like, anyone can have a problem. Anyone can use a medium to overcome difficulties. Should I dim light and deny people? . . . I understand this tradition is from the ancestors and the ancestors are from Africa. But if the tradition can help somebody, can help save somebody's life, I don't see myself saying no to somebody. I will say well, if this can help you, if you can be respectful, if you understand that this is adoption, this is not your heritage, I [say] yes, you can be part of it.[5]

Manbo Maude does not believe the healing power of Vodou can be limited to any one racial community. Pain is pain, and the spirits are a resource to address human troubles, no matter the color of the person calling on them. Although she is open to White people as practitioners, her contention that they are merely adopting the faith is tied to her belief that "Blacks belong to the tradition."[6] The spirits speak to anyone who honor them and Manbos can aid any person who needs help, yet Manbo Maude emphasizes the idea that White people are not inheritors of this religious tradition: it is not their "heritage." She expects respect from White practitioners and enough humility to understand that Black people from anywhere in the world have an inherent connection to the faith that no amount of study or enthusiasm can replicate.

Yet, respect is not a given. Manbo Maude has been forced to respond to and handle racist acts and comments by White people in her home. Behind closed doors during meetings I am not privy to, she meets with all her initiates in heated interracial conversations. Racism is called out, and Black practitioners are allowed to air their grievances. These meetings are intended to be opportunities for reconciliation, where Manbo Maude and the members of her temples can address their problems before they damage their ability to function as a religious community. Manbo Maude describes solidarity as providing the necessary cohesion for her religious community, which must appear as a unified group to guests and to the spirits during ceremonies. Interpersonal issues cannot be allowed to destroy the members' ability to execute their ritual work and serve the gods. These meetings, and even the everyday interracial interactions in her temple, require a significant investment in *emotional labor* not only by Manbo Maude but also by the members of her temples. Any spiritual community needs ongoing acts of emotional labor to function, yet Manbo

Kouzen, while possessing Manbo Maude, sulks after being momentarily disappointed by practitioners at a ceremony in Mattapan, May 2022 (photo by Eziaku Nwokocha).

Gede possessing both Manbo Maude and a Vodou practitioner (in white) while posing with members of Sosyete Nago—Manbo Gina, Manbo Carmel, Manbo Hugueline, and Manbo Cynthia—in Mattapan, November 2021 (photo by Eziaku Nwokocha).

Manbo Vante'm Pa Fyem comforts a Vodou practitioner after they were confronted by Ogou during a ceremony in Mattapan, March 2022 (photo by Eziaku Nwokocha).

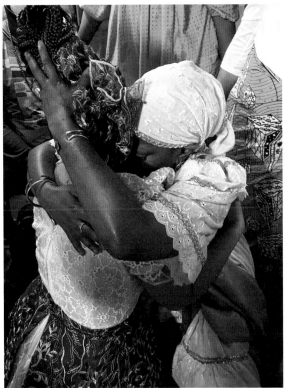

Simbi possessing Zetwal Ashade Bon Manbo while embracing Manbo Hugueline in Mattapan, March 2022 (photo by Eziaku Nwokocha).

Gede, possessing Manbo Maude, interacts with participants through Zoom in Mattapan, November 2021 (photo by Eziaku Nwokocha).

Manbo Cynthia places a cup of water on an altar during a Danbala ceremony in Mattapan, March 2022 (photo by Eziaku Nwokocha).

Manbo Hugueline and Manbo Carmel fix Manbo Cynthia's head wrap in bedroom before a Danbala ceremony in Mattapan, March 2022 (photo by Eziaku Nwokocha).

Manbo Maude looking over an assortment of trimmings at Sewfisticated in Cambridge, Massachusetts, March 2018 (photo by Eziaku Nwokocha).

Houngan Jean Marc praying to Ezili Dantò to commence her ceremony in Jacmel, July 2015 (photo by Eziaku Nwokocha).

Practitioners resting during a lull in a Gede ceremony in Mattapan, November 2021 (photo by Eziaku Nwokocha).

Kouzen possessing both Manbo Maude and Houngan Babbas as they playfully negotiate the price of produce with practitioners and audience members in Mattapan, May 2022 (photo by Eziaku Nwokocha).

Vodou practitioner adjusting Manbo Lunine's head wrap after an intense possession experience in Mattapan, November 2021 (photo by Eziaku Nwokocha).

Gede possessing Manbo Vante'm Pa Fyem during a ceremony in Mattapan, November 2021 (photo by Eziaku Nwokocha).

Gede, possessing Manbo Maude, thinks pensively while resting with one hand on his stick and the other on his chin in Mattapan, November 2004 (photo by Patrick Sylvain).

Maude's attempts to forge bonds across race (among other factors) certainly require even more time and energy.

Manbo Maude's temples are called Sosyete Nago, after the lwa Ogou, for whom she has an affinity; therefore, it is no surprise that Manbo Maude often turns to him for help in maintaining the temples. Manbo Maude believes that the racism she confronts has no place in a temple that practices Vodou, a religion born from and inherently connected to Black people—let alone one that has a strong connection with Ogou, one of the spirits summoned by enslaved Haitians as they fought for their freedom from French enslavers and colonizers. The deity's experiences combating White supremacy were literally world changing. As I discuss in chapters 1 and 2, the spirits are responsive to the lived realities—including White supremacy and racism—of practitioners. Thus, the lwa are integrally involved in her search for solutions and her attempts to maintain communal cohesion.

Manbo Maude is unwilling to let the negative comments regarding White practitioners prevent her from fulfilling her duties as a Manbo, holding firm in her belief that Vodou and the spirits have the capacity to help anyone who seeks guidance. Still, she understands the protectiveness of some Black practitioners and their reluctance to welcome people who represent grave injustices. When I asked her why some Black people are uncomfortable with White people practicing Vodou, she replied,

> Because they know that they are the colonizers and they know that they are the people who put us into slavery, they were White. . . . I know how difficult it is for somebody to accept that. My thing is that if we are preaching unit[y], can we get to a point where we say ok, I know your ancestors did that to my ancestors. And I am still feeling it and I am still dealing with it, but I am willing to kind of begin to forgive you. Not to forget, but to forgive you. . . . I don't think it's something that you can forget. But you can begin to take action to forgive, not understand, but forgive. Because without forgiveness we can never heal, because we need to heal.[7]

The belief that Vodou has the capacity to encourage forgiveness is anchored in the idea that healing is central to the faith. As Manbo Maude says, it is impossible to forget the past: it resonates too powerfully in the present to forget. And so, without disregarding past injustices, she cultivates forgiveness as an integral part of healing Black pain. While acknowledging the long history of pain wrought by colonialism and racism, Manbo Maude emphasizes the role of healing. She also believes that forgiveness demands work from White people: they should surrender to the notion that their ancestors caused harm and express a commitment to the role of being an "ally" to Black people.

Yet Manbo Maude's willingness to initiate White practitioners remains a fraught issue for some Black practitioners interested in joining her temple. For example, Babbas, a cisgender, heterosexual male Haitian initiate, was drawn to Manbo Maude's home because of her connection to Haiti and the immediate trust he felt on meeting her, but the racial makeup of her temple in Mattapan troubled him. He explained, "I was having racial conflict, I guess cultural conflict. And I had conflicts with the fact that it was so many White bodies in the space that I did not know. I was going through my own journey as a heterosexual, Black man in America as well but just as a Haitian in general."[8] Babbas foregrounds the importance of the temple as a refuge, as a religious space that offers shelter from the domination of White people in the outside world. He sees his "journey" as a Black man as not predicated on any responsibility to heal racial divides with White practitioners. Vante'm Pa Fyem echoes his sentiments, noting the historical connection between religion and resistance to oppression. She explained, "I think this is Black people finding their own space. It has been since its beginning. . . . Religion is in general people finding their own space. Black people have to do that in the context of bigotry, context of colonization, people coming—missionaries coming and throwing away their sacred objects and religious practices. All of this plays into the history of the religion."[9]

Vodou's history in many ways is the history of Haiti, which necessarily ties it to the experiences of Black people in that country. From its inception, as Vante'm Pa Fyem states, the religion has answered to their needs, providing them "space" to reckon with the legacies of White supremacist violence and to cultivate solidarity with other Black people. As central as Blackness is to Vodou, however, it is also in practice an interracial faith, especially in Manbo Maude's temple in Mattapan. Consequently, the reality of living in Boston and feeling drawn to Manbo Maude's home forced Babbas to wrestle with the conflict between his desire for a solely Black religious space and the unavoidable presence of White people. The number of White attendees made the temple less "attractive" to him, but Manbo Maude's love for the spirits convinced Babbas that they were a "distraction."[10] He could not allow their presence to prevent him from serving the divine or from recognizing her mission in Haitian Vodou, which struck him as special. "It feels like home," he shared. "My spirit brought me there."[11]

"Make Me Look African!": Fashioning Affinity through Head Wrapping

In March 2017, a year after Shori and I designed Manbo Maude's head wrap in the vignette described earlier, I was once again in her bedroom in Mattapan with other participants, getting dressed for another ceremony honoring Danbala. Manbo Maude, Shori, and I were joined by her daughter Vante'm Pa Fyem, two Haitian immigrants, and a Black American. We were changing and getting ourselves ready at around 11 P.M. in anticipation of a late ceremony, as well as watching Manbo Maude's preparations for the event. Once again, only Black women populated this space. We chatted about our outfits and people in our community using English and Haitian Kreyòl interchangeably. Manbo Maude sat on her bed in front of her dresser as she had the previous year. When she saw me, she stretched out her arm in my direction, presenting me with an emerald-green lace scarf. It had sequins and subtle yellow embroidery and was around two yards long. The length would give me enough fabric to play with and create twists, knots, movement, and height. "Okay, Eziaku," she said expectantly, "Make me look African."

I grinned and took the scarf. By asking me to tie her head wrap, Manbo Maude conferred on me a sense of cultural authenticity, enabling me to wrap her hair for the ceremony even though I was not an initiate. My African heritage, which was validated by the fact that my parents are Nigerian Igbo immigrants to the United States, gave the head wrap a connection to the continent. "There is a type of understanding that you know how to do hair because you come from the motherland," Manbo Maude explained during a phone conversation. "And I see you as an expert. . . . It's not just because you know how to wrap hair. The style comes from Africa." For centuries, head wrapping was a cultural practice in Nigeria, Senegal, Ghana, Benin, and Côte d'Ivoire in West Africa, evolving from practical use as protection from the climate into a style connected to religion and social status.[12] The meaningful use of head wrapping traveled with West Africans through the Middle Passage, changing to accommodate the social and cultural contexts of enslavement.

In the Caribbean and the United States, the head wrap was often a "mark of slavery" and simultaneously an accessory used by enslaved Black women to express their individuality and style.[13] Manbo Maude intentionally invokes the historical and cultural links between West Africa and the Americas, reaffirming those connections by calling on me to help her wrap her hair. My

Ethnographer Eziaku Nwokocha wrapping Manbo Maude's head wrap in her bedroom before a Kouzen ceremony in Mattapan, May 2022 (photo by Hugueline Fleurimond).

Igbo ethnicity seems to inspire interest in Haiti where people, on multiple occasions, broke out into song when hearing about my heritage, sharing Vodou songs that pay homage to Igbo culture. In the dressing room, I understood the interest in my ancestry to be more generalized. I am Nigerian American and therefore African, which lends me cultural credibility whether I did anything specific to earn it or not.

When I later asked Shori about Manbo Maude's willingness to allow me to participate in wrapping her hair, she said, "I think that you represent as a Nigerian woman in the house another base of knowledge that she considers sacred in its own right."[14] She contrasted my relationship to head wrapping in Manbo Maude's home with her own experience, continuing, "And then for me, I think it's more from the fact that she's seen me wear head wraps that she's liked."[15] Shori's participation in hair wrapping came about after Manbo Maude witnessed her expertise and assessed her as skillful in the craft, whereas my abilities were interpreted as being inherited from my African heritage. Manbo Maude did not know that I had spent hours watching my aunt wrap women's hair in Sacramento. Indeed, there were no clear indications that my abilities in head wrapping were unique or that the way I wrapped hair was any more "African" than the styles Shori used for the ceremonies. But my direct connection to Nigeria created a sense of cultural credibility that afforded me the opportunity to work with Manbo Maude during her preparations for the ceremony.

I was mindful of the honor of being permitted to touch Manbo Maude's head. In Vodou, the head is where the spirit lies and where mounting takes place during ceremonies. In initiation, a person's *met tet*—Haitian Kreyòl for "master of the head" and a phrase used to describe the principal spirit of protection for an initiate—is determined through the head. Moreover, the head is where the spirit resides and where practitioners dedicate themselves to certain spirits.[16] The spiritual importance of the head in Vodou derives from West Africa. For the Edo people in Nigeria, for example, "the head is the locus of reason . . . and enables a person to realize his or her destiny and potential in his life."[17] This focus on the head as central to spirituality is also present in Brazilian Candomblé and Cuban Santería.[18] Again, my Nigerian heritage granted me access to Manbo Maude's personal space and permission to touch her hair, which should not have been permitted to me as a noninitiate, "Ostensibly, there is no reason that somebody who is not initiated should be touching her head, her crown, the site of her spiritual power," Shori explained, when I asked her to elaborate on the collaborative process of head wrapping in Manbo Maude's bedroom. She continued, "I think it speaks to the trust that she's developed with you. I think that it speaks to the fact that you are African and that she regards your knowledge base as being somehow 'authentic' and beautiful."[19]

I began the process of wrapping Manbo Maude's head by draping the lace from the front of her head and tying it in the back. Watching women with head wraps as they moved during ceremonies taught me that putting the knot in the front often caused the wrap to fall off more quickly than tying the wrap in the back. Ultimately, though, there was no guarantee that the head wrap would survive any given ceremony. Sometimes, Manbo Maude's dancing and movement while mounted was so energetic that no head wrap I could create would stay in place. During those nights, I lowered my expectations and hoped that whatever material I fashioned for her would at least last for the first half of the ceremony when she welcomed guests into her home in her completed outfit. I also learned from my aunt that the texture of a woman's hair affected which materials should be used for the head wrap. Because Manbo Maude's hair had been relaxed, I had to cover her hair with a white satin fabric first so that the lace head wrap would not slip off her head. The impression she made on the people entering her home was important, and I did not want participants to be distracted during prayer or the start of the ceremony by an unkempt appearance. After five years of attending her ceremonies, I understood the image Manbo Maude wanted to maintain.

After tying a knot in the fabric at the back of her head, I used the remaining material to create height by twisting and folding it. The other women in the room nodded and hummed in agreement. Completing the head wrap required more hands than just mine. Shori held the scarf down against Manbo Maude's head and added hairpins to secure the lace. Trial and error were involved. I would twist the fabric in one direction and then would be told by one of the women that the design did not flatter Manbo Maude's face, or Manbo Maude would tell me the wrap was too high and she did not appreciate the way it looked. We started over in response to these comments. In general, Manbo Maude was satisfied by the designs I and others created, especially when there was a consensus within the group that it was beautiful. Often, her daughter's approval was all the confirmation she needed. We twisted the green lace and wrapped it around her head. White was a color used to honor Danbala, so its peeking through the green lace on top would complement the green-and-white color scheme of the ceremony. "Danbala is really showing," Vante'm Pa Fyem commented, beaming.[20]

All the hands involved in creating Manbo Maude's head wrap were Black: Nigerian American, Haitian, Haitian Dyaspora, and Black American. The head wraps created in Manbo Maude's room represent an "assembled" aesthetics, not born in a void but assembled from the cultures and histories of the Black women in the room who brought their complicated and varied heritage together in one space in the service of their shared religious practices.[21] Later, I asked Manbo Maude why she consistently asks Black women, like Shori and me, instead of the White women in the house, to help her with her head wrapping. She responded, "I think it's common sense. They're used to wrapping their own hair. They will have a sense of how to do it. It's not in White people's tradition. I wouldn't be comfortable asking them to do my hair unless I will see them perform that and I will see, 'Oh, they have some talent, let me ask, yeah.' It's just like a sisterhood thing. You know, I am sorry, it's not racism. It's just that we click better. It's sisters! [laughs out loud] We click better."[22] The Black women in Manbo Maude's bedroom create and reinforce bonds of sisterhood and solidarity not only through their conversations where they share personal information but also through the affirmation of the changing room. They offer compliments and constructive advice, seek validation and assistance, or playfully correct wardrobe malfunctions. For instance, when the zipper broke on someone's dress, other women helped pin the garment together or wrapped scarves around her waist to keep the dress closed, adding an unexpected accessory to the outfit. The bedroom is a site where sisterhood is fostered, where collective knowledge and collective memories are disseminated and expressed in a gendered space.

The changing room becomes what Robin D. G. Kelley calls an "alternative" cultural space, defined by the shared religious and cultural knowledge of Vodou and by the potential for refuge from the racism and sexism of the world beyond Manbo Maude's home.[23] Gathering in Manbo Maude's room to prepare for ceremonies is not a "clear act of resistance"; Manbo Maude and the other Black women in the room were not discussing explicitly political ideas that stood in direct opposition to the larger, predominantly White society around them. Yet this gathering constitutes a more subtle act of resistance that emphasizes survival and community building across the African Diaspora.[24] The connections built in the changing room also contribute to the care, or *intimate labor*, shown later during the ceremony as that sense of caring is maintained throughout the process of possession and the religious rituals.

The affective sense of camaraderie that is cultivated in the changing room moves into the ceremony where these same Black women surrender their bodies to the vulnerabilities of *pran lwa*, the physically exhausting dances, and the stresses of organizing and managing the ceremony. The changing room, just as surely as the ceremony itself, is a space of "spiritual empowerment," where Black women find strength and community through collectively engaging with ritual fashion and religious practice. Preparing their aesthetic appearance is a crucial element in summoning the spirits later in the night, which they perceive to have real, material effects on their everyday lives. The process of preparing ritual outfits is part of how Manbo Maude creates a sense of solidarity in her religious community. She is with her "sisters," which helps construct an idea of African Diasporic connection and creativity.[25]

During the preparation for Manbo Maude's ceremonies, Black women are principally responsible for head wrapping and aiding each other in the practice; I never saw a man of any race or sexual orientation contribute to this ritual process, although that may occur in other temples. Black women also assist White women initiates when asked. Although I never observed a White woman assist a Black woman in wrapping her hair, I did witness White women initiates wrapping their own hair. This dynamic changes during ceremonies when Black women are possessed: if a White female initiate is nearby and the possessed Black woman needs assistance fixing a head wrap that was disturbed by the exertions of the ritual, the White woman will adjust or rewrap the fabric. Moreover, White women initiates might also tie *moushwa*, ritual silk headscarves that signify which spirit is present during a ceremony, around the heads of Black women initiates for ritual purposes when calling on the spirits. These are rare occurrences because Black women outnumber White women in Manbo Maude's ceremonies. Yet, for Samentha, a Black practitioner in Manbo Maude's home, the racial makeup of the Black women involved in head wrapping is unrelated to the greater number of Black people and has a more practical purpose than creating a sense of sisterhood. Black women's involvement is about style and technique:

One could argue that it's not actually such a fundamental difference in the way that Haitian women wrap their hair. But it's done less expertly [by White women]. . . . The way that the Haitian women do it is so expertly done. It's tight! You know it's not gonna slip; it's not gonna fall. It's like *byen marle*. The word is *byen marle*, like well woven, well tied, well wrapped. You know, whereas a lot of White women, they will do the same style, but it's all loose. But part of the reason it's all loose is because they don't know how to tie it. . . . To be quite frank, seeing people wrap their hair who are White in a fashion that to me doesn't at all resemble the way that women of color wrap their hair was kind of like, yeah, this is yet one more way that you all don't quite fit in.[26]

Samentha describes a disparity between the technical skills of Black women, whom she perceives as having more experience, and White women, whose efforts are more amateur. She is concerned with the practical matter of whether a head wrap is tight enough to endure women's energetic movements during a ceremony. The gulf between the skills of White women and Black women contributes to Samentha's sense of who belongs where with respect to aspects of ceremonial preparation and participation. Her observations of the varying levels of skills in head wrapping reinforce her ideas of who does or does not belong in the room during those social moments before ritual. If White women cannot tie a head wrap tight enough to last through a significant portion of a ceremony, then essentially they do not "fit in" the preparations in Manbo Maude's room. They cannot contribute properly to those preparations or ensure that the ritual fashion would be constructed well, whereas their Black peers can. Because of the importance of fashion in Manbo Maude's Vodou ceremonies, the variation in skills is especially noticeable.

The differentiation between Black women and White women extends beyond perceptions of technical skills in head wrapping into the physical space of ceremonial preparation. As previously discussed, Manbo Maude's room was bustling with Black women. I never heard anyone explicitly request this racial stratification: it was just understood that White women initiates in Manbo Maude's community did not change in her bedroom. They changed clothes in the attic of her home or went into a room across the hall from Manbo Maude's bedroom. Usually, if I saw White women in her bedroom at all, it was to ask for help with tying their head wraps or zipping up their dresses. Their visits were brief; after they received help, they left the room. I was not sure whether the racial homogeneity of the room was purposeful. When I asked about the racial organization of the changing rooms and the people involved in head wrapping, Manbo Maude did not seem to have ever considered the matter and struggled to find an explanation: "Well, to tell you the truth, I don't know. Maybe they don't want to. I don't know, they are just not interested. I am guessing, the reason is because they are White, and the head wrapping is part of the African tradition. But they may feel uncomfortable. But they have not said anything to me. But it's just like, now that you are saying it. . . . I think that you are right. They have never asked. Because I think there is a barrier."[27] Manbo Maude also noted that the male initiates— whether White, Black, or Latinx—involved in the ceremonies often arrived in their ritual outfits: white pants and a white buttoned-up shirt. Sometimes they changed into their outfit hours before the start of the ceremony.

Non-initiates invited to the ceremony were encouraged to wear white or whatever color was associated with the spirit who was being honored. There were also Black, White, and Latinx women, initiates and non-initiates, who arrived in their ceremonial clothes and did not make use of any of Manbo Maude's rooms for preparation.

Vante'm Pa Fyem extended the differentiation of race, explaining that one's race determines the amount of work one does in the temple. *Blan*, in this case referring to White people, are usually ready for the start of the ceremony before Black practitioners are: "Of course, the Blan are going to be ready first because they don't really do anything during the day. They set up downstairs and they are pretty much done. The Black people in the house are cooking, cleaning, doing laundry. There is a different sense of obligation there. Sometimes it upsets my Mom. If we were able to spread things more evenly, ceremonies could get started sooner."[28] For Vante'm Pa Fyem, the "barrier" to participation that Manbo Maude described has a direct impact on the practical realities of the temple. Ceremonies start later because the labor is not spread evenly among the members of the home: the burden of preparing for the event falls on the shoulders of Black people. Manbo Maude and Samentha both mentioned the concept of "comfort" when attempting to describe the racial divisions in the temple. Vante'm Pa Fyem also cited "comfort" but followed up the thought by saying, "I think it's really a cultural thing."[29]

Vante'm Pa Fyem's insight is valuable. Underlying the persistent invocation of comfort and familiarity are expectations about who should be responsible for ritual preparation and who has an inherent cultural connection to those rituals. Which practitioners attend to a given task is also governed by example. The fact that Haitians dominate the kitchen space sets the expectation for new Haitians entering the home; the fact that White people commonly set up the altars encourages other White people to follow. Sometimes practitioners I interviewed described these divisions as "unintentional," the natural outgrowth of differences in nationality, race, and language that occur without anyone making a conscious decision.[30] Practitioners gravitate toward the people and duties they are familiar with. Yet, all the practitioners, Black and White, bought the needed supplies for the ceremonies, such as alcohol or food, and draw multiple *vèvè*, Haitian Kreyòl for symbols of the lwa, for the spirits on the floor of the basement.

At the Danbala ceremony I asked Natasha, another practitioner, to share her observations of the racial dynamics of Manbo Maude's home in Mattapan. Natasha is a first-generation Caribbean American woman from

St. Vincent, who was attending a ceremony with Manbo Maude for the first time. She had spent a year communicating with Manbo Maude online through Facebook and receiving spiritual readings from her over the phone, but at this time was not officially a member of the temple. Having somewhat of an outsider's perspective, she noticed the racial separation and offered her observations through a conversation with me via Skype: "There was this sort of separation. Because it felt like Manbo Maude put me on the second floor like 'You go here.' It's funny, I wasn't hyper aware of it initially until I saw people start coming down the stairs. And then I was like 'Oh . . . I'm in! I'm in!'"[31] Because Natasha was from the Midwest and had grown up in a predominantly White environment, the fact that she was included in the preparations taking place on the second floor was important for her identity as a Black woman. She told me that, where she was raised, she was often "coded as White" because of her light-skinned complexion. But in Manbo Maude's home, she was invited to join the other Black women participating in and observing the ceremony, which made her feel a sense of inclusion. For Natasha the racial separation was about what Kelley defined as "congregation," gathering with other Black women and reinforcing her sense of identity by allowing her to "construct and enact a sense of solidarity."[32] She understood the idea of "sisterhood" that Manbo Maude expressed, which was enhanced by the process of jointly preparing their clothing for the ceremony, and was pleased to be considered part of that group of women.

Earlier in the evening, however, Natasha's feeling of belonging was less secure, largely because of the religious fashion expected at Manbo Maude's ceremonies. After Shori and I finished changing in Manbo Maude's bedroom, we hovered in the foyer near the living room as other people set up for the ceremony: cooking, setting up the altar in the basement, and folding the moushwa. Natasha walked up the stairs and we greeted each other. She immediately asked me whether the length of her skirt was appropriate for the occasion. I looked down to where the hem of her simple, white cotton skirt stopped just above her ankles and told her it was suitable.[33] She seemed relieved. Later, when I asked her about dressing for the ceremony, she explained, "I was a little self-conscious because I noticed that my attire was not the same as everyone else. So, it's a little bit like 'Hmmm, am I *in* enough?' I was in a room with people like, 'Is this ok? Is this alright? It's not too tight?' Because I felt like what I was wearing was a lot tighter than what a lot of other people were wearing. They had a lot more fabric."[34] Again, Natasha emphasized the importance of fitting in with the rest of the religious community and was relying primarily on her clothing to determine whether she had accomplished this goal. She was anxious about her ritual outfit not fitting the norms set by Manbo Maude and the other members of her temple. Her worry pinpointed the effectiveness of Manbo Maude's use of fashion in her home and the pressure that prospective practitioners might feel to conform to that standard of ritual adornment.

The emphasis placed on the clothing and adornments in Manbo Maude's bedroom and among the Black women in her "sisterhood" reflects the women's understanding that the preparations taking place there are inextricably connected to the practice of Vodou in her temple. Head wraps, dresses, moushwa, and the various rituals performed throughout the night constitute what philosopher Paul C. Taylor describes as "expressive objects and practices," which are constantly at work in Manbo Maude's bedroom and in her ceremonies and are responsible for "creating and maintaining Black life-worlds."[35] These Black life-worlds can be imagined in a number of ways: Vodou itself, or African Diasporic religious and cultural formations, or the rituals taking place in Manbo Maude's temples. The head wraps participants fashion, the dresses they wear, and the makeup they put on our faces are the "expressive" means through which are formed the Black life-worlds of Manbo Maude's Vodou home and community. The relationships fostered in Manbo Maude's bedroom are practices essential to creating community and encouraging the considerate, cooperative behaviors needed to produce Vodou ceremonies.

Charged with Spiritual Energy: Ritual Clothing as Conduit and Breaker

The importance of ritual clothing in Manbo Maude's temple is undeniable, but the sentiments of the people in her home about religious fashion vary. The initiates and participants I interviewed imagine the role of ritual outfits as a connection to the spirits, the African Diaspora, and Haiti. Different aspects of ritual clothing, such as the process of getting dressed, the colors of the outfits, or the use of the clothing during ceremonies, affect the way practitioners engage with fashion in Manbo Maude's temple. These varying interpretations provide a means to examine the role of Haitian Vodou and material culture in the lives of practitioners and participants, which emphasizes how community, identity, and the spirits are imagined in an African Diasporic religious space. The lived experiences of the practitioners in Manbo Maude's home are points of inflection that create a diverse array of opinions on ritual fashion, often reflecting the geographic and cultural histories of their lives.

I spoke to Nadège, a middle-aged, cisgender heterosexual female Haitian immigrant who is an initiate and a Manbo in Manbo Maude's temple, on the phone on her day off from her job as a nurse in Boston. She described wearing ritual clothing as a form of transformation, a visceral, sensorial connection to the spirits.[36] For Nadège, donning religious clothing created "electricity":

> The moment you put those spirit clothes on, you don't feel yourself anymore. You feel like you are on top of the world because you feel the vibration on you, you feel so good. Especially when you dance, we all line up, holding the candle going downstairs. There's a vibration there. You feel the spirit with you. You feel something like electricity. Some kind of electricity from the bottom of your feet. You feel like a chill. It goes from your toes all the way up to the top of your head. You feel like you are transforming. The spirit is with you. You know you are not yourself. You feel like something on you. That means that you are surrounded.[37]

In Nadège's description, sacred clothing itself is a connection with the spirits: she experiences the physical manifestation of the divine through the ritual outfits she wears. The sensations she described, the "electricity" she felt moving through her body, reinforce her beliefs in the presence of spirits and her religious commitment. Wearing ritual outfits, whether in a ceremony or elsewhere, immediately affects her body and transforms her into a vessel for the spirits, proving the link between the clothing and the divine. During ceremonies, her religious clothing acts as a medium for spiritual connections, combining with her movement and dancing and entwining her with the divine. For Nadège, ritual outfits are inseparable from the presence of the gods. Even though Manbo Maude did not tell me about any special rituals performed on the clothes themselves, Nadège describes feeling a sense of the spirit as soon as she dons her ceremonial garments. Her connection to the dresses is derived from the presence of the lwa, within or outside the ceremonial space. For example, she shared with me that when she wants to feel close to the spirits, she wears her ceremonial dresses.[38] She has integrated this proximity to the divine into her everyday life, sporting the clothes while vacuuming and attending to other chores around her home.

The belief that ritual garments hold special power is not unique to Nadège. Babbas offered another perspective on the role fashion played in Manbo Maude's temple and in his personal experiences as a practitioner. For the ceremony honoring Danbala, Babbas wore a plain white t-shirt and pleated white pants. In past ceremonies, men wore shirts proclaiming the name of

Manbo Maude's temple, Sosyete Nago, in aerosol spray-painted words or collared buttoned-up shirts. The relative simplicity of Babbas's outfit is indicative of the current fashion in Manbo Maude's temple, which is distinctly gendered: the clothing that men wear is not as detailed or elaborate as the clothing women wear. Generally, the clothing worn in her home is decided by the person's gender presentation or personal gender identity, and their assigned sex at birth is irrelevant. As mentioned in chapter 1, fashion can be used to connote differences in status between women within the religious community, but this is not the case for men, who all usually wear the same ritual outfits: high-ranking Houngans dress the same as newly initiated ti feỳ. For Manbo Maude, the focus is on the elaborate dresses worn by women. Yet, despite the gendered stylistic differences, the men in her temples are expected to participate in every ceremony, and their clothing still holds spiritual and ritual importance.

As stated, the significance of the fashion in Manbo Maude's temple varies among the participants. Babbas's use of ritual outfits is closely connected to his emigration from Haiti and his sense of belonging. The colors of the clothes he wears at ceremonies represent his close ties to his home in Haiti. He does not feel a strong connection to Boston, so he wears white to signal not only his respect for the spirits and the ritual of the ceremony but also to represent his existence in a liminal space. "My family is not here; I didn't want to be here. I am just being honest," he explained. "I just don't feel at home. So, like I said, white is what I feel. It is what I usually wear, it is my preparation of not being home."[39] Babbas uses color to connect with people in a shared religious community and to represent his sense of dislocation, a reminder of where his true home was. White connected him to the spirits, but it also represented a transitional space. When he wore reds, blues, greens, and other colors beyond white, he was anchored to Haiti and the sensational experience of ceremonies there. Because of this sensorial and spiritual connection to his homeland, he chose to reserve the use of such colors for the ceremonies he attended in Haiti.

Babbas's thoughtful engagement with religious fashion extends beyond the ceremonies themselves: he places great value on clothes as sacred items. Like Nadège, he describes the spirits as present and real; the clothing acts in part as a vessel for spiritual energy. Because of this presence, he cannot casually or carelessly disregard this clothing, even after the ceremony ends. "I wash it, I fold it, and I am wearing this again next year," Babbas explained. "So, it's like an understanding. It's like a promise that I am not throwing it away. Or if anything happens to it, I am gonna protect it, I am gonna fix it,

I'm gonna make it better."[40] In Jacmel, Babbas's clothes are washed by the laundresses Manbo Maude employs, maintaining the gendered labor divisions in the temple. In Massachusetts, however, he is responsible for taking care of his own spiritual garments.

Babbas believes that how a practitioner cares for clothing is just as important as the ritual process as putting it on. To extend the life of these clothes, he engages in an active process of improving and repairing them. His treatment of his ritual outfits represents a "promise" between himself and the spirits, a commitment to continued reverence and devotion. The care he shows his clothing reflects his reverence for the spirits and for Vodou itself. "I hope you respect it," he said, expounding on the process of preserving ritual outfits, offering his wishes for other practitioners and participants. "I hope you carry it in a certain way. I hope you don't disrespect it, you know; I hope when you get home you don't just take it off throw it somewhere and step on it." Because his clothing is doing spiritual work, aiding in calling spirits into a ceremony, the fashion transforms into a sacred item and needs to be afforded respect. This is a practice that Manbo Maude demonstrates as well. Although she produces a large amount of clothing, she is meticulous about cleaning her pieces after wearing them, either having them dry cleaned or washing her clothes by hand. She also stores her clothing in various containers, keeping them for future use or for her own collection and inspiration, protecting and archiving the history of previous ceremonies and the ritual work the dresses enable her to pursue.

The elaborate fashion in Manbo Maude's temple can positively shape a practitioner's experiences with the spirits, but that is not always the result. The economic realities of purchasing the dresses influence Samentha's opinions on their necessity and functionality:

I wouldn't say it's necessarily my favorite part. I really like doing head wraps. And some of the dresses I like; some of the dresses I don't like. I like preparing. I like doing my little makeup and doing that with the other ladies. But I feel less enthralled by the dress itself because there are times when I don't have a dress, right? So, there are times in Boston, for instance, where I just don't have the money to do the dress that year. And because I don't have the money, I am going to be the only one who stands out, and who looks different, and who isn't a part of that inner circle. And I think it creates some differentials. And to be very honest I think it's extravagant to do a new dress every single ceremony for every single year.[41]

Samentha enjoys the preparations for the ceremony, helping other women get dressed and wrap their hair or put on makeup, but does not feel any enthusiasm for the dresses themselves. She feels they can be "frou frou" or over the top and flamboyant. She expresses much less excitement over the dresses than does Nadège, who seems to relish the role of spiritual dress in her ceremonial experiences. Moreover, whatever spiritual meaning Samentha may have experienced through the dresses is tempered by their costs or by feeling embarrassed when she is unable to afford the same clothes as the rest of her religious community.

Manbo Maude's intention to create a sense of religious unity in her home seems to have been successful, but Samentha's words reveal an obstacle to this solidarity. The failure to don the same dress as the other members of Manbo Maude's home made her feel distant from her peers, thereby negating part of the purpose of the ritual outfits. Samentha's opinions shed light on the financial resources needed to maintain the solidarity that Manbo Maude has cultivated in her communities through fashion. For most ceremonies Manbo Maude performs in Mattapan, she has a new dress made for herself and her initiates. The frequency of the ceremonies that require dresses, occurring many times a year, became financially burdensome for Samentha. Her sentiments are shared by others. The expense of becoming part of Manbo Maude's Vodou communities is an issue that she must negotiate as a religious leader interested in increasing the number of practitioners and maintaining her temples.

Trop Blan: Judging Who Adorns the Spirits

Each practitioner interprets the will of the spirits differently. As Manbo Maude makes clear, the gods do not concern themselves with race: that is the province of the people who serve them. She, along with other practitioners I spoke with, stated that the spirits use whomever they need to get the work done. Once again, it is human beings, forced to reckon with the social constructions of their earthly realm, who introduce racial divisions. I observed those divisions in March 2018 while attending a ceremony in the basement of Manbo Maude's home in Mattapan. What I witnessed did not merely suggest a contradiction between the practice of Vodou and the will of the spirits but also generated questions about how the will of the spirits is seen and felt during a ceremony and which bodies are judged as authentically connected to the divine.

The interplay between race and racial division is thorny: the hatreds, prejudices, and inequalities of race are certainly human, and yet Manbo Maude and others understand the lwa to be Black gods. Their Blackness is not questioned: they are West and Central African, which means they are Black. It is innate to them, not bequeathed to them through the perceptions of their worshippers. However, what their Blackness means and how it is expressed through Vodou are determined by the people who animate the faith: Blackness, too, is constructed. Not all Black Vodou practitioners believe that their Black gods are so willing to commune with White people or that White people have any business in the religion at all. The divine is Black, they claim, and so they are principally concerned with Black devotees.[42] Manbo Maude and others like her would argue that, although the gods are Black, their power and reach encompass the whole world and all the people in it, regardless of race or skin color. These are foundational cosmological ideas that express beliefs about the nature of Black divinities, and the conclusions reached by practitioners have consequences for how they practice their faith and whom they incorporate into their religious community.

Cosmological differences reveal themselves during ceremonies in the interactions between practitioners, the audience, and the spirits. Race, sexuality, and gender are observable fault lines in Manbo Maude's temples, despite the effort she makes to encourage cohesion. The following vignette illustrates the tensions of her diverse religious community. These divisions became clear during a ceremony for Danbala in March 2018 that was set to begin at around 11 P.M. I went down the stairs to the basement, moving past the crowd of people standing in the room. Most of the people in the house, some of whom were unaffiliated with Manbo Maude's Vodou home and some who belonged to her temple, had gathered in the basement, waiting for Manbo Maude to appear and begin the ceremony. Even though I arrived two hours early, I was fortunate to have found someone hours earlier to save me a seat. Samuel, a Black, gay American man who was a Vodou practitioner, waved me over and patted the metal folding chair next to him.[43] As I sat down, I overheard audience members speculating on what Manbo Maude was going to wear. We sat and talked among ourselves for thirty minutes until finally she, her daughter, and a female Haitian initiate walked down the stairs.[44]

Manbo Maude was wearing the green lace head wrap that Shori and I had helped her fashion and an embroidered white cotton dress that went down to her ankles. Her sleeves featured six tiers of white embroidered ruffles that stopped at her elbows. The fabric of the top half of the dress was sheer, so she wore a white tank top underneath. She had on pearl earrings, several rings, a simple, gold necklace with a cross pendant, and two gold bangle bracelets. One of the bracelets was shaped like a snake coiling around her wrist, a symbol of Danbala. She layered a green lace skirt that tied around her waist over her white dress. The skirt had a gap in the front where the white of her dress showed through, framed by the flowing ruffled trim of the green material. She wore white sandals with silver buckles on top. Unlike many of her other ceremonies, this event would not feature Manbo Maude and her initiates changing their ritual outfits. She was more flexible in her requirements for ritual outfits when honoring Danbala. Primarily, this was because Danbala was one of the first spirits to be called in the line of ritual.

During Vodou ceremonies, the lwa are called on in a particular order, and each spirit is honored with a minimum of three to four songs during this procession. One song welcomes them, the second celebrates their presence, and the third ushers them out so the group can move on to the next spirit. Any one of these songs can be sung repeatedly. With at least thirteen spirits to call on, Manbo Maude's ceremonies in Mattapan were long events; they required a significant time commitment. The other commitments of the participants also determined the duration of the ceremony: people had jobs and could not attend an event that lasted well into the next day. Usually, her ceremonies in Mattapan ended by 7 A.M., so some of the participants could be at work by 7:30. In Jacmel, the number of spirits honored in her ceremonies tripled: she could start her ceremonies earlier in the day there, which enabled her to honor additional spirits. Moreover, there were more people in Haiti who were able to sing the songs for the spirits. She could pass the microphone along to another person and rest her voice while the line of ritual continued, increasing the minimum number of songs to five to seven for each spirit.

Before the procession of spirits could begin, Manbo Maude needed to complete her ritual of Catholic and ancestral prayers and songs. Catholic prayers were often featured in Vodou ceremonies, and in Manbo Maude's rituals they were brief interludes before longer prayers dedicated to *Ginen*, which called the spirits into the *fete* and could last as long as two hours. Ginen translates to "Africa" and, in a religious context, connotes an African realm underneath the oceans that practitioners believe their souls will reach after death, joining their ancestors.[45] Ginen prayers are a universal feature of Vodou ceremonies, because they call on the lwa to be present and ask for protection and healing for the participants, although they differ in length.

Catholic prayers, in contrast, are not standard for all Vodou homes. I witnessed ceremonies in Montreal and Boston where the Catholic prayers lasted ten to twenty minutes and others where they were not recited. The inclusion of these prayers largely depends on the practitioners' personal relationship to Catholicism, how they were taught to begin a ceremony by their spiritual mothers or fathers, and their opinions on the incorporation of Catholicism into traditions that are historically African or Haitian. For some Black devotees, Catholicism represents White religious practices and can function as a reminder of French colonization, forced conversion, and the generations of Vodou practitioners who had to hide their religious practices for fear of punishment. However, for others, the blending of Catholic traditions with Vodou rituals illuminates the complexity of Vodou as a religion, which includes different traditions from many African cultures — including those of the Kongolese, some of whom had already converted to Catholicism before they were enslaved. Moreover, the inclusion of Catholic rituals reflects the religious diversity of Haiti as a nation throughout its history.

During Manbo Maude's prayers to Ginen, some people in the audience bowed their heads, and others sang along, or covertly texted, or took furtive swigs from their mostly alcoholic drinks. People clapped when they were supposed to clap and responded when the songs demanded callbacks. As Manbo Maude continued praying and singing, Samuel leaned over, glancing around the room, and whispered to me, "There's a lot of fucking White people here." I snickered, surprised that he was comfortable enough to share the sentiment even though we had only met that afternoon. I scanned the room and tried to count the number of White people in attendance, curious as to what constituted "a lot" in his estimation. I counted twelve White people, more White folks in the room than I remembered seeing at any previous ceremony in Manbo Maude's home. I counted around fifty Black people in the room, Haitian and American, and two or three Latinx people. It was not uncommon to see White people practicing Haitian Vodou; in fact, many of the White scholars making significant contributions to the study of Vodou became Vodou initiates.[46] For some, Whiteness, admittedly, acted as a barrier, preventing them from gaining insight into the opinions and rituals of Black Vodou practitioners. Therefore, becoming an initiate helped them bridge the distance and contributed to their ability to produce work about Vodou. For others, becoming initiated was a personal journey into their own spirituality. A number of White people who were initiated in Manbo Maude's home were scholars or felt a personal connection to Vodou, and they often openly discussed their reasons for practicing the religion before or after the ceremonies.

After the prayers to Ginen concluded, no drums accompanied Manbo Maude at this point in the ceremony, only the sound of her rattle. Samuel and I were facing the altar where she sat in a chair in the center of the room and prayed with her back to us. Danbala's vèvè was drawn on the floor in yellow chalk in front of her. Male and female initiates sat on her left side, listening to her prayers. Behind me, a Haitian man whispered to the Haitian woman sitting beside him, *"Trop Blan,"* Haitian Kreyòl for "a lot of White people." If he meant his comment to go unnoticed, he failed. I spoke Haitian Kreyòl well enough to understand his words. I glanced at him, and he gave me a head nod in response.

Natasha shared with me later that she perceived a certain level of discomfort among the Black participants and members of the audience because of the presence of an unusually high number of White people, particularly gay White males. She was seated next to the Black male drummers, and she watched them whisper to one another and "pass weird glances" throughout the opening prayer. She described some of these drummers rolling their eyes at the White men in the audience as they were fanning themselves because of the warmth generated in the crowded basement. It was difficult to interpret the exact cause of the drummers' discomfort: Was it the Whiteness of the men, their sexuality, or both?

The procession of spirits continued. A group of three gay White men danced two feet in front of where Samuel and I were sitting, shuffling from side to side as the drummers played. One of the men, an initiate, was especially off the beat. He was an average-sized man in his early to mid-twenties. Dancing barefoot, he wore white linen pants and a white cotton shirt. With arms folded across his chest, sucking his teeth in annoyance, and sliding down in his seat, Samuel watched the White man, saying, "Look at him. He doesn't know how to move. He doesn't know what to do. I don't know why they're all initiated, and they don't know what to do. If I were them, I would sit the fuck down." The White initiate heard Samuel's words, glancing over his shoulder at us. I was embarrassed that Samuel was speaking so loudly. The man moved away from us and closer to the other two White gay men who were dancing nearby. He kept dancing.

The Vodou practitioners then called on Ezili Freda, the goddess of love and wealth, singing her a song of welcome and praise. A Haitian Houngan called forth a Haitian woman initiate and tied a light pink moushwa, Freda's representative color, on her head, handing her an ason. Another Black female initiate stood to her right with a white cup of water, used to pour libations in the four corners of the room to conjure the spirits. The initiates poured the water three times in each corner, signifying the trilogy of the beginning, middle, and end of a human life cycle. A White male initiate held a candle and followed the two Black women as they walked to each corner of the room. Members of Manbo Maude's temple continued to dance and sing to Ezili Freda to welcome her to the ceremony. As the Black woman was finishing dousing the last corner of the room, she began dancing backward, swaying her head from side to side and rolling her shoulders. Her eyes rolled back into her head. She started to undulate to the rhythm of the Vodou drums. Her hands flailed upward over her head. She prissily chattered a series of teh teh teh noises, a sound associated with Ezili Freda when she possesses a devotee. The deity had arrived. Instantly, three Haitian male initiates ran to the altar to get the lightly scented perfume, white rum, and white lace hand fan to welcome and adorn her. One man splashed her hands and feet with the perfume, while another gave her the fan so she could cool herself. The third man sprayed her feet with rum by taking a few sips of the alcohol and spitting it out from between his teeth.

Male initiates and non-initiates, Black and White, came forth to greet Ezili Freda. Some linked both of their pinkie fingers with both of hers, raised their joined hands upward, and then touched their foreheads to their fists. This was one of the many standard greetings that signified a connection between the participant and the lwa. Others gave Ezili Freda a hug and asked for favors of money or romantic love. She returned the greetings by either kissing them on the forehead, smearing perfume on their face and neck, or splashing Florida Water cologne on their face or chest. Male initiates usually tend to Ezili Freda. This was primarily because Ezili Freda viewed other women as competition and wanted to be the center of attention. Sometimes she even shied away from greetings offered by female participants, who may not have been aware of her preference for male adulation.

Manbo Maude and two other Haitian women were also mounted by Ezili Freda during the ceremony. Initiates tied additional pink moushwa on these women's heads and arms to signify Ezili Freda's presence. Soon, all the men, both initiates and audience members, Black and White, went to one of the four Black women to receive their blessings. Three White gay male initiates were also mounted, including Liam,[47] the man sitting in the section of the room in which Samuel and I sat. We both watched as Liam shook and fluttered his hands at his sides, whimpering but smiling. Two other White gay male initiates tied pink moushwa around his head and arm. They both greeted Ezili Freda by linking pinkie fingers and pressing their fists to their foreheads. Liam walked around throughout the room during his possession. Black Haitian men who saw him smiled slightly but did not greet him as enthusiastically as they did the possessed Black women. They let him pass by.

Liam's possession did not last for very long. He fell out of possession, falling backward toward the floor at Ezili Freda's departure. The two White initiates who had helped him before caught him and assisted him to a nearby chair for rest. They fanned him and gave him water. Aiding people in the aftermath of pran lwa is a standard task for initiates in Vodou ceremonies. The Black men still attending to the possessed Black women only a few feet away from Liam were prepared to assist in their recovery but seemed uninterested in helping Liam. It is common for Ezili Freda to mount gay men: her hyperfeminine presentation is often considered compatible with them.[48] However, I rarely saw heterosexual men possessed by Ezili Freda. Being possessed by a feminine spirit associated with homosexuality risks jeopardizing men's personal sense of masculinity and the perception of their masculinity within their community. In theory, then, Liam's possession was not unusual, yet awkwardness arose, and divisions were made visible. It disrupted the *emotional* and *intimate labors* normally performed in a ceremony, which were offered only to the possessed people whom individual practitioners and audience members felt comfortable with.

The divide I observed in this moment does not occur in all ceremonies, but what is important is that it illustrates the racial, sexual, and gender dynamics of adornment and ritual. This moment captures the reality of a division in Manbo Maude's religious community that cannot be easily bridged by the fellowship encouraged by her use of fashion and aesthetics in her ceremonies. Compellingly, race and sexuality interceded in the traditional ritual use of fashion and adornment. There seemed to be a discomfort not only with the presence of White people but also with White people participating in possession. When I asked Samentha about this ceremony over the phone, she elaborated on her thoughts about the racial dynamics of Manbo Maude's ceremony:

> I think there was a divide because I think Haitians are always suspicious as to whether Blan can really be mounted by spirit. Frankly, I am too. And to be honest, [2017] was the first year that I ever seen so many Blan being mounted by spirit. It may have been the first time I have ever saw Blan who were mounted period. So, the fact that it was like raining cats and dogs of Blan being mounted seemed a little ridiculous. And I don't think that they were completely faking it. But it was a little suspect, a little suspect . . .
>
> The other thing is that in Haiti and in Haitian Vodou women can be mounted by both male spirits and female spirits. But it's pretty

unusual to see men mounted by female spirits. . . . The few exceptions that I can think of are men who are mounted by Freda who are
gay. And that still happens rarely, but if you are going to see something like that, that's typically what you are going to see. That's been
my experience. So, with that in mind, I think there was a double layer
of suspicion. And I think the cautious part was "*Ki Blan sa a k'ap pran
lwa konsa?* (Who is this White person who thinks that they have
spirit?)"[49]

As a Black woman who spent a great deal of time visiting Haiti and convers-
ing with practitioners, Samentha felt comfortable elaborating on how some
Haitians react to White people participating in Vodou. For her, race affected
the authenticity of pran lwa and the legitimacy of being connected to the spirits during religious ritual. As she stated, during the ceremony several White
people were mounted in addition to Liam, which caused her to doubt the authenticity of the possession taking place. Race was not the only factor that
gave her pause; gender also did so. She had expectations as to which gendered bodies could be taken over by which gendered spirits based on ceremonies witnessed in the past. Samentha explained that typically men were
possessed by male spirits, and women could be possessed by both male and
female spirits. As stated earlier, the typical exception to this rule is gay men
being possessed by Ezili Freda. I attended ceremonies in Manbo Maude's
temples where I observed other exceptions: Black heterosexual men were possessed by the female spirits Ezili Dantò and Gran Ezili. Notably, these spirits
are not hyperfeminine like Ezili Freda. Ezili Dantò is often characterized by
her fury and power, and Gran Ezili is a stooped old woman, ancient and shriveled in appearance. The implicit expectations around pran lwa are evidence of
persistent gender norms. Women can transgress gender lines during possession with ease, but men cross that same border carefully because their communities might see their interaction with female spirits as disparaging their
masculinity. As a result, I argue that many heterosexual men, because of the
rigidity of norms of masculinity, are deprived of the ability to experience
the full range of the Vodou pantheon during public ceremonies.

Ritual performances cannot erase the racial, gendered, and sexual dynamics visible in the room, where individuals with very different life experiences and cultures gather to honor the same deities under the guidance of
the same Manbo. The presence of lwa during possession is real, an actual
manifestation of revered and respected deities. And yet, the racialized physical bodies of the initiates being possessed affect the adornment practices

of a typical Vodou ceremony with some practitioners picking and choosing which possessed people to adorn with moushwa based on their race, gender, and sexuality. Samentha questioned whether a White person even had the ability to be possessed, placing great importance on the identity of the practitioner during the process of being mounted by a spirit. The "unusual" sight of a White gay man being mounted by a spirit, let alone a female spirit, was so jarring that it prevented Black people in the room from fully believing in the presence of the spirits. It is notable that although many practitioners are skeptical of a White person's ability to serve as a vessel, their desire to avoid interacting with the supposedly possessed person varies.

Often, White cisgender women who are possessed evoke less resistance. Fewer eyes roll toward the ceiling, the stares are less withering, and a smaller number of people feel compelled to suck their teeth in annoyance. Black men and women adorn and honor possessed White women as they would a possessed Black person. The disparity between Liam's treatment and that of White women defies full understanding, but some speculation is warranted. The combination of his race, gender, and sexuality may have heightened the doubt that many Black practitioners already held about White practitioners. Further, women are commonly understood as having a more pronounced ability to connect with the spirit world. White women's race sometimes inspires skepticism, but at the same time their gender implies spiritual potency. Doubts about the authenticity of a possession are not limited to White people or queer people. Those factors had particular power in the 2018 ceremony, but spiritual authenticity is a general issue of debate among practitioners. Black people of any gender identification or sexuality are also sometimes judged for the way they move or speak or act during pran lwa. The question, *Do White people have access to the spirit?* is part of a broader conversation about who has access to the spirit in general.

Practitioners' adornment practices in Manbo Maude's ceremonies extend only so far as their beliefs and the constraints of their perceptions. Some Black practitioners' and audience members' refusal to engage in the expected adornment rituals represents a denial of the presence of the divine: it is a tangible demonstration of how they view their own religious communities. Practitioners ultimately decide for themselves which bodies are suitable for the spirits, despite the sartorial displays that imply a broader unity in Manbo Maude's temples. In this ceremony, Black initiates and participants focused their attention on the Black women who were possessed and did not tie moushwa on Liam, despite this being a typical action during possession in Vodou ceremonies.

Arguably, Liam's race, gender, and sexuality partially ruptured the usual interaction between the Black participants and the spirits because these factors disturbed their ability to see the presence of the spirits as real when manifested in his body. The meaning derived from the framework of spiritual vogue shifts, depending on the practitioners, audience, and spirits. The interaction between these three entities is shaped by the complicated histories and identities of the people involved. Focusing on the triangulation of these influences emphasizes the malleability of spiritual vogue and illustrates how inseparable one is from the other. The Whiteness, gender, and queerness of the practitioner; the gender of the spirit; and the expectations of the predominantly Black audience shape the ceremony and affect the execution of the performance ritual. The awkwardness of these interactions raises a question: Does shunning a possessed person because of his or her body mean a practitioner is also shunning the spirit occupying the vessel? For the Black practitioners who doubt the validity of White peoples' possession, the answer is unequivocally no. If they do not believe a possession is authentic, the spirit is not actually present; not tying moushwa or spraying perfume does not disrespect the divine because the divine is simply not there.

Similarly, Natasha doubted the validity of the possession as much as did Samentha, saying, "I remember thinking to myself 'Is this thing real?' Like that was my first instinct when White boy went down. Was this even real? And I didn't feel like I could believe it because I didn't know who this kid was. You know, that didn't look like the other possession did. And I was trying to keep an open mind, but seeing all the Black people move away just like kind of [she throws her hand in air and scoots chair back] like something is weird about this."[50] Natasha's reaction to this particular possession was influenced by a variety of factors: her unfamiliarity with the person being possessed, his race, his movements and actions while possessed, and the reactions of the other Black people in the basement. She took cues from other Black people in the room on how to react to Liam's possession, relying in part on their responses to navigate a situation that made her feel uncertain. It was her first time attending a Vodou ceremony, and the behavior of Black practitioners and audience members shaped her own perceptions of what a typical possession should look like. She adapted to the religious community around her by emulating the social norms she perceived during the ceremony. Her initial reluctance to believe in the veracity of the possession was reinforced by the reserved reactions of the Black people in the room. She was confident that her uneasiness with Liam's possession was felt by others.

"You could see the room did not know how to deal with that," Natasha recalled. "People were uncomfortable."[51]

Natasha and Samentha were relatively comfortable sharing their thoughts on the possessions that took place during Danbala's ceremony. It, however, proved more difficult to get Samuel to talk to me and share his observations. I made numerous attempts to speak to him about the ceremony, eager to hear the perspective of someone I thought would colorfully articulate the discomfort I could sense from many people in the room that night in Mattapan. Ultimately, we compromised on a written response. When asked about his reactions to the White people at the ceremony, his emailed response was simple: "I suppose I was just being catty."[52] Potential cattiness aside, the perspectives of the Black practitioners I spoke to reveal that their sense of community is tethered to more than the appearance of cohesion or the technical correctness of performance rituals. Taking a cue from Bailey, a performance "acts out a role" that is legible to the audience and other participants.[53] Liam's Whiteness interrupted or even prevented the performance rituals Bailey describes as generating a sense of community. For some practitioners, Liam's whiteness meant he was ineligible to perform the role of a vessel for the lwa. Samuel rejected the performance because the movements were wrong in the context of his experience, whereas Samentha and Natasha questioned Liam's ability to perform at all—or rather they believed he was pretending, trying to take on a role for which he was inherently unsuited.

Underlying this claim that White people cannot catch the spirit is the implication that, in contrast to Manbo Maude's claims, the gods do care about which bodies they use for their work. To dismiss the potential validity of White possession suggests that those Black practitioners and audience members do not believe the spirits are indifferent to the race of their worshippers but instead are fully aware of it. Or perhaps the implication is that White people lack the capacity to call on the spirits and, as a result, are simply not an option for spiritual possession. After all, Manbo Maude has stated that Black people have an inherent connection to Vodou. Is it such a stretch to assume this innate affinity affects who can and cannot become possessed by the divine? Or is the will of the spirits being conflated with the earthly concerns of practitioners and audience members?

Although Vodou is inclusive of all races, genders, and sexualities, the presence of White people in Manbo Maude's temples is a complicating factor that divides her religious community. These fissures not only affect the ceremonies performed in Mattapan but also the preparations before the ceremony, including head wrapping and the ritual use of clothing. Manbo

Maude's careful and purposeful use of fashion cannot fully bridge these divides. These complications do not prevent Manbo Maude from completing all necessary ritual work and honoring the spirits, but fashion brings into focus the complex interplay between race, gender, and sexuality.

A Femme Wink: Clocking Queer Black Women through Spiritual Fashion

The clothing in Manbo Maude's temples is notably gendered: dresses and skirts for women and pants for men, with only occasional exceptions. Her initiates meet her expectations for feminine sartorial presentation, yet Manbo Maude does not attempt to wield control over what all practitioners and audience members wear in her ceremonies. Wearing dresses does not appeal to every woman in her temple: masculine-presenting lesbians who refuse feminine clothing present a clear alternative to Manbo Maude's ideas of female style. A few Black queer women are part of her spiritual home: most are femme presenting, and one presents as both masculine and feminine or androgynous. At the time of my writing, no woman in her temple presents as masculine.

The presence of queer and lesbian Black women during ceremonies does not cause the same discomfort and division as Liam did in Mattapan, no matter their style. Homophobia and prejudice are overt and covert currents in both of Manbo Maude's temples, yet the sexualities of Black women do not provoke other practitioners to question their ability to channel the spirits. They, unlike Liam, are female and Black, and this combination allows them to operate in Manbo Maude's ceremonies with little disruption to performance rituals and possession. The trifecta of influences that define spiritual vogue—the audience, the practitioners, and the spirits—operate smoothly, uninterrupted by Black women's sexualities or gender presentations. No one questions whether Black queer women are capable of pran lwa.

Scholars of African Diasporic religions have long discussed the origins of the notion that women are more open to possession than men and therefore are holders of great spiritual power. As J. Lorand Matory explores in his work on Candomblé, the term "mounting," used to describe being ridden by the spirit, has sexual connotations. Intercourse, in its basic heteronormative conception, involves women being penetrated as the passive partner. This role as the more passive partner who is penetrated is analogized to explain women's capacity to take on the spirit, to be mounted.[54] They are inherently porous, primed for possession. The sexuality or race of cisgender women does not change their natural receptivity to possession by the spirits. Cisgender queer Black women and White women, because of their bodies' perceived penetrability, are suited for pran lwa.

Exploring expressions of Black women's femininity and masculinity provides an opportunity to examine what is a neglected realm of study in African Diasporic religions: much of the scholarship around queerness focuses on gay men as the primary source of rupture in normative paradigms of gender and sexuality. The relative invisibility of Black lesbians and Black queer women reflects a preoccupation with maleness stemming from the sexism and misogyny inherent to Western societies. Women of all sexualities are conforming to, contesting, and negotiating the gendered expectations in Manbo Maude's temples and in African Diasporic religions generally.[55] Questioning how and why women, no matter their sartorial self-presentations, are figured into the gender dynamics of Vodou ceremonies produces still more questions about queerness, visibility, and gender fluidity. The observations I offer about Manbo Maude's homes are not meant to explain the nearly limitless diversity of Black women's gender and sexual identities but do explicate some of the complexities of their experiences in ceremonial spaces.

Within her own ceremonial spaces, Manbo Maude emphasizes hyperfeminine dresses in her religious fashion, but she does not foreclose other possibilities for herself or other practitioners. The practitioners who are not enamored with her elaborate dresses rework the stylistic expectations of Manbo Maude's temples to suit their own connection with the spirits, embracing her enthusiasm for fashion while respecting their own sensibilities. Women in her temple are allowed to alter the designs as they please, so long as they have the required ceremonial colors, fabrics, and patterns for a given spirit. If a woman decides to forgo dresses altogether, she can wear the shirt and pants designed for male practitioners. Vin Pouwe, a queer Haitian-born initiate in her mid-forties who moved to Boston with her family when she was three years old, has been in Manbo Maude's home since 2018. She was a Vodou practitioner for many years before she became an initiate under Manbo Maude. Her self-presentation has changed over time, and now she defines herself as androgynous, containing "masculine and feminine energies."[56] She learned quickly that she prefers simpler dresses: "I didn't want any lace and puffiness and the ruffles. I wanted just a traditional like . . . very simple blue and red [for Dantò]. She has made me send her the money and I wanted two white dresses; one was a plain simple white dress. The other one had poofy little flowers over it, and I told her I didn't like it. Now I [have] dresses made for me, and I want it simple as possible. . . . If it is extreme femme, I am not interested in that."[57] The dress Vin Pouwe described as "poofy" was made for her initiation into Manbo Maude's temple. She hated wearing the fluffy, ruffled outfit. Yet, although she felt unlike herself and unattractive when wearing it, she understood the dress as important to the ritual she participated in. She is glad she joined Manbo Maude's home, although the clothing's "extreme" femininity taught her it is necessary to tone down the designs for her own comfort. Still, it is important to Vin Pouwe to maintain the integrity of the stylistic vision in Manbo Maude's ceremonies and represent the cohesion of the members, so she wears simplified versions of the dresses everyone else dons, without the lace and ruffles. As a certified K–12 school psychologist and associate professor in education at a private university in Florida, Vin Pouwe connects self-presentation to the emotional and mental well-being of practitioners. The ability to serve the spirits while dressed in a personally satisfying way is crucial. However, she also understands the importance of stylistic expectations in Manbo Maude's home: "I do think there are certain things you agree to when you go to this type of initiation at her house."[58]

Fashion in Manbo Maude's temples is always a point of negotiation, not only with the spirits but also between practitioners. The range of stylistic expression has its limits. Even women who dress in a feminine manner must adhere to certain norms of what is proper: dress length, the amount of cleavage revealed by a neckline, the neatness of a head wrap. The changing rooms in Mattapan and Jacmel, spaces for bonding and congregation, are simultaneously places where sartorial expectations are conveyed and reinforced. These expectations also affect the ceremonial space and flow from the type of religious cohesion Manbo Maude envisions through her fashion. "She encourages; she doesn't obligate," Vin Pouwe explained when I asked her whether she and other practitioners were supposed to wear Manbo Maude's designs.[59] Vante'm Pa Fyem classifies the ability to drastically modify the dresses as a privilege largely enjoyed by practitioners living in the United States; they have access to more money and fabric than those in Haiti. Practitioners in Haiti mostly work with what Manbo Maude provides. "It's not a dictatorship," Vante'm Pa Fyem told me. "But my mom is paying for it." She also explained the differing expectations for gender presentation and ceremonial beauty in Haiti and the United States:

[In Haiti] I have never heard, "Oh I want my dress toned down." It's a cultural thing as well. . . . Wearing spiritual clothing is a chance to be beautiful and not wear your everyday clothing. You are seen as something more, something greater, something more positive. Essentially in Haiti they want the opportunity to dress up. Whereas, in the United States the notion of toned-down femininity is a very Western thing. The idea that you can still be a woman and not wear a dress or not wear a skirt—notions of femininity are different. . . . [In Haiti] you don't really see the example of not conforming to those notions of femininity.[60]

That Manbo Maude pays for the dresses for many of her practitioners in Haiti translates into more authority over the uniformity of their ceremonial outfits. Practitioners from the United States who pay for their own clothes have more latitude in interpreting their sartorial presentation. But Vante'm Pa Fyem's comments do not solely address the disparate financial realities of practitioners; they also explain the importance of Manbo Maude's vision of femininity to other Haitian women, who regard her garments as an opportunity to "dress up." Vante'm Pa Fyem diagnoses the "Western" impulse toward "toned-down femininity" as one that is not aligned with the celebratory and performative nature of Haitian Vodou ceremonies. Manbo Maude's aesthetic sensibilities are generally antithetical to a "toned-down femininity": she deliberately displays the almost boastful femininity of her spiritual clothes through her own understanding of beauty and grandeur. Although consultation with the spirits is necessary, Manbo Maude's fashion is also undoubtedly shaped by the cultural notions that Vante'm Pa Fyem described. Moreover, as a religious leader it behooves her to design garments that excite and please her communities, which contain many Haitian practitioners and audience members. Some Haitian women in Jacmel and Mattapan are so enamored with Manbo Maude's feminine dresses that they add fabric and ruffles to increase their glamour.

The popularity of her designs among Haitian women is doubtlessly encouraging, yet Manbo Maude has visions of bursting out of the standards she has set and broadening the stylistic choices in her temples. Occasionally, Manbo Maude wears a suit to honor a spirit like Gede or Ogou, bending ceremonial gender norms. Her choices are unique and innovative, though in these instances she is the only one in her home to wear the suit. Most of the practitioners still wear dresses. Recently, Manbo Maude began incorporating pants into her designs for Kouzen and Gede, which she and her daughter wore. The pants are underneath a long skirt with an opening in the front.

This change is another manifestation of Manbo Maude's inclination to push some gender boundaries in her temples, though so far, she has only experimented with pants when honoring male spirits. According to Manbo Maude, this is only a temporary truth, a result of limited funds and not a reflection of any constraints she has placed on her own religious garments: it is just that suits are more expensive to make. She is eager to design a suit to honor Ezili Dantò in the future. "Wait until I have money," she told me playfully. With time and money, Manbo Maude is confident her designs will grow to challenge more gender expectations.[61]

As a queer, femme-presenting woman, I am able to navigate the gendered expectations for ceremonial fashion in Manbo Maude's temples. I wear skirts and wrap my hair. I apply eyeliner and lipstick and hang gold hoops in my ears. The more feminine I look, the better the reception I receive from the practitioners and audience members. Underneath the determinedly ladylike designs of Manbo Maude's garments, the sexualities of female practitioners are assumed to be heterosexual. Despite the presence of numerous queer people and Manbo Maude's openness to queer people in her temples, the ceremonies in Jacmel and Mattapan operate under heteronormative expectations. Most of the flirting that occurs during ceremonies is between men and women. Men can be aggressive with their advances, at times reaching out to touch women's behinds or standing rigidly in the way of women as they walk by them, forcing their bodies to brush against each other to pass. The behavior is common though often contentious. Sometimes women order men to leave them alone. Some men censure other men for their actions toward women, including making occasional threats of violence. Expressions of same-sex desire are typically much more covert.

At a ceremony honoring Ogou in Jacmel in 2018, I dressed up and received an enthusiastic reception from the people gathered in Manbo Maude's temple. They invited me to dance in the circle of practitioners that formed in front of the drum players and shared their drinks with me. It was a new experience that I credited to the time I spent primping in the mirror in my hotel room. I was thoroughly outdanced by a middle-aged Haitian lesbian practitioner, whom I call Manbo Eve, as I tried and failed to keep up with her easy command of the drumbeat and her own body. Manbo Eve is a staple at Manbo Maude's ceremonies, a frequent and invited guest who leads her own temple in Jacmel. I do not have an accurate count of the number of Vodou homes in Jacmel, let alone the number that are queer friendly. Many of the temples operate quietly, refraining from advertising their religious practices for fear of discrimination or ostracization. However, I do know that Manbo Eve's home is known around Jacmel as an LGBTQ space. She is also open about her own sexual identity as a lesbian and often brings her partners to ceremonies in her own temple and Manbo Maude's. Out of respect, affection, and hospitality, Manbo Maude provides spiritual dresses for Manbo Eve to wear while attending her ceremonies. Manbo Eve is feminine presenting, so the dresses do not conflict with her personal sense of style or identity.

After I eased away from the thick of the crowd to catch my breath and observe, I hovered near the chairs set up for the convenience of the gathering practitioners and audience members. There, a dark-skinned, masculine-presenting woman wearing a stylish tracksuit and sunglasses sat next to another woman, her arm slung around the back of her chair. She had cornrows and a pleasant face. She was a visitor, a worshipper from other temples or from the local community. Her clothes were entirely red in honor of Ogou. The outfit was far removed from anything Manbo Maude had designed for her own initiates up to that point, yet the woman was also showing her respect for the deity.

Normally I would not blatantly transgress the heteronormativity of the ceremony, but I was still elated after dancing with Manbo Eve, and the woman in the tracksuit was cute. Feeling playful and confident after being showered with compliments on my appearance, I winked at her. Typically, I only dared to flirt with men if I flirted at all. I thought the wink was subtle, a small gesture of acknowledgment between two queer women that implied, "*I see you*." As I started to walk away, the woman began balling up napkins in her hands and tossing them at me. I turned to look at her. She waved her hand in an obvious invitation to join her. The people around me were immediately amused. They had not seen my wink, only her noticeable reaction. I was shocked, embarrassed, and disappointingly scared by her lack of discretion. As a queer femme, I benefit from moving invisibly. By *invisible*, I mean that in Jacmel I am read as heterosexual. Growing up in Nigerian American and Black American communities taught me to be discerning about revealing my sexuality in the company of strangers, wary of the possibility that my queerness might be met with homophobia. In Haiti and in many other foreign countries I visit, I refrain from sharing my sexual identity. Yet the woman at Manbo Maude's ceremony called my bluff and openly broached a truth I had been unprepared to admit to in front of an audience. Startled and anxious, I pretended I had no idea why she was trying to speak with me. The confidence I felt dancing with practitioners by the drums receded. As present as lesbians are in the ceremonial space, there is still a worry that latent prejudice will manifest as real danger in the outside world after the ceremony's end. I could not assume that I would be afforded the same latitude as Manbo Eve.

Black queer and lesbian women do not disrupt possession or ritual work, and yet that truth did not translate into a broad sense of total acceptance within the temple in Jacmel. Using the frame of spiritual vogue reveals uninterrupted ceremonial practices and the easy interaction between practitioners, the audience, and the spirits, and yet the social life of the ceremony has underlying tensions that cannot be resolved through a shared faith in Vodou. I still felt the unease that often accompanies being queer in heteronormative spaces. The fact that same-sex desire is expressed covertly, despite the presence of queer and lesbian women, speaks to the sometimes jarring discontinuities of the ceremony. Queer and lesbian women practitioners and audience members do not complicate the spiritual work of the ceremony and can in fact operate as highly regarded spiritual authorities in the community, but their desires are eclipsed by the general heteronormativity of the temple and remain largely unspoken. This does not preclude the kinds of blunt ruptures represented by the masculine woman confidently attempting to gain my attention. For her and perhaps for Manbo Eve, the heteronormativity of the ceremonies may feel less suffocating.

Negotiating with sexual and gender conventions is an unavoidable reality for women in any religion, not only in Manbo Maude's homes. Vodou is shaped by the needs of its practitioners, yet those needs change over time and from person to person. Managing the complexities of religious ritual and the constantly evolving understandings of gender and sexuality within her temples requires an extensive amount of labor, yet Manbo Maude is not expected to address this work alone. The spirits themselves share her responsibilities, participating in rituals that create direct access between the divine and devotees.

CHAPTER FOUR

Making Love to the Spirit

Sex and Dreams in Spiritual Marriages

In July 2015, I spent my nights sleeping in the master bedroom in Manbo Maude's home in Jacmel, among the barrels of ritual clothes she kept stored next to the bed. Some of the clothes were from past ceremonies, and some she kept for other practitioners for upcoming events. There were packages of food and water along the wall, and under the bed were baskets filled with sacred *koulie* or "beads," *moushwa* or "scarves," and *ason* or "sacred rattles" for initiation rituals and ceremonies. I shared the room with a practitioner and people came in and out all day and night to grab clothes or food, take naps, or gossip with one another. One of the ceremonies Manbo Maude and her practitioners were preparing for was a spiritual marriage for an initiate named Zeta who had moved to a different Vodou home but was excitedly preparing for the marriage being performed in Manbo Maude's temple. Zeta is a cisgender, heterosexual Black American woman in her mid-thirties with a heavy southern accent, whose ancestry is rooted in Louisiana and Texas. Zeta's marriage was one of the first spiritual marriages that I witnessed in Jacmel. She married seven male spirits, including Kouzen, the spirit of agriculture. Spiritual marriages take months and possibly years to prepare for, but because of her specific circumstances, Zeta had only three months to obtain the needed clothes and undergo the required ritual preparation.[1] After the ceremony, she shared with me the experience of getting married:

> It was all going so fast! So it was like a blur. People had to zip me up
> on the back and throw me back out to get married to spirits. I had
> so many costume changes I felt like a model! Overall, it was a good
> feeling. I couldn't see how I looked like because there was no mirror.
> The spirit was waiting for me, and people were rushing me back
> downstairs. Although I had no mirror, I could see the spirits face
> looking back at me and he [Kouzen] was smiling. And he commented
> on how good I looked. You can see it on his face. [The spirits] look you
> over. They are excited to see you. Although I felt flushed, they were
> happy. And that's all that matters.[2]

Manbos flaunting wedding rings that represent their marriages to male spirits in Mattapan, March 2021 (photo by Eziaku Nwokocha).

Without a mirror, Zeta is unable to see her own reflection, yet the audience and Kouzen affirm her appearance through their approval. Their "sacred gaze," conveyed through the social experience of the ceremony, reflects the ritual validity of her outfit in service of her marriage.[3] Kouzen's gaze and his pleased smile confirm the effectiveness of Zeta's sartorial efforts and her worthiness as a spouse. The gazes of the audience and the spirits confer on Zeta's marriage the necessary religious authenticity, cementing her connection to

Kouzen. This ritual reality illustrates spiritual vogue, emphasizing the multiple dimensions of sight and its importance to Vodou ceremonies. Zeta dresses for the *lwa* and the audience, incorporating her African Diasporic identity as a southern Black American in Haitian Vodou; in turn, the spirits and the audience offer their approval after witnessing her ritual performance and her garments. As a result, she is able to publicly declare her affinity for the spirits and continue asking for their favor, honoring them in many ceremonies to come.

In her marriage ceremony Zeta donned a two-piece outfit for Kouzen, standing tall inside the temple awaiting the spirit's arrival. Her light-blue denim blouse was plaid, with a prominent ruffle that flowed down to form a wide boat-neck collar. White cotton trim accentuated the ends of her sleeves and blouse. The plaid cotton and denim were arranged in a checkered pattern on her blouse, which reached her mid-thigh. The cotton skirt underneath was long enough to brush along the dirt floor: it had a gradual overlay of flounces in midnight blue emerging after the abrupt stop of the blouse's patchwork pattern. She also wore a layered necklace with four strings of pearls, a bracelet made of three rows of pearls, and large pearl earrings in tribute to her heritage as a "southern belle."[4] "He's country, like me!"[5] Zeta explained, associating Kouzen's country or agricultural identity with her southern heritage. Kouzen reflected pieces of her own heritage, representing the embrace of her ancestral connection to the land. The spirit's visual and cultural significance to Zeta's familial past echoed his clear link to a similar past in Haiti, where millions of enslaved Africans toiled on plantations. By claiming Kouzen's history as her own, Zeta instinctively created this Diasporic connection.

Zeta described the denim fabric of her dress as hot and heavy.[6] Her dress cut a bigger profile than most in the room: it had more fabric, more ruffles, and more layers, all to accentuate her status as a Manbo and to emphasize that this was her wedding day: it was her time to shine.

Manbo Maude and other practitioners sang Vodou songs to call Kouzen and welcome him into the ceremony. Kouzen arrived and mounted a Haitian female initiate. Practitioners loosely tied a royal blue moushwa around her neck and handed her a straw satchel. When Kouzen looked at Zeta, he was overjoyed and gave her a kiss on the cheek, inspecting the ring on her finger, which was a silver band with a red jewel imbedded into it. Zeta had the ring made for her marriage to Kouzen. He smiled and kissed her hand multiple times, embracing her in appreciation. Zeta and Kouzen took each other's hands and walked to the altar, where a *prèt savann* or "bush priest" in

Haitian Kreyòl, and several witnesses awaited.[7] As a prèt savann, the priest is not ordained by the Catholic Church, yet he sometimes dons the vestments of an actual priest and usually wears a cross around his neck. Though prèt savanns are not ordained, they still have religious responsibilities during the weddings, such as officiating the event and repeating traditional Catholic and Vodou prayers and blessings. The prèt savann is a Haitian innovation that arose after the Revolution when the Vatican ceased sending priests to the country. Prèt savanns filled the resulting religious vacuum, performing rituals that were previously the province of ordained Catholic priests.[8]

The prèt savann aiding in Zeta's wedding gained his religious knowledge in childhood, spending years as an altar boy at a Catholic Church.[9] Manbo Maude has worked with him for several years; he has officiated at some of her spiritual marriages and baptisms for newly initiated practitioners in her temple in Jacmel. Manbo Maude is capable of performing all the rituals the prèt savann carries out during weddings. She officiates at weddings in both Mattapan and Jacmel; however, she has more people to help in her role as a Manbo in Haiti and prefers to have a prèt savann officiate so she can focus on other religious responsibilities.

During the ceremony, the priest took off Zeta's ring and blessed it with Florida Water cologne, which participants used to cleanse ritual objects and bless participants and spirits during ceremonies. The scent of the cologne was also useful in attracting the spirits. To please Kouzen, the altar featured tobacco and food that had been prepared earlier in the day, including corn, avocados, bananas, and cassava. Because Zeta was marrying seven spirits, their food, alcohol, and ritual objects were also displayed on the altar. The priest asked Zeta and Kouzen if they wanted to take each other's hands in marriage. They both agreed. He presented them with a spiritual marriage contract, which stated the promise being made between the spirit and the practitioner, as well as the obligations they would need to fulfill as a part of their union. Both Zeta and Kouzen had to sign the contract. It included the signatures of two witnesses. The witnesses could be anyone who was a part of Zeta's spiritual home. After they signed the contract, they kissed each other on the cheek. Manbo Maude and her practitioners sang a song to usher Kouzen out of the ceremony and out of the body of the initiate he had mounted. As the initiate was recovering, Zeta left the temple to change into another outfit for the next spirit she would marry. When she returned to the temple, the process started anew.

Spiritual marriage, or mystical marriage, is a sacred institution that creates an allegiance between the practitioner and the spirits. It is a symbiotic relationship that establishes a ritual commitment; the spirit will aid the practitioner, and in turn, the practitioner will serve the spirits. The unions formed through spiritual marriage can be polyamorous, with people marrying multiple spirits and the spirits marrying multiple people. Scholarship on spiritual marriage is scant and largely explores basic ritual elements of the tradition.[10] Examining these rituals carefully and in more detail reveals that, through the mechanics of ritual, spiritual marriage is a way to connect spirit and practitioner and that this union is facilitated by fashion. In Manbo Maude's temples in Jacmel and Mattapan, establishing legitimate unions relies on the interconnectedness of the spirits, the practitioners, and the audience. Her traditions, however, do not represent the full spectrum of spiritual marriage in Vodou: rituals vary across temples and practitioners.

In chapter 2, I emphasize the role of labor in Manbo Maude's temples. Spiritual marriage affects the labor she is required to do in her religious community by relieving her of some of her responsibilities. As a Manbo, she is continually engaged in educating practitioners and initiates about Vodou and its many rituals. She provides guidance to the people in her home on both religious and personal matters by communicating with spirits through spiritual readings and other ritual services. When practitioners marry spirits, Manbo Maude no longer needs to function as a primary mediator, because members of her home can consult with the spirits directly, thereby reducing the *emotional labor* she performs. Practitioners "become more confident," Manbo Maude explained. "They don't have to consult with me all the time because the spirits start taking over. I have less work to do with the person."[11] Doing less work with her practitioners reduces not only her responsibilities but also her income. She usually charges for the spiritual readings and ritual work she does, but when practitioners communicate directly with the spirits more often, she loses this revenue. However, Manbo Maude is invested in facilitating the spiritual journeys of practitioners and initiates who are spiritually independent and confident in their abilities within Vodou. She maintains a commitment to passing on the knowledge of Vodou and its rituals and understands this to be a fundamental aspect of her role as a Manbo. Moreover, when she ushers members of her community into a more self-reliant relationship with the spirits, she can spend more time with newer members and with her own immediate family. Spiritual marriage facilitates ongoing exchanges of *emotional, intimate, aesthetic,* and *negotiatory labor* between practitioners and spirits.

The marital ritual performed in Vodou ceremonies combines African and Christian religious elements that include dancing, saluting the spirits, a religious ritual contract, witnesses, and an officiator. It is a multisensorial practice involving the smell of food on the altar, the donning of clothes, the touch of hands and lips, and the rhythmic sound of ritual drums. Practitioners and spirits communicate directly as they make religious commitments to one another, and the audience and other initiates confer legitimacy of the union by acting as witnesses. Spiritual vogue exposes the ceremonial conventions of this practice, especially regarding the role of gender because of the expectations placed on women and their fashion and adornment choices. Ultimately, the ritual depends on the interconnectedness of the spirits, the practitioners, and the audience, which are tied together by devotional garments. When practitioners beautify their bodies, they wear the evidence of their meticulous efforts to please the spirits, proving their reverence for them and inviting them into the ceremony. The spirits' approval is clear when they land in a ceremony, reveling in their own exaltation, accepting rings at the altar, and committing to practitioners who have honored them. The religious fashion involved in spiritual marriage extends beyond ceremonies into the everyday lives of practitioners through the ongoing use of ritualized clothing and adornment, signaling a personal connection with the divine, aiding ongoing communication, and facilitating the crucial possibility of sexual contact between practitioners and spirits.

Sexual interactions, which happen *nan dòmi*, Haitian Kreyòl for "in dream," emphasize the commitment between practitioner and spirit and play a significant role in enabling intimate labor in spiritual marriage. Importantly, sex is not mandatory; whether to engage in it is a point of negotiation between the divine and their worshippers. These sexual relations cannot be reduced to mere tawdry affairs: they are expressions of care, pleasure, and adoration that reaffirm the affinity between spirits and practitioners, a sensual and ecstatic acknowledgment of the good work completed by the faithful *en sèvi*, Haitian Kreyòl for "in service" of the divine. Sexual encounters also occur outside spiritual marriages, often acting as an indicator of which spirits a practitioner has a special connection with. For the purposes of this chapter, however, I focus on how sex functions within ritual unions. Nan dòmi encounters are detached from the trifecta of spiritual vogue; they do not engage an audience. They are not public-facing ceremonies but private affairs defined by the intimate connections between spirits and their devotees.

As I made clear in previous chapters, the lwa meet practitioners where they are, and practitioners are resourceful and determined in their efforts to serve the divine. If they cannot have their needs met in one home, they often Vodou hop and search out another that can. In spiritual marriages, queer practitioners' quest for a temple with the capacity to satisfy them can be fruitless. Yet the lack of institutional support in the waking world does not foreclose queer people's ability to devote themselves to the spirits: it just pushes some unions into dreams. I argue that nan dòmi is a realm where the spirits can commune with queer practitioners who are unable to find a Manbo or Houngan willing to marry them because of their gender or sexuality to the deities for which they have an affinity. I contend that marriages nan dòmi illustrate the spirits' disregard for earthly prejudices about gender and sexuality and suggest the inherent queerness of lwa. These spiritual marriages, although not performed in a ceremony or presided over by a spiritual leader, are as consequential as any other. The bonds formed in dreams influence practitioners' daily existence, where they adorn themselves with clothing and jewelry that mark their commitment to the gods.

Put a Ring on It: Gendering Presentation in Devotional Adornment

If practitioners expect the gods to help and protect them, then they must show their dedication and commit themselves to the spirits. In exchange for protection, the gods expect to be shown favor by the practitioners they wed. During an evening phone conversation, Manbo Maude emphasized the mutual obligations created through spiritual marriage, saying, "Spiritual marriages are done because it places the responsibilities on spirits. Letting them know that they owe you protection. They owe you stability. . . . They know they have you. They know they can invest in you."[12] This investment carries with it a lifetime commitment, which alters the everyday choices of practitioners, infusing their actions with spiritual significance. I do not know how long spiritual marriage has been in existence nor does Manbo Maude, who told me, "This is what we do. This is what I have been taught."[13] She described spiritual marriage as a practice with roots in Haitian culture, history, and the traditions passed down by her spiritual mother.

In service of the spirits, practitioners adorn themselves with rings and devote days of the week to the spirits they marry. Wearing a ring is an adornment practice for both female and male initiates, who often purchase it at a jewelry shop or have it custom made by a jeweler. Practitioners are not required to spend an exorbitant amount of money on these rings, though many do. For those who do not have the means, their rings need only appear to be made of precious stones or valuable metals, but they do need to be durable. Some practitioners forge family heirlooms into spiritual rings through ceremonial rituals that involve fire—but only rings that meet certain criteria can be turned into spiritual items. The type of metal and jewels used in the ring design depends on the preferences of each spirit, and each ring can represent one or multiple spirits.

On the days that are dedicated to the spirits, practitioners dress in the colors that are traditionally associated with the spirits they married, abstain from sex with any nonspiritual partners, light candles at their altar, and engage in ritual prayers. Practitioners also expect to receive messages from the spirits they commit to on the days designated for them.

In my time observing spiritual marriages in Haiti and the United States, I found that it is typical for initiates to marry at least two spirits during a single ceremony. In Manbo Maude's home, they often marry more, perhaps three to seven spirits in one ceremony. She explained that initiates marry multiple spirits because it creates balance. She also offered a more practical reason:

> I know for a fact that women when they are getting married, they should marry Danbala, that's the first spirit, Danbala, Ogou, and Kouzen Zaka. So that's the norm, that's what I know. But, because there is so much money that goes into a spiritual marriage, it's not something that you want to keep on doing. Like you know, you do one today, and then the next time you do another one. It's better to look, to search for who wants to marry the person. So, what I do, I will ask questions before. I will do divination, or ask with just a candle, and say, "Can you tell me now because I don't want you to tell me after the person already gots the ring and stuff to get married, can you tell me now?" So that's how I search, I look.[14]

When Manbo Maude speaks of "the norm," she is acknowledging that much of what she knows about spiritual marriages came from her spiritual mother and what she learned while an initiate in her temple. The grouping of Danbala, Ogou, and Kouzen Zaka reflects the importance of the idea of balance through the combination of *Petwo* spirits and *Rada* spirits, which establishes equilibrium by balancing their cool and hot temperaments. Danbala, the serpent spirit of wisdom, and Kouzen, the god of agriculture, are both *Rada* spirits. Ogou, the god of iron and war, is a *Nago* or Yoruba spirit and can be *Petwo*, moving between the categories depending on the version that manifests. Ogou is a warrior spirit who is sometimes depicted as handsome and heroic and, conversely, as a violent drunk capable of destroying himself and others. He has a potentially countless number of incarnations reflecting an array of personalities.[15] Because of Ogou's capacity for anger and war, he often needs to be balanced by the cooler, calmer *Rada* spirits. This balance between the personalities of the spirits aids initiates with decision making in their everyday lives.

Manbo Maude also encourages initiates to marry all the spirits they have an affinity for in one ceremony out of concern for the expense of spiritual marriages. She uses divination, which usually consists of card readings and other rituals I am not privy to as a non-initiate, to seek out the spirits that are connected to a given initiate so they will not have to go through the marriage process again. Manbo Maude also has numerous conversations with initiates about their dreams, past ceremonies where spirits demanded rings, and life experiences that suggest an interest from specific deities. Traditionally, Manbos and Houngans determine the spirits a given practitioner should wed within their spiritual home.

Manbo Maude emphasizes the expense of spiritual marriages because she is constantly concerned not only with the finances of her temples but the financial responsibilities placed on her practitioners and initiates. She considers having more than one marriage ceremony an unnecessary financial burden. Getting married requires paying for the labor of fellow initiates, the musicians, the animals involved, and the food and drinks being served, in addition to the costs of traveling to Haiti for protégés outside the country. When the marriages are combined into one ceremony, the initiate only has to pay once for these elements. For example, the purchased pork, beef, rum, and wine can be offered to all the spirits being called down for the ceremonial marriages.

Another important consideration is the expense of the dresses that female initiates don for the marriages. Zeta, for instance, married seven spirits—Danbala, Ogou, Ogou Ferray, Kouzen, Agwe, Simbi, and Gede—and had to plan outfits for each. Zeta purchased or repurposed five outfits for her marriage. In addition to the checkered garment I described her donning for Kouzen, Zeta wore a white dress with silver sequins and ruffled short sleeves for Danbala that glimmered in the light of the ceremony. She used the same dress for her marriage to Agwe but wore a glittery, aqua-blue head scarf to honor his presence. In the service of Ogou and Ogou Ferray, her dress was royal blue with a red trim along the seams of her sleeves and the flowing hem, which whirled around her as she danced through the room. A red sash was tied around her waist, and her hair was wrapped in a sparkling, sequined red fabric. A red beaded necklace hung around her neck. In her marriage to Gede, Zeta wore a black-and-white dress that opened in the front to reveal a purple skirt underneath. Small black-and-white roses were sewn onto the dress in large clusters that nearly formed a polka-dot pattern. A purple sash cinched her waist, and her hair was covered by a sequined black wrap.

The clothing worn in Manbo Maude's temples varies greatly by gender not only in style but also in cost. Depending on a female practitioner's status as a Manbo or the closeness of her relationship to Manbo Maude, extra fabric and trimmings are included on the dress, which can increase the price. For male practitioners, style does not change according to status: a senior Houngan often wears the same clothes as other male *ti fèy* of the temple. The cost of ritual clothing can be significantly lower for male practitioners because their outfits, usually a shirt and pants, are less complicated and require less fabric. This difference in ritual clothing applies to spiritual marriages as well. As previously mentioned, Zeta wore several dresses for the spirits she married. Because she did not regularly attend ceremonies in Mattapan or Jacmel, she had to spend more on the creation of her dresses than many other initiates did.

Although I did observe a spiritual marriage where a female initiate who frequented ceremonies in Mattapan and Jacmel was able to use dresses made for past ceremonies and only had to purchase one new dress, the stylistic expectations for ritual clothing generally are higher for women than for men. Manbo Maude makes sure her female practitioners have the dresses necessary for their marriages. She asks them which dresses they already own and which ones will need to be made in preparation. If female practitioners do not have a dress for a particular spirit, Manbo Maude sends their measurements, possible dress styles, and fabric to her seamstresses in either Mattapan or Jacmel so that the outfit will be ready for their wedding. The cost of ritual dresses usually ranges from $50 to $300; if an initiate cannot afford one for her wedding or for a ceremony, Manbo Maude sometimes dips into her own savings to help pay for the outfit.

Marriage ceremonies are not divorced from the gender politics of everyday life that stem from larger cultural and societal constructions of gender. When considered through the lens of spiritual vogue, the gendered dynamics of spiritual marriage reveal the malleability of the interactions among the audience, practitioners, and spirits during ritual practices in Haitian Vodou: these interactions vary depending on the identities of the practitioners. The spiritual marriages in Manbo Maude's homes depend on female practitioners presenting a particular vision of femininity to the audience and the spirits. Zeta and other female practitioners like her are marrying men, even if those men are spirits, and this carries traditional expectations of gender presentation. In my time in Manbo Maude's temples, I did not see any female practitioner wear anything other than an elaborate dress. These practitioners are wearing what scholar of feminist studies Marcia Ochoa calls "symbolic resources," which are the indicators of glamour and beauty that are used to connote femininity.[16] To please the spirits and the audience, Zeta and other female practitioners must dress and adorn themselves beautifully, and in Manbo Maude's home, beauty is signified by elaborate feminine dresses, makeup, and jewelry.

In Manbo Maude's temples, spiritual marriages are also heteronormative: female initiates marry male spirits, and male initiates marry female spirits. This holds true for all initiates, whether heterosexual, homosexual, or transgender. Although Manbo Maude performs heteronormative weddings, she has initiated transgender people according to their gender identity. For example, she initiated a transgender man as a Houngan. However, when this same initiate was spiritually married, he married male spirits because Manbo Maude believes that initiates need to be married in relation to their assigned sex at birth. "I am not going to marry a man to a man, because that's how the tradition was," she explained when I interviewed her. "If it's changing, I don't like to change tradition like that; it's not up to me to do that."[17] Manbo Maude learned how to perform spiritual marriage from her spiritual mother and wants to maintain those traditions. She asserted that Manbos and Houngans who married male initiates to male spirits and female initiates to female spirits were practicing the ritual incorrectly.

I discussed this topic with her on numerous occasions, largely because she embraces queer and transgender practitioners and participants and allows gay men to perform rituals during ceremonies that are traditionally performed by women. Manbos and Houngans choose how they want to honor tradition in their spiritual homes, and for Manbo Maude, heteronormative spiritual marriages are a tradition she continues to maintain. Her adherence to some heteronormative traditions goes against my earlier statement that the spirits are queer. Thus, Manbo Maude's insistence on honoring the precedent set by her spiritual mother arguably defies their natures. Ezili Dantò, for example, protects lesbians and is often regarded as lesbian and sometimes intersex herself, yet Manbo Maude does not allow female practitioners to marry her.

Spiritual marriage, like all rituals in Vodou, involves ongoing negotiatory labor between the divine and those who *sèvi lwa*, between the supernatural and the practical realities of everyday human life. These negotiations produce ambivalences and inconsistencies. Manbo Maude welcomes gender and sexual diversity in her practitioners but still holds onto heteronormative ideas about marriage in her temples, all while believing she is honoring the spirits and their needs. No spirit has come to her in a dream or during a ceremony to censure her for how she performs spiritual marriage, so perhaps she and the spirits have found an agreement. Negotiations in other temples reach different conclusions. Practitioners who are called to marry spirits of the same gender can find spiritual homes that allow queer marriages, though they are in the minority. Practitioners choose spirits just as surely as spirits choose them. If one spirit stops aiding them, practitioners abandon them and concentrate on honoring another that offers clearer guidance and favor. The same choice applies to spiritual homes. A spiritual home is only valuable to practitioners if it meets their needs. When a temple ceases to enrich practitioners' connection to the divine, they move on to another.[18]

The gender of the spirit determines how the audience and the practitioners view the body and personality of the mounted person throughout Vodou ceremonies. In Manbo Maude's homes, this gendered perception solidifies not only spiritual marriages but also their heteronormativity. At first glance, spiritual vogue operates to reinforce the perception of a heteronormative marriage through the interaction of the spirits, audience, and practitioners, who are engaging in the marriage ceremony as though the body of the practitioner is immaterial. During Zeta's marriage, Kouzen, a male spirit, was mediated by a Haitian woman that he had possessed. I asked Zeta if she cared that the body that Kouzen rode was female. She explained, "You have to remember that when I look at Kouzen, I don't see the female body, I see him. I am marrying a male spirit. Also, there were not a lot of males present for Kouzen to take over."[19] Zeta's comment derives from the idea that, in Vodou, the bodies of practitioners are vessels during *pran lwa*. Therefore, the gender of the mounted practitioner during a spiritual marriage ceremony is irrelevant and overwritten by the gender of the spirit possessing them. This idea is typically articulated through the possession of female practitioners; it is less common to see men become possessed by female spirits, and so their genders are displaced by spirits in far fewer instances. Zeta was seeing the spirit, not the body it inhabited, because of the ritual and adornment practices she and other practitioners engaged in during the ceremony.

Without questioning the validity of Zeta's account and her experience with marriage, further contemplation reveals a complex interplay among gender, pran lwa, fashion, and performance. Spiritual vogue unveils the multiple concurrent meanings within a given ceremony. On one hand, the interaction between the spirits, practitioners, and the audience appears to present heteronormative marriage traditions that remain firm, no matter the people and spirits involved. On the other hand, spiritual vogue also reveals the inverse: a fete rife with contradictory meanings about gender and sexuality where the relationships between practitioners, the audience, and spirits actually undermine heteronormative marriage traditions. Much of this contradiction is centered on female bodies, which are often understood as simultaneously powerful and still somehow able to be ignored. A person who is assigned female at birth is seen as especially available for spiritual possession because of her body's perceived penetrability; yet is that person so permeable that her body is overwritten completely in the eyes of practitioners and the audience?[20] As previously discussed, the physical body cannot be discounted so readily. During a marriage ceremony, a possessed woman leaning over to kiss a female practitioner on the cheek or lips to solidify their union does not inspire speculation about their sexual orientations, as it might between two cisgender men. This perception not only indicates the spiritual availability of female vessels but also signifies disregard for, or even the invisibility of, the sexual identities of women.

The rituals of spiritual marriage during ceremonies uncover pran lwa as a gendered performance ritual, animated by body language, movement, intonations of voice, and adornment. Zeta's possessed partners for the marriage ritual varied. Some were cisgender Black men, and others were cisgender Black women. A few of the possessed men and women were queer, though I cannot account for the variety of sexualities that may have been represented during the ceremony. During Zeta's marriage to Ogou, the audience and the practitioners understood that Ogou was present through his loud voice, stern facial expressions, demands for his sword, and expansive body language, including flexing and strutting around the room. Possessed practitioners also donned red and blue moushwa, which were tied around their arms and chest. This adornment solidified the presence of Ogou and communicated his existence to other practitioners and the audience in service of the marriage ceremony. The gender of cisgender men, heterosexual or queer, is affirmed by the presence of Ogou and other male spirits whose gendered bodies reinforce the masculine display performed by the divine.

For women, wearing moushwa and gesturing with ritual items signify that the bodies of possessed practitioners are no longer fully defined by their sex or gender but by the gender of the spirit mounting them; the ritual and adornment items represent this shift in identity and perception during a ceremony. The differing colors of moushwa and their positions on the body indicate which version of Ogou has arrived at a ceremony.[21] Ogou is hypermasculine, which aligns with his connection to war. He reflects the strengths and weaknesses of this brand of manhood; sometimes, he is an uncontrollable drunk who is perpetually angry or he is hypersexual, and at other times he is a noble warrior and protector.[22] This image of masculinity is not the only one represented by the Vodou pantheon. Kouzen does not perform an aggressive masculinity but instead has mannerisms that are courtly and calm. His voice is typically even and calm, and his body language is composed. His presence is also indicated by his straw hat, his *makout*, and the blue or red moushwa that is loosely tied around his neck, indicating his role as a farmer. He converses with the audience and practitioners, a result of his roots in the marketplace where negotiation is necessary for business. This does not mean Kouzen is incapable of anger, but his primary display of masculinity is humble and level-headed. Unlike the ceremonies celebrating the hyperfemininity exhibited by Ezili Freda, in which mostly women and gay men take part in pran lwa, all people can engage in Ogou's and Kouzen's masculine behavior without fear of recrimination. The multisensorial performance of gender during spiritual marriages determines the multiple meanings the audience and practitioners generate through viewing and interacting with the possessed person, allowing for some to disregard the individual's gender in favor of that of the lwa.

In Manbo Maude's home, flexibility in gender presentation does not usually extend to the marriages performed for male initiates; in these ceremonies, female spirits almost always possess female practitioners. It is common and acceptable for women to be mounted by male spirits, but it is unusual and potentially uncomfortable for a male to be mounted by a female spirit during a marriage ceremony. The actions taken by a possessed practitioner during spiritual marriages, such as kissing, are socially unacceptable if the practitioner is a man mounted by a female spirit, offering these signs of affection to other men. This suggests the human body still plays a role in how gender is represented in spiritual marriage. In pran lwa, gender is not anchored to the body, which challenges some elements of Manbo Maude's thinking on heteronormative marriages. This inconsistency between the enforcement of genders assigned at birth during spiritual marriage versus that during the act of possession, which routinely invites practitioners to flout the borders between genders, highlights the complications of gendered representation in Vodou ceremonies.

If the body were truly irrelevant, more male practitioners would be possessed by female spirits in spiritual marriages. The fact that this is a relatively rare occurrence suggests that the body of the devotee is not completely immaterial to the audience and the practitioners. I witnessed men who were mounted by Dantò and Freda in ceremonies other than spiritual marriages, which is why I argue that both male and female spirits are unconcerned with the gender of the bodies they ride. Even when these female spirits possess men, they align with normative ideas of masculinity. Dantò, because she is commonly characterized by wrath and power, mounts men easily. Embodying aggression by raging through a ceremony brandishing a dagger is acceptable for heterosexual men because her combative femininity aligns with broader perceptions of masculine behavior. Freda, however, is a different matter. She is hyperfeminine and expresses this persona through gestures of femininity: a soft wave of the hand, batting eyelashes, swaying hips, and demands for perfume and powder. When Freda leaves a male body, her actions create a lingering sense of suspicion that threatens to follow male practitioners beyond the ceremony. The community of practitioners and audience members may question whether Freda's ability to mount a supposedly heterosexual man hints at some latent homosexuality. It is more common to see homosexual men possessed by Freda, although that tradition is also made to answer to the realities of human interaction. In a marriage ceremony between Freda and a male initiate, a homosexual man might opt out of participating for fear of the consequences of publicly expressing desire for another man. The fact of their possession would not necessarily shield them from potential repercussions: Freda's presence during the ritual is not enough to convince others of the immateriality of the mounted male body. Women are given more latitude to express same-sex affection. They are allowed to openly kiss and caress both men and women. The everyday lives and experiences of practitioners and audience members influence how pran lwa and spiritual marriage function: the beliefs of the practitioners and the audience affect religious rituals, and religious communities cannot exist outside these societal and cultural perceptions.

Ezili's Kisses: Consecrating Commitment on a Spiritual Wedding Day

Eddie was a twenty-seven-year-old cisgender, heterosexual native of Somerville, Massachusetts, when, in 2015, he decided to marry five spirits in Manbo Maude's temple in Jacmel. He was raised in a public housing project in Somerville and had been familiar with Vodou his whole life thanks to his Haitian parents, who were practitioners. His grandparents were also *Vodouizans*, practitioners of Vodou, as were their ancestors, stretching generations back in his family lineage. Although he grew up around the religion, it was not a meaningful part of his life until he was an adult, when he endured a nearly fatal experience. The event altered his perspective on his faith and his commitment to the spirits. When I first met Eddie in Jacmel, he was preparing for his marriage, and a week after we met, I was there to witness the ceremony. The spirits he remembered most vividly from the ceremony were the Ezilis: Ezili Freda, Ezili Dantò, and Metres Ezili. When we spoke years later in 2019 through WhatsApp, they were the marriages he described in the most detail. "There are others," Eddie explained. "But it's mainly the three."[23]

Several days before the marriage ceremony took place in Jacmel, Eddie underwent a ritual bath for good luck, while others planned a ritual designed to prepare him for the wedding and to rid him of any negative energy. Members of Manbo Maude's home brought a half-dozen hens into the temple and tied a small string to their legs, attaching them to nearby chairs so they could not escape the room. The hens needed to stay in the temple for a few days and nights, and they clucked and crowed the entire time. The time they spent in the temple made them holy, designating them as animals to be used in ritual services and showcasing them for the spirits. Sacred foods, rum, ritual objects, and elaborate fabrics were also placed on the altar in the temple. In the afternoon before the marriage, Manbo Maude performed a preparatory ceremony. She and all her practitioners wore simple white clothes. During this ceremony, the hens were moved by practitioners into the open-air area adjacent to the temple, rubbed with water that had been mixed with sacred herbs and leaves, and fed cornmeal.

Haitian female initiates cleansed Eddie with the hens by wiping them against his body and making circular motions above his head and feet. When the hens flapped their wings, they rid him of negative energy. The more they flapped their wings, the more negative energy escaped. During this ritual, two Haitian men tied a massive pig to the *potomitan*, or sacred center pole, in the center of the outside area and cleansed it with the sacred herbs and leaves. Previously, the pig had been tied to the sacred Mapou tree for two days, which made it holy. After the pig was brought into the temple, Ezili Dantò was called into the afternoon ceremony by practitioners. She possessed several female practitioners, including Manbo Maude and Eddie's mother. Red and blue moushwa were tied around their arms, head, and waists to signal Dantò's presence. Mounted practitioners rode the pig to show Dantò's acceptance of and appreciation for it. While possessed by Dantò, Manbo Maude was handed a dagger and mimed stabbing herself and the air around her. When Eddie's mother was possessed, she approached him, and he knelt on the ground. She saluted him by pouring rum on his head and pressing her head against his. Eventually, the hens and the pig were cooked and placed on the altar as offerings during the wedding. The wedding ceremony started at 10 P.M. that night inside the temple.

Eddie described it as an exciting event, saying, "It's vivid. It's a dance. It's a party. It's a celebration."[24] Eddie wore all white, with his long, freshly retwisted, waist-length locs pulled back into a bun. He wore a short-sleeved buttoned-down shirt, with all the wrinkles pressed out, and white jeans cuffed at the ankle. Unlike Zeta, he did not change his outfit to suit the different spirits he was marrying. Because he wore all white, he still met the requirements of honoring multiple spirits for his marriage, because white is an appropriate color for all the spirits. Yet I never observed a female initiate who wore only white during her marriage ceremony. The gendered expectations of religious fashion in Manbo Maude's temple did not demand that Eddie wear anything elaborate, and the focus was on the overall neatness of his appearance. The spirits and the audience required a far less extravagant sartorial display than what was expected for female practitioners like Zeta; this reduced the expense of the ceremonial preparations. As previously discussed, within spiritual vogue, the interaction among the audience, the spirits, and practitioners is shaped by the identities of the people involved, which includes their gender. He tied moushwa of various colors around his neck to indicate the spirit he was marrying. Dantò, one of those spirits, arrived at the ceremony at around 1 A.M. after the initiates welcomed her with a song and drumming. Manbo Maude was the vessel through which Dantò made her presence known.

After mounting Manbo Maude, Dantò was adorned with red and blue moushwa and handed her sacred dagger. Dantò began to dance in front of the drums and inside the Vodou circle. Other practitioners were pran lwa as well, most of them female. There was a notable exception: a Black gay man from Manbo Eve's temple. As a gay man and as a man mounted by a female spirit, his possession made some people uneasy. I caught sight of his possession taking place across the room, my focus straying from the giddy exchange of alcohol and laughter among the crowd around me long enough to see Manbo Eve's ti feỳ begin twitching, his eyes rolling: both recognizable signs of spirit possession. Simon, an especially uncomfortable cisgender, heterosexual Black Haitian man, was standing nearby, eyes trained on the same sight while his hands curled into fists at his sides.[25] "Sak Pase?" I asked, Haitian Kreyòl for "What's happening," and he immediately replied, "He better not do it."

I squinted in confusion, "Do what?"

Simon kept glaring at the possessed man, "He better not pran lwa by Dantò. I won't allow him. They do that so they can kiss men. I won't allow him to kiss my friend."[26]

Simon was angered by the prospect that his friend Eddie might be approached by the possessed man and be kissed under the guise of Dantò's affection. Queer men are sometimes mounted by female spirits in Manbo Maude's communities but usually do not offer kisses to other men outside the safe territory of the forehead; more often they embrace other men with hugs, and they are rarely brought to the altar during marriage ceremonies. For many practitioners, gay men possessed by female spirits do not transcend the realities of their earthly bodies or identities, and so a man pran lwa by Dantò would not be expected to stand at the altar next to Eddie. The peck on the lips often exchanged during nuptials might become scandalous if both persons were male, though there is little to no concern when two women kiss. Manbo Eve's ti fèy was also an outsider, so perhaps some of Simon's hostility resulted from the assumption that he was unfamiliar with the tacit understandings governing Manbo Maude's temples.

Hoping to defuse Simon's temper while remaining wary of his negative attitude, I playfully hit him in the chest, saying, "Be cool." Simon was unfazed and continued to glare at the Black gay man across the room. Interestingly, another male practitioner—a member of Manbo Maude's home, heterosexual, and Simon's friend—was mounted by Gran Ezili, an elderly female spirit. He crouched on the ground, hunched and shaking, making his body small to approximate the shriveled form of Gran Ezili. He held his stiff hands close to his chest, wrists bent and fingers tucked toward his palms, emulating the lwa's arthritic immobilization. Eddie showed Gran Ezili his reverence by embracing her and pressing his forehead against the possessed practitioner's forehead in welcome. Simon had no reaction to the display, watching the proceedings as though they were normal. I cannot discern all the factors that contributed to his angry reactions to men being mounted by female divinities during Eddie's wedding. Yet his disquiet directed my attention, once again, to the ongoing complications of being a queer person in Vodou spaces, where one's sexuality and gender, if known, are constantly affecting ceremonial performance rituals and even, as with Simon, may arouse the specter of violence. The man possessed by Gran Ezili—perhaps because he was heterosexual, or because Simon knew him, or because he was a member of Manbo Maude's temple, or all that and more—was completely unthreatening to Simon's sense of masculinity and the masculinity he was attempting to protect on Eddie's behalf. Gran Ezili is old and so withered she is devoid of sexual connotations, and that too may have added to Simon's blasé reaction to her presence within the body of a man.

Whatever Simon's opinions about Gran Ezili might have been, his reaction to Manbo Eve's ti feỳ was so vitriolic that I must return to the factor I believe was key to his anger: the man's homosexuality. The hypervisibility of any queer Black man who is perceived as feminine was a continuing source of discussion during the ceremonies I attended and in my casual conversations with practitioners. No one ever told me that they doubted the validity of the possession experienced by queer Black men, as they did with White people; yet, they also suggested that queer Black men might be more open to pran lwa by female spirits because of the potential for same-sex kisses, as though this possession offers an excuse for physical affection with other men. By interpreting their motivations as purely sexual and denying the religious motivations that are ascribed to Black male heterosexual practitioners, that assumption hypersexualizes queer Black men. There is no corresponding concern about the motives of Black heterosexual men who are taken over by male spirits and may become overly enthusiastic in showing their appreciation for women: their displays of affections are routine and rarely provoke reproach. Yet, no one who expressed these beliefs to me would agree to have their comments attached to their name or even to a pseudonym. Their clear apprehension about the issue and Simon's open displeasure are evidence that the nexus between queerness and possession needs further exploration.

While his friend attempted to vigilantly guard his masculinity, Eddie continued with his ceremony, saluting Dantò, who was still mounting Manbo Maude, through a short routine of ritual footwork. She watched with a dagger pointed at her navel. A male initiate flicked Florida Water onto Eddie during the salute and while he knelt. Dantò placed her dagger flat against his head and then tapped it on his shoulders. She moved the dagger around and across his body while dancing in circular patterns around him. She poured Florida Water around him in a circle. Dantò tried to light her dagger, which had been doused in cologne, on fire by holding it over a lit candle that sat on the potomitan. A Black male practitioner rushed over to assist her and lit her dagger on fire. Together, they set the circle of cologne that surrounded Eddie on fire. She went back to dancing and was greeted by other male initiates who were married to her. She looked happy to see Eddie and danced over to where he still was kneeling on the ground. The fire is symbolic of Dantò's Kongolese origins and the fact that she belongs to the *Petwo* pantheon of spirits, whose temperaments are volatile and intense.[27] Moreover, as art historian

Robert Farris Thompson wrote, fire signifies the "*Petwos*' power to make things burn in a positive healing sense . . . [and] powerfully reflect this notion of salvation through extremity and intimidation."[28] When mounting practitioners during ceremonies, *Petwo* spirits are given to robust displays of strength, which reflect their ability to channel awesome forces in the service of their followers. Anthropologist Karen McCarthy Brown described how to nourish their passionate personalities, stating that *Petwo* spirits "are offered rum mixed with ingredients such as coffee, hot pepper, and gunpowder" along with "cracking whips and shrieking police whistles" during ceremonies.[29]

The prèt savann then stepped into Dantò's path and gestured to her, telling her without words that she was there to marry Eddie. The only visible indicator of his status as a priest and officiator was the large silver cross hanging around his neck. At this ceremony, he was not wearing any Catholic clergy clothes but instead wore a white t-shirt with a large Vodou symbol printed onto it. He looked at Dantò, waved his hand toward Eddie, and then raised his eyebrows at Dantò, as though asking for her approval for the marriage. Dantò smiled. The priest instructed Eddie to get up by beckoning him with his hand. Eddie rose and Dantò took his hand and admired his ring before they linked and then released their pinkie fingers, one of the standard greetings between practitioners and spirits. She spun him in clockwise and counterclockwise circles with their fingers still connected. Dantò flung more Florida Water onto Eddie. She spoke to him, gave him a kiss, and joyfully danced with him. Eddie followed her lead through the room toward the altar while they both grasped her dagger. The prèt savann held up their marriage contract, a lit candle, and a small white porcelain plate with two rings on top of it. One of the rings was for Dantò, and the other for Metres Dantò. Because both spirits were manifestations of Dantò, he did not have to marry them in separate ceremonies, and Eddie would be placing both rings on his fingers. Eddie and Dantò sat in two chairs placed in front of the decorated altar, after Eddie guided her into her seat. The prèt savann stood in front of them and held out the plate with the two rings. "Other people wear silver," Eddie recalled "But mine is white gold with the red ruby; that's for Dantò. Metres is white gold or silver with a blue stone."

Dantò pressed her hand against her chest in surprised delight at the sight of the rings. She looked to Eddie and the prèt savann, saying, "*Pou mwen?*" Haitian Kreyòl meaning "For me?" The prèt savann recited the marriage vows in Haitian Kreyòl, holding the lit candle above the plate and asking them if they accepted the union. They accepted, and Dantò poured Florida Water onto the rings. The prèt savann then used his candle to light the rings on fire.

Dantò swirled the rings, the cologne, and the fire around the plate with her fingers. This ritual transformed the rings into spiritual items. After the fire died out, she inspected the rings. Once she was satisfied, she placed the rings on the index and ring fingers of Eddie's left hand. The prèt savann asked Eddie whether he was prepared to do what was needed to serve the spirit. Dantò ran her dagger across her chest in the sign of a cross to signify her own commitment to protecting him. She took his hand and pressed it to her heart. She kissed his ring and pushed his hand back toward him, so Eddie could kiss his own ring. Then Dantò put her arm around his shoulders and kissed him chastely on the mouth three times. They hugged each other while the prèt savann made the symbol of a cross over their heads with his hand.

Eddie remembered this moment fondly: "I love how [the Ezilis] embrace me and they love me and they [were] hugging me and kissing me. I had the food out for them. They came. It was like a great time. It was a legit wedding, but it's almost like they were there. There's no denying that they are there. You had a legit marriage."[30] Other initiates joined them at the altar, giving them the food that had been offered to Dantò. It consisted of plantains, fried pork, and *pikliz*, which is a Haitian condiment made from pickled cabbage, carrots, and bell peppers. Eddie fed Dantò the plantains, and then she started to eat her fill at will. Dantò tipped a bottle of rum to Eddie's lips for him to drink before taking a swig for herself. The prèt savann gave Eddie and Dantò the marriage contract. They signed their names, and then he gave the contract to witnesses to sign as well. I was one of the witnesses, along with some initiates. Later, Eddie kept the marriage contract and brought it home with him to keep as a ritual object on the altar he maintained in his apartment for Dantò.

After they got married, Dantò returned to the broader ceremony, linked arm and arm with Eddie, and blessed other male initiates. Together, they circled the potomitan. A few moments later, she separated from him and danced around the room alone. Eddie waited on the other side of the room. She looked toward Eddie and then abruptly sprinted across to him, jumping into his arms. She continued dancing while in his arms. Dantò left, releasing Manbo Maude, and she slumped in Eddie's embrace. Several initiates, male and female, rushed over to help Eddie place Manbo Maude onto a chair to recover.

When I asked him what he remembered most vividly about it, he described the support he received from his friends and family: "It's new to me. So, when you [Eziaku] are there, and I see you and you are supporting me. Shori is supporting me. I am nervous. It's like a real wedding. You are making a commitment, you are doing something, and you see that your family is there. You got people that say, 'You can do this; you got this.' That's how I took it as. The key thing was the support. Nothing felt better than turning around and looking at the corner and feeling like I got people who got my back."[31] His recollections helped me understand that my presence, and the presence of other audience members and observers, shaped his wedding and his spiritual commitment. For Eddie, they were a physical reminder of the support for his spiritual marriage. Our presence was a key element signaling the legitimacy of the ceremony taking place, emphasizing the role of the audience in spiritual vogue, and illustrating the constant interaction among the audience, practitioners, and spirits. The union between the spirit and the practitioner is strengthened by the presence of the audience, who make up the broader religious community that essentially sanctions and facilitates the marriage. The rings, which are ritual adornment items, symbolize the marriage and are placed on the practitioner's hand in front of witnesses. The spirit, in this case Dantò, placed the rings onto Eddie's fingers in front of the prèt savann, other practitioners, and the audience, who bore witness to their spiritual marriage. Having witnesses at the wedding solidified the commitment Eddie and Dantò were making to one another, not only because they were making their promise in front of their religious community but also because that same community was facilitating their ability to make that commitment through their physical presence and by participating in and preparing for the ceremony. By serving as witnesses during the wedding ceremony, the audience became a significant part of the ritual service, grounding the demonstration of devotion between practitioner and spirits in their religious community.

Eddie's commitment to the spirits he married extends beyond the ceremony officiated in Jacmel. When Eddie reflects on his marriage, he emphasizes how the commitment has changed how he lives his life and interacts with the world. The unions of spiritual marriage are lifelong, and continuing devotion is expressed through engaging in numerous ritual practices. He spent $4,000 for each of the three rings he wears for the Ezilis he married, which he had custom made by a private jeweler in Somerville. He designed the rings according to what suited the spirits; for example, "Freda is a gold band; you can put diamonds on it or not. I chose diamonds to make it look pretty."[32] When I asked why he was concerned with making one of the rings especially pretty for Freda, he answered as if that question needed no explanation: "Well, it's Freda, and two, I am just a pretty dude so I like everything really pretty."[33]

Eddie's impressions about what type of ring fit specific spirits are shaped not only by Manbo Maude's guidance but also by information he finds on the internet. Manbo Maude often encourages members of her house to look up information online about Vodou rituals and history, and she also posts information on her Facebook page about proper Vodou etiquette. Her videos on YouTube provide additional guidance for practitioners.

Eddie began saving for the significant expenses of his spiritual marriage a year in advance, after being told that he needed to get married during a spiritual reading he had after being initiated in Manbo Maude's temple in 2012. He had to pay not only for the rings but also for the ritual materials that would be necessary for his wedding ceremony and for the labor provided by the cooks and the initiates assisting during the wedding. Eddie credited the spirits with his ability to save money and attributed his economic success to their blessings. Some initiates paid for their weddings in installments throughout the year. Eddie paid for his ceremony all at once because he was able to save the needed money.

Eddie also designates particular days for particular spirits, as he explained: "Saturday is for Ezili Dantò, Tuesday is for Metres, and Thursdays are for Freda."[34] On the days he dedicates to the spirits, he lights a candle on his altar and wears the rings he had custom made for them and dons clothes in the colors associated with them—pink for Freda, red and blue for Dantò, and white for all of them. "White is what I usually go with," he explained, "White goes with everybody."[35] Eddie does not wear clothing that was specially made for Vodou, but everyday clothes in the proper colors, such as t-shirts and blue jeans. Although these clothing items were not created for Vodou ceremonies, the intent with which he wears them illustrates his devotion to the spirits and his commitment to their marriage. Neglecting this practice after committing to the spirits or forgetting to honor them on their days can bring bad luck. Eddie also prepares his body in the ways he believes will please the spirits, such as bathing before going to sleep and wearing cologne, not only with the expectation that he might meet them nan dòmi but also to remain clean and pure in honor of the spirits.

Eddie described a recurring dream he had on nights dedicated to the Ezilis: "I've had days where I see that I am dating like three different sisters, and they are fighting over me. Where one would go to the kitchen and the other would go the room, and they would tell me that they secretly like me and they would fight over me and it would pretty much be like your wives fighting over you, like they are jealous. Pretty much things like that."[36] In dreams such as this, the spirits communicated their continued commitment to him and to their marriage through this vision of heterosexual, polyamorous domestic partnership. In his dreams, Eddie was living in his home with his wives as the center of their affection and sexual desire. He described the three spirits fighting over him and vying for his affection. The playful interactions connoted a relationship built on mutual affection and respect. He was honoring them properly and therefore maintained their affection.

Before his spiritual marriage, Eddie used to have spiritual readings with Manbo Maude once a month. After the marriage, he only visited Manbo Maude for spiritual readings once a year. He credited this change to his stronger relationship to the spirits and the confidence he gained after marrying them. Eddie also understood his marriage to the spirits as preparation for marrying a human woman, saying, "They've helped me because I used to doubt if I could commit to a woman if I really get married."[37] He views the commitment he made to the spirits as an opportunity to learn lessons about himself and how he relates to other people, particularly women. "Now, if I found a woman that I truly love I can be dedicated and not cheat on her," he explained. "I know what's expected. [Spiritual marriage] teaches you self-discipline."[38] His dedication to the Ezilis and his resulting willingness to stay faithful to them prove that he can dedicate himself to a woman in the physical world.

When the Spirit Cums: Consummating Divine Intimacies in *Nan Dòmi*

Dreams are an inescapable and crucial aspect of Vodou.[39] They play a significant role in spiritual marriage by conveying messages and consummating the marital commitment. This dream state is often referred to as nan dòmi, the lucid dream state between conscious and unconscious where spirits connect with practitioners.[40] The messages received in dreams can be abstract, in which case the practitioner must decipher the meaning, or they can be quite literal, conveying clear messages from the spirits. In either case, these dreams are often shared within a practitioner's religious community where a spiritual guide or family member can help decode the messages to determine how best to please the spirits. Sometimes the dreams and messages are kept private: a practitioner might understand the messages without help or choose to find meaning through his or her own analysis. Thus, dreams, like possessions, can be interpersonal and intrapersonal experiences within a spiritual community. The lucid nature of nan dòmi explains why practitioners can recall their dreams in such vivid detail and why the decisions they make in the dreams regarding their relationships to spirits hold sway over their actions in the conscious world.

The dream world is held in high esteem because it is one of the avenues used to converse with the spirits and to negotiate with the divine. Fashion and adornment, either in nan dòmi or in preparation for it, fosters communicative relationships between practitioners and spirits, opening a space for the negotiation and reaffirmation of commitment. Nan dòmi is not only a space to learn about the unknown but is also where practitioners discern the desires of the spirits, respond to demands for material offerings, make commitments, and experience real, multisensorial contact with the divine. Away from the crowd and noise of the ceremonies, the spiritual encounters nan dòmi are not defined by the presence of a broader community of witnesses. Dreams offer an intimate space of connection between practitioners and spirits, often providing an opportunity for the sexual expression of marital commitment.

Eddie invited the spirits to communicate with him nan dòmi by dressing and bathing for the ones he married before going to sleep. Eddie, as well as other practitioners, dons specific clothing or colors for sleeping in anticipation of sexual encounters with certain spirits, which foster a continued devotion to and communication with the spirits. For Eddie, these dreams were a visceral, pleasurable experience that remained vivid on awakening: "I actually had a full wet dream. . . . It was crazy. And a couple nights ago, I actually, I almost had the same thing happen, but it was almost like I woke up and I was like, 'What the fuck am I doing?' Like I was humping the shit outta this bed. But it felt so real. There were times that it feels like I was with this person."[41] I asked Eddie how he knew which spirit he was having sex with, and he explained that he knew through their physical appearance. When he saw a woman with a dagger, he interpreted it to be Ezili Dantò because the dagger is a symbol commonly associated with her. A light-skinned woman, in contrast, represented Ezili Freda, who is often depicted as having fair skin.[42] Moreover, if two women appeared together and they were bickering, then they were the Ezilis, who have a contentious relationship as sisters. The Ezilis can be interpreted as sisters because they are part of the same family of spirits.

The sexual encounters like the one Eddie described are one key outcome of spiritual marriage. Although sex with spirits is not reserved only for those who marry the divine, it is commonly expected and helps curry continued favor from the spirits. Yet, it is not a mandatory obligation for initiates who marry; the spirits can communicate through numerous avenues. But for those who do engage in sex with the deities, that experience reaffirms their connection to the divine and can bring good fortune. Manbo Maude described the significance of sexual relationships with spirits as being an exchange of energy and compared it to sex with human partners. Sex with anyone, human or spirit, is "divine," Manbo Maude professed. "Your body is your temple. . . . It's spiritual when you have relationships with people."[43] Spirits and initiates give and take energy from one another during these experiences.

Eddie refrained from having sex with nonspiritual partners or himself on Tuesdays and Thursdays, the days reserved for the Ezilis. He would wait until sunrise on the following day to even think about having sex, after being scolded by the Ezilis nan dòmi in the past for having sex too soon after their special days ended. Engaging in sex almost immediately after midnight, when the day was technically done, was viewed as disrespectful by the deities, who felt slighted by his rush to leave them.[44] The fashion Eddie donned to honor the spirits, wearing white or the color associated with the spirits he married, as well as his rings, enabled this multisensorial sexual encounter nan dòmi. For Eddie, this fashion and adornment were part of the ongoing ritual work of spiritual marriage and a necessary aspect of communicating with the spirits. Eddie was able to touch, see, and hear the spirits. The adornment and fashion choices practitioners make to prepare their bodies facilitates a multisensorial sexual interaction that reinforces their faith and their surety that the spirits are a tangible presence in their everyday lives.

Though Manbo Maude emphasized the importance of heteronormative spiritual marriages, there are practitioners who have affinities for same-gender spirits and have sexual relationships with them as well, inside and outside her spiritual home. In Manbo Maude's spiritual homes and in many other Vodou temples, the gender conventions on display during spiritual marriages are often explained as based on tradition, but there are also cultural and societal reasons for these ritual preferences. When I interviewed a Houngan and scholar of Haitian studies whom I call Joel, he argued that the widespread reluctance to embrace same-gender spiritual marriages in Vodou was rooted in homophobia in Haiti: "People would be horrified if we had a ceremony, and I was going to marry Ogou Ferray and Ogou Badagri. People would be very offended. A Haitian would be very offended because they are homophobic. . . . I blame Christianity for that. Because this is where they learn to discriminate against homosexuals."[45] Joel described homophobia as being widespread, yet some temples embrace same-gender marriages. In Jacmel, there are Vodou homes that allow same-gender spiritual marriage and permit transgender people to marry according to their gender identity. In 2018, I Vodou hopped to a spiritual home that was run by a gay Haitian man who had spiritually married initiates and spirits of the same gender. Although I did not witness these ceremonies, I was told about them by Manbo Maude and by initiates in her home. Spiritual marriages are mostly officiated publicly during ceremonies, but Joel asserted that his marriage to Ogou and the Ezilis happened in the dream state.

Finding practitioners willing to openly discuss sexual encounters with spirits is often difficult, including among practitioners in Manbo Maude's temples. In private, people shared the details of their sexual relationships with spirits but only with the expectation of complete secrecy. For that reason, I continue to share Joel's experience, even though he is not a member of Manbo Maude's religious communities. His story of sex, marriage, and the spirits offers a valuable point of contrast with some of the traditions stipulated by Manbo Maude and emphasizes the intimate connections between practitioners and the lwa. The interconnectedness of the spirits, practitioners, and audience is not required to establish a valid union. Barred from having his marriage recognized in many temples because of his and Ogou's gender, Joel relies on the bonds formed nan dòmi to reinforce his commitments. In dreams, the homosexuality of their relationship is a non-issue. The promises made nan dòmi carry into Joel's daily life, where he understands the marriage to be legitimate.

When I interviewed Joel over the phone, he described his sexual encounter with two versions of Ogou: Ogou Ferray and Ogou Badagri. He had a strong connection with Ogou, even though he had never formally committed to him during a public marriage ceremony. The sexual encounter was proof of their devotion to one another and of the tacit truth that spirits could have same-gender desires, as shown in this interview excerpt:

> JOEL: I am married to two Ogous as a matter of fact. As a matter of fact about fifteen years ago, I woke up about five o'clock in the morning, and I was covered with sperm and it was not my own. And I woke up and I went to a pile of CDs which I had never opened, that I had purchased and never played, went to the middle of that pile, pulled out a recording by a Haitian band. [I] put on my CD player, and here was a song that Ogou was singing to me in the dream. I have never heard that song before. . . . I went straight to that CD and played the song that they were singing to me.
>
> EZIAKU: So you woke up to sperm that wasn't yours?
>
> JOEL: No.
>
> EZIAKU: How did you know that it wasn't yours?

JOEL: Because I know it was not mine, because I know mine.

EZIAKU: Because you know yours. Was the smell different?

JOEL: Yeah. And because I was making love all night to the two Ogous.

EZIAKU: Oh wow. So, the two Ogous, what did they look like? Were they dark-skinned, light-skinned?

JOEL: Well, it's interesting, when I see those Haitian spirits I see them as light brown. Typically light brown. He comes to me from time to time and he is light brown. Or medium brown and green eyes.

EZIAKU: And so, you had sex with the Ogou.

JOEL: It was *very* wonderful.[46]

During our interview, I repeated my questions because I wanted to make sure I understood the spiritual experience he was describing. His detailed description of his encounter with the two Ogous illustrates the intense, pleasurable sexual experiences that are possible nan dòmi. The residues of the dream are the evidence of spiritual presence, a mark left behind by the spirits to communicate their mutual affection and belonging. Joel also told me that Ogou gave him a ring as a gift during his dream to signify their commitment, another symbolic material offering signifying their union. In an earlier dream state, he had a wedding ceremony where he married Ezili Dantò and Ezili Freda and engaged in all the rituals that were described during Eddie's marriage. The Ezilis gave him rings to honor their commitment as well. In the waking world, Joel does not wear any rings for the deities on his fingers but considers the adornment that took place nan dòmi to be as fully binding as anything he might have done during a full ceremony in the presence of other practitioners. Because nan dòmi is a lucid dream state, he recognized the commitment he was making and the resulting consequences in the conscious world. In his home, he has altars dedicated to the spirits, and he sets aside days to honor them. He also wears colors dedicated to the spirits he serves. Joel places very little significance on the type of marriage ceremonies Manbo Maude performs for her initiates, instead emphasizing the direct connection between a practitioner and a spirit during the dream state. "I don't have to do it in a ritual and spend that kind of money,"[47] he concluded. His perspective on spiritual marriage and sex between practitioners and spirits provides an avenue through which to explore the reality of same-gender encounters. Nan dòmi, spirits can circumvent the heteronormative boundaries placed on them by temples in the physical realm.

Manbo Maude, like Joel, has an affinity for a same-gender spirit: Ezili Dantò. As previously mentioned, the Ezilis are some of the primary spirits who influence her innovative relationship to religious fashion. To honor her connection to Dantò, Manbo Maude wears a ring and specific dresses during ceremonies. Moreover, she has married male spirits who are affiliated with Dantò, such as Ogou and Simbi, a freshwater spirit and healer. "I married them to show her my commitment toward her men,"[48] Manbo Maude explained. "She won't be jealous that I am with her men. She will collaborate with me [because I am] taking care of her men." Thus, Manbo Maude's relationship to Dantò is mediated through her marriage to male spirits who represent this important connection through their affiliation with Dantò. When Manbo Maude said "her men," she was referencing larger ideas within the Vodou ethos that pair various spirits with one another in sexual or familial relationships. Dantò, for example, is said to have taken Ogou as a lover and given birth to his children, and she has also had a sexual relationship with Simbi. Instead of marrying Ezili Dantò directly, she wears a ring and married the male spirits associated with her. Ogou and Simbi are not substitutes or stand-ins for Dantò but represent the broader family of spirits she is dedicated to and who help her perform spiritual services. It is also possible that the rigidity of the marriage traditions in Manbo Maude's home necessitates this arrangement, that her connection to a female deity could only be ritualistically established through male spirits. Ultimately, the adornment practice of wearing a ring to show dedication to the spirits connects Manbo Maude to male and female deities whether she has married them or not, binding her to the spirits who have had the most impact on her life and religious communities.

When I spoke with Manbo Maude in 2016 about her connection to Ezili Dantò, she told me how she came to acquire a blue ritual dress that was made especially for the spirit. During a dream she had in the early days of her tenure as a Manbo, Dantò came to her and sexually propositioned her. Manbo Maude reacted defensively, forcibly shoving her away. After having that dream, several strange misfortunes befell Manbo Maude, and her spiritual mother advised her that the bad luck was the result of Dantò feeling disrespected. Her spiritual mother prescribed performing a series of rituals to regain Dantò's respect. Manbo Maude followed the instructions, and after performing the rituals, which included lighting a candle and saying a series of prayers, she encountered the deity in a second dream. Nan dòmi, Manbo Maude observed Ezili Dantò in a stream, engaging in sex with Ezili Freda. Dantò had both a penis and a vagina—a common, though not universal, description among the practitioners. Manbo Maude recalled the sexual encounter in great detail, describing the sight of ejaculate in the river. "I saw when she reached the climax," Manbo Maude said. She found the entire scene alarming and was frightened when Dantò looked to her for her next tryst. She wanted to flee but feared disrespecting Dantò a second time and so stood by the water, petrified.

When Dantò and Ezili Freda were done having sex, Dantò ascended from the water and approached Manbo Maude. The spirit spoke with compassion: "I know you are not that way, and I will not do those things to you, because I know you don't like it. I will never do that to you because I know you don't like that. But I need you to know that you are mine, and you belong to me, so wear this dress."[49] Dantò handed Manbo Maude a blue dress. When Manbo Maude awoke she remembered the dress and sought out fabrics that mirrored the appearance of the garment nan dòmi. She created an elegant blue dress for Dantò and immediately wore it for seven days. Later, she donned the same outfit during a ceremony dedicated to the spirit. "She never came onto me that way again," Manbo Maude recalled. "I was blessed after that, and I stopped having problems."[50]

As previously discussed, sex is a common means through which the spirits communicate with those devoted to them. Although Manbo Maude was not married to Ezili Dantò, the offer of sex represented a possible avenue of connection and favor. When Manbo Maude indicated that she was not interested in sex, Dantò shifted to fashion as another means of communication. The dress symbolized the nonsexual relationship between Dantò and Manbo Maude while still indicating their dedication to one another. This encounter illustrates the ongoing negotiation between spirits and practitioners nan dòmi and the importance of fashion as a conduit for such conciliation. The negotiatory labor necessitated by Manbo Maude's encounters with Dantò nan dòmi allowed the two to find a mutually beneficial relationship. Though Manbo Maude was unwilling to engage in sex with Dantò, she accepted the compromise, creating in the real world the dress Dantò demanded in the dream, thereby solidifying their connection. This compromise was also reached through the emotional labor Manbo Maude engaged in, negotiating with Dantò face-to-face in her dreams.[51] She needed to mediate the tension between herself and the deity to stay in Dantò's favor and avoid the bad luck associated with disobeying a spirit. For Manbo Maude and Dantò, clothing marked their mutual affection and commitment. The decision to make a dress nan dòmi had real consequences in Manbo Maude's religious practices, just as the rings offered to Joel in his dream established real-world connections with the spirits.

The spiritual dreams that Manbo Maude, Eddie, and Joel recounted were defined not only by a sense of intense intimacy. Within their stories lie a clear attempt by the gods to claim them as devoted supplicants through sex and adornment. Both the deities and the practitioners demonstrate a belief in mutual belonging, articulated through ritual items like rings and clothing and meetings nan dòmi. Within ceremonies, possessions allow for various gendered expressions to occur, yet women are clearly afforded a wider array of masculine and feminine expressions of the divine, as well as nonbinary manifestations. As a result of the social confines that permeate religious rituals, and often in contradiction of the nature of the divine, the possession performances of male practitioners are limited. I argue that cisgender heterosexual men are prevented from obtaining a fuller connection to the divine because they have to operate within patriarchal expectations. Negotiations with restrictive social mores curb the full expression of Vodou and the potential egalitarianism of ceremonies such as spiritual marriages. Although Manbo Maude and members of her temples have pushed some gender boundaries, they also invest in gender norms in their ritual practice. This contradiction is embodied in young practitioners who are continuously pushing the borders of beliefs, challenging and maintaining the status quo. Manbo Maude's daughter is a part of the next generation of Vodou practitioners who will determine how the faith interprets its traditions. The following chapter explores the intergenerational nature of Vodou with Vante'm Pa Fyem at the forefront, shaping her own relationship to fashion and adornment. Like her mother, Vante'm Pa Fyem has a unique connection with the spirits and maintains the legacy started by Manbo Maude while beginning to cultivate her own stylistic tastes in service of the divine.

Dènye Panse
Fashioning Lineages into Vodou Legacies

Ezili Dantò chose Vante'm Pa Fyem. When Manbo Maude became pregnant with her, she was already overwhelmed with the effort of raising two other children. The strain on her finances was so great she considered seeking an abortion to spare herself and her family the burden. That same night, as though summoned by Manbo Maude's instinct to terminate the pregnancy, Dantò came to her *nan dòmi*. The spirit told her to keep the baby. Manbo Maude expressed her worries: she was exhausted, and another baby would further drain her depleted resources. Dantò was insistent. The child belongs to her, the deity said; the child was special. *You need to keep her. I will provide for you.* Manbo Maude was never one to refuse the will of the spirits, not when they reached out so purposefully. If Dantò's words were true, her child was favored by the divine. Since that night, Manbo Maude says she never again suffered dire financial difficulties. Dantò kept her word.[1]

Ezili Dantò's history in Vodou is closely tied to the Haitian Revolution. Stories tell of a gruesome mutilation performed to ensure she would keep confidences: her tongue was cut out of her mouth, either by Black people who wanted to ensure she would never share the secrets of revolutionaries with enemies or by White people who wanted to hobble the massive rebellion. Centuries after the Revolution's end, she is still incapable of speaking: her recognizable *k kk kkkk kkkk* sounds are only decipherable by practitioners through the aid of translators who follow her around the ceremony. In legend, Dantò has a cherished daughter named Anais who acts as her mouthpiece to the world, speaking the words her mother can no longer articulate. In ceremonies, the practitioners who keep close to Dantò, conveying her messages, play the role of her divine daughter. The story of a celestial daughter speaking for her mother resonates in the earthly realm of Manbo Maude's temples, where Vante'm Pa Fyem often communicates Manbo Maude's words and needs to others. Vante'm Pa Fyem frequently acts as one of the translators when Manbo Maude and others are mounted by Dantò, verbalizing whatever messages the deity is miming toward practitioners and audience members. She becomes Dantò's mouthpiece.

Manbo Vante'm Pa Fyem and Manbo Maude posing in their spiritual dresses before a Danbala ceremony in Mattapan, March 2016 (photo by Eziaku Nwokocha).

Vodou en Vogue is my own attempt at translation—not of the words of a singular deity or Manbo but of the intricacies of the public ceremonies I witnessed and the stories I was told. Concluding with a neat statement seems ill-fitting for a book filled with stories about a Black woman as innovative as Manbo Maude and spirits as varied and dynamic as the Vodou pantheon. They are too lively to be captured fully within the confines of any conclusion. Instead, I offer a few *dènye panse*, Haitian Kreyòl for "last thoughts," that articulate not only the knowledge my work has produced but also a sense of the inescapable shifts within Vodou itself. Vodou changes over time, just as all religions do; its practitioners and rituals cannot be held in stasis. Traditions are passed down through spiritual lineages, and with each successive transition they shift, accommodating new places, people, and experiences. Thus, these last thoughts cannot represent a definitive end for Manbo Maude or her communities, just a snapshot of where they are in a particular moment and the foreshadows of where they might go from here.

Throughout *Vodou en Vogue*, I emphasize the interplay between the spirits, practitioners, and audience, offering a new interpretation of the relationality within African Diasporic religions through the concept of *spiritual vogue*. It pulls together multiple influences—materiality, religion, race, queerness, sensation, and performance—that are arguably individually inherent to African Diasporic ceremonies yet together offer fascinating insights into the relationship between the people and spirits that bring life and meaning to religion. I make plain that the fashion showcased during Vodou ceremonies is indicative of an interactive process, the meaning of which is only evident through considering the practitioners, spirits, and audience as dependent on one another for successful ritual work. Material culture strengthens the beliefs of devotees and facilitates communication with the gods, a cyclical exchange that satisfies the spirits and guides practitioners. In addition to revealing the negotiations between deities and their devotees, spiritual vogue also underscores the practicalities of ceremonies, the friction caused by the intersection of faith and everyday social, economic, and cultural mores. Vodou ceremonies are animated by performance rituals that, through the lens of fashion, reveal fissures within the religious community, generating complex portraits of gendered possession practices, sexual intimacy with the divine, faith labor, and racial, sexual, and gender identities.

The concept of spiritual vogue, as well as the entirety of *Vodou en Vogue*, is rooted in the notion that religious fashion cannot be dismissed as a mere manifestation of conspicuous consumption. A simplistic dismissal of the material culture in Vodou and other African and African Diasporic religions misses vast cosmological traditions anchored in the everyday practices of lived religions and would ignore crucial conduits to the gods. The anecdotes, interviews, and theories I explore throughout this book clearly show the centrality of transnational material culture to Black practitioners' ability to forge intimate and spiritually meaningful connections with the divine and with one another.

At the beginning of my research, that nexus between performance and fashion, alongside the valuable insights drawn from queer Black and Brown people in Ballroom culture, brought me to spiritual vogue. The communal systems shaping expressions of race, sexuality, and gender in Ballroom also appear within the structure of Vodou ceremonies, where performance rituals convey normative beliefs around gender, sexuality, and sex while simultaneously creating ruptures in those same perceptions. Spiritual vogue is not dependent on public-facing ceremonies—those are simply the religious events I had access to as a non-initiated researcher. The lack of insider access, far from restricting my work, narrowed my focus to the core intricacies of ceremonial spaces, directing my attention to the crucial connection between practitioners, spirits, and the audience. Instead of chasing the secrets of the initiated, I sought the overlooked knowledge on display in crowded temples, full of practitioners ready to speak with the spirits and one another. The triangulation of practitioners, spirits, and the audience is also applicable to more private affairs that still involve performance rituals carried out in front of witnesses within a religious community: certainly, the concept expands beyond Vodou into other African and African Diasporic religions such as Ifá, Candomblé, and Santería. At its center, the concept describes the ritualized performance of identity and piety in front of an audience, an idea that is expansive enough to elucidate the role of sensation and material culture in many religious traditions beyond Haitian Vodou.

For more than a decade I attended Vodou ceremonies, in and outside Manbo Maude's homes, building relationships with devotees and learning the purpose and practices of performance rituals. Focusing on Manbo Maude and her temples led me to the idea that the gods speak to their devotees through avenues they can understand, making room for the talents practitioners can then incorporate into their religious practices. Manbo Maude's devotion shows in every seam, trim, and ruffle she dons during ceremonies. Her garments are evidence of her ability to communicate with the divine and a material tool through which she facilitates continued connection to the spirits for herself and other practitioners. The role of fashion in her religious practices is so foundational she has built it into the structure of her ceremonies, introducing stops and starts to show-case spiritually inspired outfits. My observations, theories, and conclusions are grounded within the communities that were generous enough to let me step into their temples.

Throughout *Vodou en Vogue*, I think largely within Black participants' own words and descriptions, allowing my work to follow wherever their practices and stories led. Inevitably, the time I spent in Manbo Maude's temples led me, again and again, to her youngest daughter Vante'm Pa Fyem. Of Manbo Maude's three children, all of whom are initiated, Vante'm Pa Fyem is the most integrated into the workings of the temples. Her spiritual authority and her wealth of knowledge are rooted in her connection to Manbo Maude, a rela-tionship that is often reinforced during ceremonies through their intentionally similar outfits. Tellingly, these clothes are similar, not identical. In part, this is a result of Manbo Maude's more powerful position within the temples. Yet it also reflects the fact that Vante'm Pa Fyem is in the process of cultivating her own opinions on Vodou, fashion, religious ritual, and com-munity that are influenced not only by her mother's lifelong tutelage but also by her personal experiences as a young woman in the Haitian *Dyaspora*. She is an increasingly knowledgeable Manbo in her own right, learning from her mother while developing her personal understanding of how to serve the spirits. Her burgeoning opinions, potentially deviating from Manbo Maude's, are indicative of Vodou's essential capacity to change over time.

Vante'm Pa Fyem's ability to innovate reflects the core characteristic that drew me to Manbo Maude's temples at the start of my research. Manbo Maude's homes caught my attention and held it, compelled by the distinc-tive use of fashion and how those expressions of material culture underline truths about African Diasporic religious practices and spiritual connection far beyond the thresholds of the temples in Jacmel and Mattapan. Manbo Maude, as individual as she and her communities are in their particulars, is indicative of concepts, principles, and trends that are occurring nearly ev-erywhere Vodou is practiced. Sustaining both her temples for more than twenty years has given performance rituals the time to grow and evolve, re-flecting changes within her life, her relationship with the divine, and the many people who seek meaning through her ceremonies. Spiritual garments are the physical manifestation of those changes, archiving Manbo Maude's shifting perceptions on the proper way to serve the *lwa*: they are also one of the primary elements that have kept her temples alive for two decades. Vante'm Pa Fyem is also key to their survival and will be even more so in the future.

Manbo Maude chose Vante'm Pa Fyem to inherit her temples, yet the knowledge she is transferring to her daughter is not reserved solely for her biological descendants. All her *ti feỳ*, the initiates and practitioners who seek her guidance, are part of her legacy, perpetuating the traditions she passed down from her own spiritual mother, to whom Manbo Maude was not biologically related. Every time she designs a spiritual garment and dresses up with her practitioners in front of an audience, she both offers her beliefs about how to serve the spirits and facilitates communication with them. Manbo Maude preserves and articulates the foundations of Vodou through her religious practices while also innovating by embracing her creativity and the will of the spirits, crafting material items in conversation with the divine. Visual and material culture—the physical manifestations of the traditions being passed from one generation of practitioners to another—is integral to the propagation of religious belief. Vante'm Pa Fyem, in addition to playing a key role in the operation of Manbo Maude's temples, is representative of the broader transference of knowledge, continuing her mother's legacy. The fashion they share is one manifestation of their connection and is an essential part of how Manbo Maude is attempting to construct her legacy. That legacy has consequences not only for Vante'm Pa Fyem's future but also for the people in Jacmel who rely on the funds generated by spiritual work, the Black practitioners and audience members searching for a genuine link to their African or Haitian heritage, and for the practice of Vodou. The spiritual children Manbo Maude trains may one day come to develop their own performance rituals, creating new traditions that bear the mark of her influence.

Vodou's history as an oral tradition can give rise to the erroneous impression that it is a religion without structure, especially when it is simplified within binaries between written and oral customs. Comparing Vodou to the formally institutionalized hierarchy of the Catholic Church, for instance, distracts from the fact that the faith has rules, some of which are described in this book. Even when rituals and gods vary across region in Haiti, the same underlying standards and concepts hold everywhere, proving both the resilience and the organizing principles of the traditions disseminated through generations. At the same time, Vodou changes and adapts to the needs of its practitioners. The passing along of knowledge inevitably leads to change. Manbo Maude, for example, learned to perform rituals and serve the spirits from her spiritual mother, while also developing her personal ideas about the importance of style within those traditions. Her spiritual mother provided her with the structure of her religion, but once she was imbued with spiritual authority, she experimented, building her capacity to communicate with the divine on her own terms. Vante'm Pa Fyem and Manbo Maude's other ti feỳ are set to trek that same path.

The first time I met Vante'm Pa Fyem was in 2012 when she was twelve years old, acting as a translator for her mother. During my conversations with Manbo Maude in Mattapan, she would often linger around us and help figure out the correct way to describe rituals and experiences in English when her mother had difficulty. Vante'm Pa Fyem speaks plainly and honestly with people. She feels protective of her mother, sometimes believing she is too kind. When interpersonal conflicts arise in the temples, Vante'm Pa Fyem will speak on behalf of her mother to help resolve the issue, deploying her directness on behalf of Manbo Maude. She has pushed her mother to handle her religious services and clients as transparently as possible. She learned from watching the occasional client cheat her mother out of money and is careful to clearly outline the costs of services for practitioners as a result.[2] Vante'm Pa Fyem even convinced her mother to begin using written contracts for some of her spiritual work, like initiations or spiritual marriages, which demand a significant amount of time and resources to complete. The money that flows in and around Manbo Maude's homes is not pursued for its own sake: participants donate funds for the upkeep of her temples, for her services, and for the exchange of ritual items like clothing. These contributions, along with the money she saves from her career as a mental health clinician, also help her support community members in Jacmel.

Manbo Maude does not proclaim the importance of wealth during ceremonies or counsel her practitioners about a doctrinally defined connection between material wealth and the spirits: money itself does not equal faith or ensure the favor of the divine. She does, however, pursue her argument that the spirits are royal, grand entities deserving of lavish praise.[3] An investment in her and in her practitioners' spiritual dress is also an investment in their continued relationship with the gods, and therefore the future of Manbo Maude's temples. The relative wealth on display during Manbo Maude's ceremonies—manifested in bright, sparkly, or voluminous spiritual clothing—is not merely a celebration of individual prosperity but is also a demonstration of the potential for communal survival and opportunity. By serving the spirits in the manner she claims they deserve, Manbo Maude also demonstrates, in front of a crowd, that she has the capacity to take care of the people who choose to be a part of her temples. Vodou's ethos is, at its base, about that sense of community, about caring for others just as well as one must care for oneself. Individual skills, weaknesses, and eccentricities are parts of a larger whole, of a broader religious community: they mirror in many ways the pantheon of Vodou spirits, who are characterized by a nearly countless number of personalities and powers yet together reflect the cosmological foundations of the religion. Within that ethos, the adornment practices of Manbo Maude and her practitioners cannot be understood as solely a reflection of their personal wealth or aesthetic preferences; they, and their fashion, are constantly in communication with the spirits, other practitioners, and the audiences that constitute their community.

This constant communication reflects the fact that Manbo Maude's temples, and arguably all Vodou temples, only function through the collective efforts of many people and deities. Manbo Maude has obvious authority within her homes, but she relies on the counsel, aid, and labor of other participants and the spirits. Vante'm Pa Fyem is intimately aware of the necessity for collaboration because she has been immersed in her mother's Vodou temples since childhood, even before she was initiated. Vante'm Pa Fyem grew up with Vodou, surrounded by the gods, easily oscillating between watching television and hanging out with her friends like any child and managing complicated religious rituals in her mother's temples. She knew Vodou songs by the age of three, singing them in her home, and by nine she was speaking with the spirits. Living in Mattapan and around Boston, with its sizable Haitian populations, provided Vante'm Pa Fyem with opportunities to learn about her heritage even when she is not on the island. For example, from ages seven to twelve, she learned Haitian folk dances from a Haitian instructor in Massachusetts and still uses what she learned in those lessons during Vodou ceremonies. As a child, Vante'm Pa Fyem found the intensity of ceremonies frightening, especially after her mother was injured by a spirit.

In Mattapan in March 2004, Ezili Freda broke Manbo Maude's foot, even though she was trying to honor the deity and wore a dress specifically made to please her. Earlier that year, Manbo Maude had canceled a ceremony without asking the spirits about it. Vante'm Pa Fyem describes this as booking an appointment and then bailing, which irritates the spirits, who expect to be consulted. Manbo Maude's lack of communication with Ezili Freda prevented the audience, the spirits, and the practitioners from interacting successfully. Her special dress was not enough to assuage the insult of forgetting to seek the advice of the gods.[4] As a result, Manbo Maude could not foster the desired relationship with the divine.

In Vodou, when a practitioner is injured during *pran lwa*, it can occur for several reasons. It may indicate that a person is not fully possessed by the spirit or cannot manage the intensity of the spirit. Or the spirit may be displeased with the offerings of a ceremony. Finally, it may act as a warning to the injured practitioner, telling them that they disrespected the spirit during the ceremony or in their day-to-day life. The injury is the spirit's way of reciprocating that disrespect. Vante'm Pa Fyem was scared by the knowledge that deities were willing and able to harm her mother and any other practitioner during possession. The fear dissipated with time and continued communication with the spirits. The fright Vante'm Pa Fyem felt as a child and the seriousness with which Manbo Maude and others take injuries experienced during possession result from an understanding of the spirits' tangibility—their anger, their desires, their very presence is real.

The spirits are real entities in *Vodou en Vogue*. Manbo Maude and the practitioners told me the gods spoke to them, and I do not have the power or the will to claim otherwise. I took them at their word and incorporated the presence of the spirits into my theories. Dismissing the divine would have prevented me from seeing the commonplace negotiations and intimacies between the lwa and their devotees. The divine is intertwined with Manbo Maude's temples even beyond the rituals of ceremonies. Spirits directly affect people's lived realities: their financial decisions, interpersonal relationships, and mental and physical health. How practitioners describe the manifestation of the divine is inescapably connected to their own worldviews and their own experiences. Therefore, accepting the presence of the spirits in the lives of practitioners, far from obscuring the social and economic circumstances of ceremonies, throws them into stark relief. The spirits' ubiquity pulls them into nearly every conversation in the temples: they are ready advisers for questions about finances and romance, or messengers relaying important information about a family members health, or willing companions offering solace during difficult times. As a result, interactions between the gods, practitioners, and audiences are points of constant negotiation.

There are moments, as when Ezili Freda broke Manbo Maude's foot, where the will of the divine may seem clear. The consequential line from her actions as a Manbo to the actions of the spirits during a ceremony appear unambiguous. Certainly, Vante'm Pa Fyem's interpretation is, for her, conclusive. Yet discerning the intentions of the gods is sometimes fraught with difficulty and cannot be fully separated from the perceptions of the people calling on their favor. The spirits' very presence, particularly during public ceremonies, forces tensions within religious communities to rise to the surface, making clear people's perceptions about who can or cannot become possessed by which spirits. In Manbo Maude's temples, for example, when cisgender women of any sexual orientation or race are possessed by gods of any gender presentation, they do not draw the suspicion of other participants because of the perceived spiritual power of their bodies. Cisgender heterosexual men, however, are rarely possessed by female spirits, reflecting a concern over damaging their masculinity in front of others. Gay men are commonly mounted by female spirits, and in Manbo Maude's temples, race emerges as still another complicating factor. White people in general are sometimes understood to lack an inherent connection to Black Vodou gods and as therefore incapable of serving as their vessels. Those perceptions do more to illuminate the social conventions of ceremonial spaces than to reveal the will of the divine, which I argue is unencumbered by human fears and prejudices about sexuality and gender. That potential truth became clear only by acknowledging the presence of the spirits, because the practitioners I interviewed describe gods capable of marrying and sharing intimacy within queer spiritual partnerships. Practitioners also tell of spirits with a wide range of gender and sexual expressions, which manifest during ceremonies and in the cosmology of Vodou. The deities' range of gender and sexual expressions and the stories from practitioners who report queer interactions with the divine make clear that homophobia, misogyny, and patriarchy in Haiti and the United States are limiting, confining forces within Vodou, deterring many people from embracing the full potential of the religion and its pantheon of lwa.

The earthly rules placed on interactions between practitioners and the spirits, such as heteronormative expectations in spiritual marriages or conventions about who can be possessed by which spirits based on traditional notions of masculinity and femininity, cannot be sourced to the will of the divine. Instead, they reflect the structural and social prejudices of the societies surrounding them: practitioners bring their social realities with them into their temples. Vodou cannot be truly safe for queer participants until those social realities are changed. Nor can those who identify as cisgender heterosexual men truly experience the breadth and depth of Vodou until social realities are changed. The spiritual authority of all women cannot be truly reflective of their power and respect in the world beyond the temple until those social realities are changed.

Passing down Vodou Legacies

Vante'm Pa Fyem now considers herself lucky to have grown up in the faith. She told me that so many people come to the religion after years or generations of disconnection, rediscovering a heritage that was left behind. In contrast, Vante'm Pa Fyem describes herself as a "legacy" child, imbued with the spiritual capacity to connect with the divine and to understand herself in relation to the world: she is a fortunate beneficiary of the spiritual knowledge passed down by her mother and the tireless efforts of Manbo Maude to create an easier path for her children. Her mother works hard, Vante'm Pa Fyem explained, so that all her children have to do is maintain the foundations she has already built.[5]

At age eighteen, Vante'm Pa Fyem was initiated. Practitioners are allowed to become initiated at any age, including during childhood if they are confident about their need and ability to walk with the divine. Often, the spirits tell people that they need to undergo initiation rituals for their health, to ward off bad luck, or to make up for ancestors who may have failed to *sèvi lwa* and thus endangered the spiritual wellness of their descendants. Vante'm Pa Fyem was told to pursue initiation many times. For example, when she was fifteen, Kouzen informed her during a ceremony that engaging in the process was a necessity, especially if she was expected to take over for her mother in the future. That same year, Ogou claimed that her *met tet*, or head spirit, would be placed on her before the age of twenty, a description synonymous with being initiated. She listened, waiting for the right moment. The age of eighteen suited her because she wanted her initiation to coincide with the transition into adulthood, so she would assume responsibilities as a burgeoning spiritual leader and as a young woman at the same time. The specific initiation rituals Vante'm Pa Fyem underwent are important to her and her mother, but there is another vein of thought in Vodou that places much less significance on those formal rituals and emphasizes education under the guidance of an elder. For those practitioners, ancestral lineage and mentorship from experienced elders are necessary, but time in a *djevo*, for example, is not required for initiation.

Vante'm Pa Fyem continues to balance her faith and her aspirations outside the temples; she graduated from college and wants to become a human rights attorney. Like her mother, she is cautious about when and with whom she shares her faith in anticipation of a possible backlash. Revealing her connection with Vodou to the wrong person might cost her opportunities in the United States. There, to avoid potential suspicion, she claims her Catholic faith and does not disclose that she visits Catholic churches in service of Vodou. In Haiti, her affiliation with Vodou is well known; she worries less about the stigma around her religion on the island, despite Manbo Maude's continued wariness. Vante'm Pa Fyem describes the split between her explicit religious identifications as living a double life. "I'm living a Hannah Montana life," she says, relating her existence in Massachusetts and Haiti to the Disney character who lived as a normal girl while hiding her secret identity as a famous musician.[6] As Manbo Maude gains prominence, so does Vante'm Pa Fyem.

One way that Vante'm Pa Fyem's expertise is revealed during ceremonies is through her extensive knowledge of Vodou songs and dances, which she loves performing. Her and her mother's conviction that fashion is crucial in honoring the spirits is reflected in some of these songs, which plainly state the divine's interest in being honored through aesthetics. She sang a song to me over the phone that is performed before officially calling on the spirits and welcoming practitioners and audience members. She also provided the English translation.[7]

ala fre timoun yo fre, ou pa we manman yo la e x2
hounsi la yo, la men fo e x2
ala fre ti moun yo fre, ou pa we manman yo la e

look at how fresh the kids are, don't you see their mother is here x2
the hounsi, give me a hand
look at how fresh the kids are, don't you see their mother is here x2

The "mother" is the Manbo, and the "kids" are the initiates of her home. When the words are sung in Manbo Maude's home, the term *manman* is used. In a different home led by a Houngan, the term *papa*, or "father," would be used instead. Even before Legba, the lwa of the crossroads, is asked to open the doorway to the spiritual world, the song espouses the importance of aesthetics, celebrating how "fresh" the devotees look as an indicator of how well their Manbo looks after them. "Their mother is here" acknowledges the role of the Manbo; if she has done her duty, her initiates will be prepared to meet the divine. The song essentially tells everyone gathered for the ceremony, *"We are ready."*

As these song lyrics show, Manbo Maude did not invent the connection between Vodou and adornment. Fashion is embedded in the songs and rituals of ceremonies. Yet Manbo Maude and her daughter continue to act as innovators within this space, accentuating and enhancing that connection. They center style as a foundational element in Vodou, catering to the vanity of the gods in service of their communities, their religious power, and their beliefs. The interplay of the spirits, the audience, and the practitioners is key to what Vante'm Pa Fyem continues to love about Vodou. "It's interactive," she explained. "You are praying, and you get results. And you can talk to the entities, and have a friendship, like a real relationship with the entity you are talking to, the spirits, your ancestors and God. It's kind of a reciprocal interaction."[8]

As I describe throughout the book, Vante'm Pa Fyem, along with the audience, the practitioners, and the spirits, is a source of inspiration for Manbo Maude, challenging her to consider designs she otherwise might have overlooked. Sometimes she sketches Manbo Maude's designs for her because she has a better hand for drawing, and they consult each other on what looks stylish and on the details of a given outfit. Manbo Maude incorporates her daughter's suggestions, like the visible straps of a bralette in the back of a dress or the daring flash of a bare shoulder in between ruffles. Vante'm Pa Fyem also helped her mother create a dress for Kouzen Zaka in May 2018. The dress was yellow and pared down compared to many of Manbo Maude's other garments, lacking the usual array of ruffles and layers. Vante'm Pa Fyem was inspired by the dresses she saw women wearing in Martinique and Guadeloupe: together, they created an outfit that gestured to multiple cultures in the Caribbean. Vante'm Pa Fyem takes pride in the fashionable home her mother has built, which she helps maintain. "I think we are trendsetters in terms of fashion," she says. "I mean the imagination is there; [my mother] has a mind in design. She has the ability to execute what she wants."[9] She is not shy about claiming the power of their innovations or the quality of their implementation. "I mean we are the only ones who think of these things—I mean we might not be the only ones," she continued. "But we are some of the only ones who have the opportunity to execute [it] well."[10]

She and her mother have developed a collaborative working process. They have a mutual understanding that the fashion in Manbo Maude's temples must meet a certain standard of quality and they work together to meet those expectations: they know that the clothing worn during ceremonies ultimately affects both their reputations. They believe the fashion in their temples distinguishes them as a religious community and facilitates communication with the gods. Vante'm Pa Fyem, like Manbo Maude, often converses with the spirits nan dòmi. She describes her close relationship with the divine as a "psychic awareness" that is derived from the openness of her "third eye." Fashion is a tool Vante'm Pa Fyem uses not only to express herself but also to concretize the messages she receives in her dreams and through her innate psychic gifts. Religious garments are the spiritual made physical. The ritual clothes in her mother's temples are the material manifestations of their shared commitment to Vodou and to the divine.[11]

Stitching Vodou Roots from Ancestral Cloth and Found Fabric

The reputation of Manbo Maude's temples and their emphasis on fashion draw good and bad attention in Manbo Vante'm Pa Fyem's direction. She knows that her appearance and behavior are seen as reflections on her mother. Her hair texture and skin color are the subject of frequent comments, some of it negative. She categorizes her hair as 3c/4a, and it is long enough to touch the middle of her back. Her hair, given her reputation as Manbo Maude's daughter, has attracted negative attention from some practitioners and audience members. If she combs or braids her hair outside her mother's home in Jacmel, for example, she gets stared at by members of the community. She is accused of thinking of herself as superior to others because she is brown-skinned instead of dark, reflecting some of the hierarchies in Haiti that are shaped by class and color. Underneath the attention to her looks is the sentiment that Manbo Vante'm Pa Fyem is privileged in both those spheres. Moreover, she is an American, a *Blan*, with the ability to leave Haiti whenever she pleases. In the United States, the commentary on her appearance is plainly insulting. Americans have told her she's "too pretty to be Haitian" or assumed she is racially mixed.[12] Being the target of comments in both countries has made her cautious. When she gets a haircut in Haiti, for example, she collects whatever hair has been shorn so that she can throw it away or burn it.

In the past, hairdressers have expressed envy of her long hair, and hair can be used to put *jok* on a person. Jok is a source of fear for many Haitians: it means bad energy, or a curse placed on a person by someone with malevolent intentions. Manbo Maude is one of the few people whom Manbo Vante'm Pa Fyem lets touch her hair. Her mother is protective of her and concerned with the energy around her daughter. Once, after styling her hair in front of others and receiving unfriendly stares, Manbo Vante'm Pa Fyem began losing her hair, suggesting the influence of jok. Because the head is the seat of spiritual energy, the negative attention directed at her hair is especially worrying. Periodically, Manbo Maude performs spiritual baths to remove the jok from her daughter, washing away the negative energy.

Despite the drawbacks of her and her mother's visibility in Haiti, the country remains a source of joy for Manbo Vante'm Pa Fyem. She travels to Haiti to participate in her mother's ceremonies and to connect with her extended family, bonding with her cousins and other relatives. She is a U.S.-born member of the Haitian Dyaspora who lives most of her life in the United States. The summers and occasional winters she spends in Haiti are cast in

Manbo Vante'm Pa Fyem posing with her spiritual godparents Houngan Ramoncite, Manbo Silvanie, and Houngan Jean Raymond in Jacmel, July 2018 (photo by Eziaku Nwokocha).

an almost idyllic glow—not because she thinks the country is perfect, but because it offers a reprieve from the pressures of living in the United States. She told me,

> I think growing up and understanding the American culture . . .
> made Haiti an escape to be honest. It was an escape from social media
> and everything happening in the US. More I needed that break from
> feeling trapped, with what's going on in social media, other people's
> lives, the news. I feel like it's draining, especially this past summer
> with George Floyd and Breonna Taylor and all the protests; being on
> social media was tiring. But you feel like you need to be on social
> media because you are in [the United States] and need to know. In
> Haiti you don't need to see that . . . especially being from Jacmel, it's
> more peaceful and not the robust city. It's very peaceful to me.[13]

Haiti is a Black country. Manbo Vante'm Pa Fyem may have to contend there with issues of color, crime, and class, but she can also escape the specific pressures of living as a Black person in the predominantly White United States for a few months at least. She sees these trips as opportunities to disconnect from social media, thereby avoiding the gossip and relentless news reports on White supremacist violence committed against Black people like George Floyd and Breonna Taylor.[14] Manbo Vante'm Pa Fyem needs to know about these events when she is in the United States, both because they influence her daily and understanding them is important to her. However, no graphic videos or accounts of Black deaths from the United States are allowed to be part of her time in Haiti. She dedicates herself to her community and to Vodou, deliberately avoiding all else, knowing she will be plunged right back into that reality when she returns home. Haiti is a place where she immerses herself in faith, community, and ancestral worship. Her mother's temples are at the center of this place of dedication, as she both participates in and contributes to Manbo Maude's sartorial practices. For years, Manbo Vante'm Pa Fyem has operated as a translator in Haiti for American practitioners who cannot speak Haitian Kreyòl and for Haitians who cannot speak English. Over time, more members of the home have learned Haitian Kreyòl or English, so she is no longer the only one to play that role. There has also been an increase in the number of Haitian Dyaspora people who have been initiated in Manbo Maude's home and who help Americans, Black or White, communicate with Haitian people in Haiti about their ritual needs or when any disagreements arise.

Manbo Vante'm Pa Fyem is enthusiastic about connecting with her "roots" and her "ancestors," which she considers a primary benefit of traveling to

Haiti. She knows Haitians who leave the country or are part of the Dyaspora and never return even when they have the opportunity to do so. In her calculation, this is a mistake. It contributes to people disconnecting from and even "demoniz[ing]" their culture. Traveling back and forth between Haiti and the United States affords her a thoughtful appreciation of her heritage. "You can love something and be critical of it," she explained, and loving Haiti also means "acting in ways that can change it for the better." Manbo Vante'm Pa Fyem's dedication to Haiti and representing Haitian culture is derived not only from her heritage but also from her vision for younger Haitians and the future. "We are the sons and daughters of our land," she told me. "We will be the ones to bring forth change."[15]

Manbo Vante'm Pa Fyem's frequent travel back and forth, and her determined insistence that she belongs in Haiti just as surely as she does in the United States, left me a little envious, wistfully imagining how my life might have been different had I a comparably strong link to my ancestry. Her ability to retain a connection to her culture, both by returning to Haiti and maintaining close ties with Haitians and the Haitian Dyaspora in the Boston area, forced me to reckon with my own connection—or lack thereof—to Nigeria, a country I visited only once as a teenager. She and I are first generation (or second generation, in sociological parlance); our parents were born outside the United States, yet my grasp of my parents' native language, Igbo, is distressingly shaky compared to Manbo Vante'm Pa Fyem's mastery of Haitian Kreyòl.

In the Sacramento area of northern California where my family lived, there is a vibrant Igbo community. Many members of my parents' generation had, like my father, served in the Biafra War, a civil war in Nigeria between the government and the Republic of Biafra, an Igbo secessionist state that was vying for independence. The war, which lasted from 1967 to 1970, ended in military and humanitarian disaster for the Igbo people, including years of mass starvation. The actual number of people lost in the conflict is unknown, but it is estimated to be as high as one to three million, most of them Igbo. My parents and others in our community left Nigeria because of these terrible circumstances, seeking safer, healthier lives for themselves and their children in the United States. The war was discussed often by those who experienced it or its harrowing consequences, generating a sense of communal connection rooted in Igbo history.[16] My parents were diligent about attending church, weddings, parties, funerals, and other gatherings. However, cultivating fluency with the Igbo language was not emphasized, and Indigenous religious beliefs were generally abandoned in favor of Christianity. Some parties featured masquerades, a traditional Igbo celebration in which men wear large colorful costumes meant to symbolize the ancestors, yet the meaning of the custom was presented as purely cultural. The gods were not discussed.

Indigenous Igbo gods and cosmologies were relegated to the past, to a time before our people converted to Christianity, and I grew up with very little knowledge of them. My parents could not afford to take my six siblings and I to Nigeria on a regular basis. When we finally made our way there, I was often referred to as an *oyibo*, a term similar to Manbo Vante'm Pa Fyem's description of the word *Blan*. *Oyibo* meant I did not quite belong; I could not claim native Igbo culture as mine and expect my Nigerian cousins to fully accept it. In their eyes, I was inescapably American. I arrived in Nigeria expecting to feel a greater connection to my heritage, in part due to a full embrace of my natural hair. My cousins greeted my appearance with confused disapproval. I could have gotten my hair done at any point, they said, so why did I arrive in such disarray? At the time, the level of disconnection wrought by only one generation of living outside Nigeria surprised me.

The physical and cultural distance between my family and my parents' native land created a sense of dissonance familiar to many who are first generation or have emigrated to the United States. Manbo Maude frequently compared our experiences with extended family and community and the resulting feeling that we were constantly being pulled in multiple directions. "Eziaku, *you* already know how this goes," she told me, shrugging off the endless demands on her personal finances, the expectation (one she willingly shoulders) that she must send money and supplies back home. She wants to aid her community, yet that does not mean those responsibilities are easy. Her perception of our similarity influenced my ethnographic work, along with my Igbo heritage, my Blackness, my femaleness, and the countless hours I spent within her religious communities in Mattapan and Jacmel. That investment of time, in combination with my identity and heritage, gave me access to spaces that would otherwise have been closed to me as a noninitiate. Conducting a Black feminist ethnography means understanding and reflexively acknowledging that the identity of the ethnographer inescapably shapes the resulting study. There is no objective observer, no invisible scholar who can integrate themselves into a community without influencing those around them: even the choices of which communities to work with and what questions to ask emerge from the specific subjectivity of the ethnographer.

Undeniably, the envy I felt about Manbo Vante'm Pa Fyem's connection to Haiti made that aspect of her story stand out to me. Initial envy drew me to her story, but with time I realized I am not destined to remain detached from my parents' native country—and, more importantly, that my research is not evidence of my disconnection but rather proof of my ongoing desire to build a relationship with my heritage. The Igbo influence in Haiti and in Vodou is a motivating one, offering glimpses into the gods and beliefs that were so often obscured in my childhood. Christianity veiled my family's connection to the divinities of our ancestors, but in Haiti they are honored. The country holds traces of my heritage, too, and every Vodou song about Igbo people or ceremonial offering to Igbo lwa brings me closer to it. Babbas, an initiate in Manbo Maude's home, sang songs about Igbo people to me on a few occasions. The first time he heard of my heritage, he gleefully sang,

> Sim te la lè grann mwen te la
> Sim te la lè grann mwen te la
> Sim te la le grann mwen te la li ta montrem danse Ibo!

> If I was there when my grandmother was there
> If I was there when my grandmother was there
> If I was there when my grandmother was there, she would have
>   taught me the Igbo Dance![17]

He was not the only person to share this song with me. I heard it and other songs about Igbo people in Haiti and in Vodou communities in Montreal. Hearing them repeatedly and seeing the ease with which practitioners recite them emphasizes how vital Igbo customs are to Vodou's foundations. This song explicitly evokes not only the passing of cultural and religious rituals from one generation to another through familial ties but also the potential loss of such knowledge. Babbas told me the words are meant to describe Igbo identity and "blood memory," the traditions that were carried in the minds and bodies of ancestors and are now expressed through the voices and movement of their descendants.[18] The lyric, "If I was there when my grandmother was there," whether about the presence of Igbo forebears in Haiti or in West Africa, implies a longing for a deeper connection with bygone ancestors. It recognizes the importance of this Igbo grandmother yet also suggests her distance: *if* the singer had been there, they might have learned her dance. That desire to conjure "blood memory" from departed ancestors honors the Igbo lineage of Vodou and of many Haitians.[19] Scholarship on Vodou has highlighted the impact of cultures from Benin, Congo, and Nigeria, centering their combined influence on the genesis of the religion. The exploration of Nigerian influence is commonly understood through Yoruba culture. The pervasive impact of Igbo performance rituals, material culture, and spirits in Vodou is largely unexplored, yet it has the potential to provide endless insights into the depth and complexity of the religion's African Diasporic roots.

The song Babbas shared emphasizes the inheritance of knowledge, a process I describe as active and ongoing in Manbo Maude's temples. The successful transmission of tradition is due in part to the array of ages present in her communities, which allows older members to share their accumulated expertise with younger ones. The temples contain many young practitioners, ranging in age from their early twenties to mid-forties. A smaller number are in their fifties or older and are considered the elders. Manbo Maude's legacy as the head of her temples relies on this group of elders and their ability to teach others. Young practitioners are the driving force behind the activities in Manbo Maude's temples, in which Manbo Vante'm Pa Fyem plays a central role. Because of her lifelong connection to Vodou, she has total command of the dances and songs performed for *Nago* and *Petwo* spirits and teaches them to other members of Sosyete Nago. She learns dance moves from her cousins and her elders as well and brings them into the ceremonies. Her skill and passion have earned her spiritual authority among community members of all ages, who call on her for ritual advice and ceremonial preparation. That constant flow of spiritual knowledge—between Manbo Vante'm Pa Fyem and her mother Manbo Maude and her practitioners, the elders and the younger generation, the spirits and their devotees—is central to Manbo Maude's legacy and her mission to build a foundation for all her spiritual children to thrive on.

This foundation, as much as it depends on Manbo Maude's ability to showcase her stylistic creativity, her spiritual potency, and the contributions of other practitioners, also needs the wisdom and favor granted by the divine. It seems fitting to return to Dantò, the spirit that personally intervened to ensure Manbo Vante'm Pa Fyem's birth and who relies on her faithful daughter Anais to communicate her knowledge. I only ever heard Anais's name invoked in the same breath as her mother Dantò; she is forever linked with the formidable goddess, relegated to stories where she speaks for a legendary warrior who no longer can. Manbo Maude and Manbo Vante'm Pa Fyem are not their mirror images, even as their close connection invites comparisons to divine mothers and daughters. Manbo Vante'm Pa Fyem is willing and able to speak for her mother when she thinks it is necessary, but she also speaks for herself. That is true for all Manbo Maude's spiritual children. It is also, in a sense, true of Manbo Maude and any other practitioner who invites the spirits into every aspect of their lives.

When spirits make themselves known during a ceremony, mounting the body of a practitioner, seeing through their eyes, feeling through their skin, moving through their limbs, and speaking through their mouth, they, like Dantò, are relying on ti feỳ to communicate with others and to keep them figuratively alive through performance rituals. Anais's devotion may appear to be the natural duty of a daughter, but it is actually a choice, one that underscores the role of support within Vodou that is also reflected in the mutually beneficial exchange between spirits and practitioners. Practitioners serve the spirits, and in return they are granted access to the wealth of knowledge commanded by lwa. Manbo Maude listened to the spirits and those around her when they told her to rethink her ceremonial garments; when she pursued that advice, the spirits remained invested, appearing in her dreams to provide their often-blunt clothing requests. Their guidance is not purely altruistic. Manbo Maude's increased effectiveness as a Manbo ensures their satisfaction during her ceremonies, and her success ultimately translates into more attendees and more offerings during the rituals held in their honor. Vodou temples like Manbo Maude's, as beneficial as they are to the religious communities they support, also keep the spirits fed, clothed, and relevant. They thrive only so much as their believers do.

By choosing to welcome the gods into her life, her dreams, and her homes, Manbo Maude has cultivated a Vodou community that stitches together the divine, practitioners, and audiences through religious spectacles that honor the spirits while emphasizing her uniqueness as a Manbo. In her home, all participants and the divine are invited to indulge in elaborate sartorial displays, fostering a sense of community within Vodou. While drafting this book, I was anxious about Manbo Maude creating new outfits that might eclipse my descriptions of her fashion. She is constantly searching for ways to change her designs, incorporating new ideas from the spirits, her daughter, her seamstresses, or some unpredictable flash of inspiration from her everyday life. Her innovations are what drew me to her temples as sites of research, inspiring the creation of spiritual vogue, yet it is difficult to keep up with the pace of her stylistic transformations. No publication can match the tempo of change in faith communities, Manbo Maude's temples included. The makeup of these communities fluctuates, members come and go, and the opinions of interviewees shift over time.

So, *Vodou en Vogue* is not intended as a comprehensive summation of Manbo Maude, Manbo Vante'm Pa Fyem, the ti feỳ, their spiritual homes, or Vodou. Instead, it is an attempt to capture moments of truth that illuminate the dynamism I witnessed firsthand in ceremony after ceremony; it is an attempt to explain the complicated negotiations among spirits, practitioners, and audience members that animate Manbo Maude's use of fashion. *When* Manbo Maude decides to innovate her style in some way I could not have predicted, making an anecdote or even several obsolete, I hope my work provides an explanation as to how she got there and why she, her spiritual fashion, and Vodou continue to matter.

I already expressed reservations about uncritically ascribing motivations to lwa, yet I feel I can make one more claim with confidence: the spirits help their adherents thrive. The gods have been a critical part of Manbo Maude's journey, offering advice and support while she continues to build her temples and her reputation as a spiritual leader. That support not only appears nan dòmi or through rituals and cosmological principles—the gods have also had an impact on her finances. They assist in relieving enough of her financial worries to allow her imagination to stretch past what it takes to survive. With her everyday economic needs met, she can provide for others and take the time to innovate in her service to the lwa, which ultimately contributes to the financial stability of her temples. In addition to the gods and Manbo Maude's own determination, her temples also benefit from the transnational community of people around her. Their aid in completing the labor necessary for every *fete* also gives her more time to contemplate which fashion statement she wants to make next, allowing her to distinguish herself as a trendsetter in religious fashion. Together, Manbo Maude, the spirits, and the people supporting her temples maintain complex religious spaces that will have lasting impacts in Vodou communities in and beyond Mattapan and Jacmel.

If I had walked into another temple or felt compelled by another Manbo, the story that unfolded in the preceding pages would have been profoundly different—not in the broad religious traditions and histories I describe but in how they take shape in the world, how they manifest in the practicalities of a ceremony. Manbo Maude is one part of a larger story about the people who practice Vodou and channel their passions into Black deities born of West and Central Africa and Haiti. Her innovations in ceremonial fashion are indicative of changes taking place in modern Vodou communities around the world, energized by African and African Diasporic practitioners and supported always by the Black gods who inspire them.

Notes

Preface

1. Manbo Maude, interview by Eziaku Nwokocha, phone interview, August 11, 2020.

Introduction

1. *Ezili Dantò*, who belongs to the *Petwo* nation, is a renowned lwa in Haitian Vodou. She is held in such high regard that people sometimes explain that the blue on the Haitian flag is dedicated to her spiritual greatness. She is known as the spiritual mother of Haiti.

2. Fieldnotes, August 3, 2016.

3. Yanvalou drumming is a type of Vodou drumming with origins in what is now the country of Benin.

4. In Haiti, there are nuanced reasons for people to suck their teeth: in frustration, as approval, or to get someone's attention.

5. I am indebted to Pérez, *Religion in the Kitchen*, which was an inspiration in studying African Diasporic religions through the senses.

6. I found Renne, *Cloth That Does Not Die* and *Death and the Textile Industry in Nigeria*, about Yoruba textiles and how they are used and made meaningful in a variety of social contexts helpful when examining the intersection of dress and religious practice.

7. Max Beauvoir, interview by Eziaku Nwokocha, in-person interview, Port-au-Prince, July 19, 2009.

8. For work on the connection between French colonization and the dress worn in Haitian Vodou ceremonies, see Hammond, "Decoding Dress," 85–90; Tselos, "Dressing the Divine Horsemen," 46–49.

9. Critical archive studies is another field that my work engages, because Manbo Maude is doing similar work in a way that ties "sensational" religion to critical archives. For more on archives and African Diasporic religions, see Otero, *Archives of Conjure*.

10. Some scholars who study fashion, such as Malcolm Barnard in *Fashion Theory*, note that although fashion is often understood as a part of global and largely Western capitalism, it is also a creative and social experience that contributes to the creation of identities. Therefore, fashion is complementary to ideas of dress and adornment. Barnard, *Fashion Theory*, xi.

11. Hume, *Religious Life of Dress*, 1.

12. Hume, 2, 5.

13. Hume, 1.

14. Promey, *Sensational Religion*, 3, 5.

15. I am influenced by David Hall's concept of "lived religion" that centers the everyday actions that animate religious belief. Hall, *Lived Religion in America*. I am also inspired by scholar of religion Charles Long who writes, "The religion of any people is more than a structure of thought; it is experience, expression, motivations, intentions, behaviors, styles, and rhythms." Long's emphasis on lived experiences as dynamic parameters of religion, as well as his investment in the connections to African religious traditions, makes his arguments broadly applicable to African Diasporic communities and to Manbo Maude's temples in particular. Long, *Significations*, 7.

16. Scholars of African and African Diasporic studies have explored the connection between religion and race. Please see Long, *Significations*; Higginbotham, *Righteous Discontent*; Olupona, *Beyond Primitivism*; Oyěwùmí, *Invention of Women*; Johnson, *The Myth of Ham*; Orsi, *History and Presence*; Weisenfeld, *New World A-Coming*; Asad, *Genealogies of Religion*, 72–77; and Price-Mars, *So Spoke the Uncle*.

17. See Olupona, *African Spirituality*, xx.

18. Tracey Hucks provides a detailed history of the significant ethnographers of African Diasporic religions during the twentieth and twenty-first centuries. These scholars, such as Zora Neale Hurston, Katherine Dunham, Melville Herskovits, George Eaton Simpson, Roger Bastide, Pierre Verger, and Alfred Métraux, were innovators in the field of African Diasporic ethnographic historiography. See Hucks, "Perspectives in Lived History," 1–17.

19. See Oyěwùmí, *The Invention of Women*. The gender debate on Yoruba religious culture between Oyèrónké Oyěwùmí (1997) and J. Lorand Matory (2005) was discussed at the 1999 "Globalization of Yoruba Religious Culture Conference" at Florida International University in Miami.

20. Promey, *Sensational Religion*, 3.

21. McDannell, *Material Christianity*, 2.

22. *Collins-Robert French-English, English-French Dictionary* (London: Collins, 1978).

23. "Consumer Magazines," Alliance for Audited Media, January 23, 2017.

24. The people in Manbo Maude's community identify using a variety of terms. I use the word "queer" as a broad identifier for sexualities and genders that are not both heterosexual and cisgender. If a person specifies a preference for a different term such as lesbian, gay, bisexual, transgender, or nonbinary, I use that term.

25. Bailey, "Gender/Racial Realness," 369.

26. Bailey, 372.

27. Bailey, *Butch Queen Up*, 128.

28. These scholars were incredibly helpful in thinking about the use of rituals and performance. Byam, "Communal Space and Performance in Africa," 230; Turner, *Anthropology of Performance*, 75; and Bailey, *Butch Queen Up*, 144.

29. For more on homophobia in Haiti, see Aljazeera America, "Haiti's Fight for Gay Rights"; Discover Thomson Reuters; "Leading LGBT+ Activist Found Dead in Haiti"; Human Rights Watch, "Haiti Events of 2019; Migraine-George, "From Masisi to Activist," 8–33.

30. Cohen, "Punks, Bull Daggers, and Welfare Queens," 437–85.

31. Beaubrun, *Nan dòmi*, 48.

32. Johnson and Henderson, *Black Queer Studies*, 136–38.

33. Johnson and Henderson, 138.

34. Turner, *Anthropology of Performance*, 24; Covington-Ward, *Gesture and Power*, 17.

35. For more on spirit possession, see Brown, *Mama Lola*; Beaubrun, *Nan dòmi*.

36. Strongman, *Queering Black Atlantic Religions*, 3.

37. Morgan, *Sacred Gaze*, 3.

38. Morgan, 3.

39. For more on religious tourism, see Raj and Griffin, *Religious Tourism and Pilgrimage Management*.

40. See Herskovits, *Myth of Negro Past*; Raboteau, *Slave Religion*; and Hurston, *Tell My Horse*.

41. For more work on the transatlantic slave trade, see Sharpe, *In the Wake*; Hartman, *Scenes of Subjection*; and Brown, *Reaper's Garden*.

42. Manbo Maude does not focus on the Indigenous Caribbean aspects of Vodou. However, there are scholars who have mentioned the Indigenous influences in Vodou, such as Deren, *Divine Horsemen*; Hurston, *Tell My Horse*; and Karen McCarthy Brown's *Mama Lola*.

43. Brown, *Mama Lola*, 209.

44. Edmonds and Gonzalez, *Caribbean Religious History*, 53.

45. Michel and Bellegarde-Smith, *Vodou in Haitian Life*, xix; Edmonds and Gonzalez, *Caribbean Religious History*, 59.

46. Mobley, "Kongolese Atlantic."

47. For more on Central African and Kongolese Catholic traditions in the Black Atlantic, see Vanhee, "Central African Popular Christianity"; Rey, "Kongolese Catholic Influences"; Bay, *Asen, Ancestors, and Vodun*; Stewart, *Three Eyes*; Heywood and Thornton, *Central Africans*; Brown, *African-Atlantic Cultures*; Thornton, *History of West Central Africa*, "On the Trail of Voodoo," and "Revising the Population History of the Kingdom of Kongo," 201–12; Thompson, *Flash of the Spirit*; and Mobley, *Kongolese Atlantic*.

48. Long, *Significations*, 4.

49. Johnson, *Diaspora Conversions*, 11.

50. Wilcken, *Drums of Vodou*, 23–25.

51. See Tselos, "Dressing the Divine Horseman," 48; Thompson, *Flash of the Spirit*; and Blier, "Vodun," 61–87.

52. Matory, *Black Atlantic Religion*, 5.

53. Thompson, *Flash of the Spirit*, xvii; Gilroy, *The Black Atlantic*, 4.

54. Matory, *Black Atlantic Religion*, 3.

55. Interestingly, in African American literature, novelists writing about the Harlem Renaissance such as Vechten, *Nigger Heaven*; Wright, *Man Who Lived Underground*; and Ellison, *Invisible Man*, all use the basement as the principal scene to discuss experiences of Black communities, especially Black music. Scholars of Vodou such as Brown, *Mama Lola*; Richman, *Migration and Vodou*; and Bellegarde-Smith, *Breached Citadel*, have noted that many Haitians in the Diaspora hold ceremonies in the basements of their New York, Miami, and Montreal homes. I further assert that we ought

to consider the basement as a liminal space and an important sacred site for Vodou communities. Additionally, the work of Maldonado-Estrada, *Lifeblood of the Parish*, on Catholic devotion in New York City also considers religious constructions in the basement and how masculinity is upheld in these spaces.

56. Boston, "US Census 2010." Cantave, "Incorporation or Symbiosis: Haitians and African Americans in Mattapan," 107–23; Jackson, "After the Exodus," 191, and "The Uses of Diaspora among Haitians in Boston," 135.

57. Global Boston, "Haitians," https://globalboston.bc.edu/index.php/home/ethnic -groups/haitians/, *Chronicle*. Boston, English, weekly. January 9, 1932–April 9, 1960. Microfilm: Boston Public Library. *Guardian*. Boston, English, weekly. July 26, 1902–November 15, 1913; January 7, 1939–April 20, 1957. Microfilm: Boston Public Library.

58. Kelley, *Race Rebels*, 47.

59. The Haitian language, Haitia Kreyòl, is a French-based Creole language with roots in various African languages; it is most commonly described as "Haitian Creole/ Haitian Kreyòl." Some scholars, like Michel Rolph Trouillot, call the language "Haitian." He argues that the use of the term "Creole" is racially coded and is often used only to describe languages spoken by Black people throughout the African Diaspora. Trouillot, *Silencing the Past*, xxii. My time at the summer language initiative of the University of Massachusetts, Boston, greatly enhanced not only my ability to speak Haitian Kreyòl but also my understanding of Trouilott's and other similarly minded scholars' position on the language's nomenclature, because my instructors there were equally insistent on calling the language "Haitian." My Haitian professors Marc Prou, Patrick Sylvain, Jean Lesly René, Lunine Pierre-Jerôme, Leslie Rene, and Joel Théodat in the summer initiative explained that all languages are mixed, or "Kreyòl," and draw from many languages to establish their vocabulary and syntax. They argued that defining Haitian as Kreyòl is a remnant of colonial attitudes, which made European languages the standard and labeled other linguistic traditions as derivative. Although I am cognizant of this argument about this distinct linguistic system, within this book, I choose to describe the language as Haitian Kreyòl because most of the people whom I interviewed in Jacmel and Boston call the language "Kreyòl" or "Haitian Kreyòl," with rare instances of saying "Haitian." I stand by the move to redefine Haitian or Haitian Kreyòl as a distinctive language that stands as firmly in its history and nationality as any other language. I think it is important, however, to heed the phrasings everyday people use to define their language. As an outsider, I respect their preferred usage while acknowledging the equally significant efforts on the part of scholars to shift the language's name in a manner that attends to its unique linguistic character.

60. Manbo Maude, interview by Eziaku Nwokocha, in-person interview, Mattapan, June 6, 2015.

61. I am grateful to the many fruitful conversations with Dr. Heather Williams and her insistence that traveling to back to Haiti was an essential aspect of my work.

62. World Population Review, "Population of Cities in Haiti," https://world populationreview.com/countries/cities/haiti; and Britannica, "Jacmel, Haiti," https:// www.britannica.com/place/Jacmel.

63. The members in Manbo Maude's home asked for varying degrees of anonymity. Some like Vante'm Pa Fyem provided their Vodou names. Some told me their actual names. I gave pseudonyms to others.

64. Nwokocha, "'Queerness' of Ceremony," 71–90.

65. I am so grateful to the many practitioners who aided me, especially anthropologist Lorand Matory, with whom I spent countless hours in conversation about my work in Haiti.

66. See the following Black feminist anthropologist and religion scholars who center Black women in their work; Bolles, *Sister Jamaica*; Mullings, *On Our Own Terms*; Cox, *Shapeshifters*; Davis and Craven, *Feminist Ethnography*; Casselberry, *Labor of Faith*; Hucks, "Burning with a Flame in America," 89–106; McClaurin, *Black Feminist Anthropology*; Ebron, *Performing Africa*; and Covington-Ward, *Gesture and Power*.

67. Many scholars have done work on this topic, including Long, *Significations*; Olupona, *African Spirituality*; Pérez, *Religion in the Kitchen*; Jesús, *Electric Santería*; and Orsi, *History and Presence*.

68. Cox, *Shapeshifters*, 31.

69. Allen, *¡Venceremos?* 9.

Chapter One

1. Unless otherwise noted, all quotes and descriptions from Manbo Maude are from my in-person interview with her in Mattapan on January 6, 2018.

2. For more on Haitian peasantry, see Sheller, *Democracy after Slavery*; Mintz, *Sweetness and Power*; and Brown, *Mama Lola*, 37.

3. Tselos, "Dressing the Divine Horesmen," 46–49; Thompson, *Flash of the Spirit*, 206.

4. Wilcken, *Drums of Vodou*, 25.

5. Manbo Maude, interview by Eziaku Nwokocha, phone interview, Philadelphia, August 28, 2020.

6. In Pérez, *Religion in the Kitchen*, 27, she draws a description from Dana Rush's (2013) concept of the "Vodun Vortex," which explores the dynamic aesthetic and material elements that organize Vodou and other Black Atlantic religions like Lucumí.

7. Hansen, "The World in Dress," 369–92; Tselos, "Dressing the Divine Horsemen"; Hume, *Religious Life of Dress*; and Deren, *Divine Horsemen*.

8. Regarding the nature and importance of religious dreams, see Heo, "Divine Touchability of Dreams," 436; Renne, "Dressing in the Stuff of Dreams," 120–35.

9. Beaubrun, *Nan dòmi*, 48.

10. Beaubrun, 276.

11. Richman, *Migration and Vodou*, 119.

12. Brown, *Mama Lola*, 296.

13. For more work on Ezili je Wouj, see Brown, *Mama Lola*; Richman, *Migration and Vodou*; Dayan, *Haiti, History, and the Gods*; and Tinsley, *Ezili's Mirrors*.

14. Brown, *Mama Lola*, 228–29.

15. Brown, 228–29.

16. See Brown, *Mama Lola*; Richman, *Migration and Vodou*; Bellegarde-Smith, *Breached Citadel*; and Maldonado-Estrada, *Lifeblood of the Parish*.

17. Brown, *Mama Lola*, 329.

18. Hurston, *Tell My Horse*, 105; Dunham, *Island Possessed*, 58; Deren, *Divine Horsemen*, 73; Brown, *Mama Lola*, 269; Dayan, *Haiti, History, and the Gods*, 173.

19. Scholars such as Joan Dayan (1995), Karen McCarthy Brown (1991), and Patrick Bellegarde-Smith (2004) have explored Gede and the spirit's roots in Haiti.

20. Brown, *Mama Lola*, 95; Dayan, *Haiti, History, and the Gods*, 104.

21. For more work on the *Gede* nation, see Dayan, *Haiti, History, and the Gods*, 263–66.

22. Brown, *Mama Lola*, 96.

23. Some scholars have found links between the uses of tobacco in Haitian Vodou and Amer-Indian influences. For more, see Deren's *Divine Horsemen* and Brown's *Mama Lola*.

24. Wilcken, *Drums of Vodou*, 24. Manbo Maude, invited lecture via Zoom for Professor Eziaku Nwokocha's "Spirit Possession in Caribbean Religion" course, Princeton University, October 27, 2021.

25. Dayan, *Haiti, History, and the Gods*, 104.

26. Miller, *Slaves to Fashion*, 15.

27. Brown, *Mama Lola*, 360; Strongman, *Queering Black Atlantic Religions*, 74.

28. For more on spirit possession, see Brown, *Mama Lola*, and Beaubrun, *Nan dòmi*.

29. See Collins, *Black Feminist Thought* and *Black Sexual Politics*, for analysis on African enslavement in the United States; Edmonds and Gonzalez, *Caribbean Religious History*, for Caribbean religious history; and personal conversations with the late historian and women's activist Florence Bellande-Robertson (July 2010) about Black American and Caribbean religious history.

30. Bailey, "Gender/Racial Realness," 369.

31. Scholars who have studied pran lwa, like Karen McCarthy Brown (1991) and Katherine Dunham (1969), have documented the process of possession and how it can be a conscious or unconscious state.

32. Bailey, *Butch Queen Up*, 167.

33. YouTube, "Sosyete nago 2019 Fet simbi."

34. For more work on these topics, see Cunningham and Marberry, *Crowns*; Miller, *Slaves to Fashion*; White and White, *Stylin'*; and Chauncey, *Gay New York*.

35. Miller, *Slaves to Fashion*, 198–99.

36. Conversation with Amber Drumgoole, religion scholar, October 19, 2019; she informed me that in Afro-Protestant churches, people often use the offering portion of services to show off their best Sunday outfits. That is when they will speak to the elders or church mothers while showcasing their outfits in a born-again church in Nashville Tennessee. There are many churches where this is the case. Cunningham and Marberry, *Crowns*.

37. Miller, *Slaves to Fashion*, 87.

38. White and White, *Stylin'*, 210–13.

39. Manbo Maude, interview by Eziaku Nwokocha, phone interview, Philadelphia, April 8, 2021.

40. Manbo Maude, personal conversation, July 23, 2015.

41. Thompson, *Flash of the Spirit*, 164.

42. Manbo Maude, personal conversation, July 26, 2015.

43. The Mapou tree is a sacred tree with symbolic importance in many Vodou ceremonies.

44. I am focusing on the triangulation of the participants, spirits, and the audience, but further research should be done on the importance of nature to the ritual practices of Haitian Vodou.

45. Renne, "Cloth That Does Not Die," describes similar practices of wrapping fabric around tree trunks within the Bunu, Yoruba in Nigeria.

46. This discussion is greatly influenced by the insights of Ochoa, *Queen for a Day*.

Chapter Two

1. For more on wealth and religion, see Barro and McCleary, *Wealth of Religions*.

2. McDannell, *Material Christianity*, 6.

3. Manbo Maude, invited lecture via Zoom for Professor Eziaku Nwokocha's "Spirit Possession in Caribbean Religion" course, Princeton University, October 27, 2021.

4. Bui and Shakun, "Negotiation Processes," 339–53.

5. Casselberry, *The Labor of Faith*, 6.

6. Casselberry, 6.

7. Bellegarde-Smith and Michel, *Haitian Vodou*, xx, explain that Haitians often used the phrase *sèvi lwa* to avoid the negative connotations surrounding Vodou, refusing to explicitly name their religion.

8. Casselberry, *Labor of Faith*, 6.

9. Casselberry, 6–8.

10. Casselberry, 8.

11. Casselberry, 6, 107–11.

12. Casselberry, 6, 127–30.

13. Casselberry, 168.

14. Personal communication with Elizabeth Perez about economic exchanges and labor in Lucumí in Miami, October 29, 2021.

15. In 2017, NPR reported that one-fourth of Haiti's GDP came from remittances. November 5, 2017, https://www.npr.org/sections/parallels/2017/11/05/561922898/we-want-to-stay-haitian-immigrants-in-u-s-fear-end-of-temporary-protected-status. The Dialogue, "Remittances to Latin America and the Caribbean in 2019." In 2019 Inter-American Dialogue, https://www.thedialogue.org/analysis/remittances-to-latin-america-and-the-caribbean-in-2019-emerging-challenges/#:~:text=Family%20remittances%20to%20Latin%20America,growth%20that%20began%20in%202017, March 20, 2020, reported that more than $3.3 billion in remittances were sent to Haiti from Haitians abroad.

16. Shori, personal conversation, July 28, 2015.

17. Pew Research Center, "Through an American Lens," June 5, 2017.

18. Brown, *Mama Lola*, 160–63, describes the practitioner Mama Lola's transition from working part-time jobs into working full-time as a Manbo, which ultimately jeopardized her ability to remain financially stable.

19. Bailey, *Butch Queen Up*, 104–17.

20. Bailey, 5.

21. Cultural in Development, "The Voodoo Priest," January 7, 2011, http://www
.cultureindevelopment.nl/News/Heritage_Haiti/681/The_Voodoo_Priest:_Mass
_burials_were_a_desecration, and The Grio, "Haitian Earthquake Unleashes Ani-
mosity against Voodoo," March 3, 2010, https://thegrio.com/2010/03/03/haitian
-earthquake-unleashed-animosity-against-voodooists/.

22. Fabienne is a pseudonym.

23. Tselos, "Dressing the Divine Horseman," 50; Desmangles, *Faces of the Gods*, 18, 121.

24. Tselos, "Dressing the Divine Horseman," 50.

25. Tselos and Thompson have written about the makout's derivation from early Span-
ish ownership of the island when it was called Hispanola. It is derived from the Iberian
alforja, a similar bag that features red trim and tassels at its bottom. It is also derived
from the Ki-Kongo word *nkutu* that describes "a small cotton bag on the shoulder."

26. For more detailed information on Kouzen, see Brown, *Mama Lola*, 36–78.

27. For more information on the history of plantation labor and colonialism in
Haiti, see Dubois, *Avengers of the New World*; James, *Black Jacobins*; Dayan, *Haiti, History,
and the Gods*; Mintz, "The Caribbean as a Socio-Cultural Area," 912–37; Sheller, *Democracy after Slavery*; Brown, *Mama Lola*; and Trouillot, *Haiti State against the Nation*.

28. For more on Haitian peasantry, see Sheller, *Democracy after Slavery*; Mintz, *Sweetness and Power*; and Brown, *Mama Lola*, 37.

29. Zombies and their role in Haitian Vodou have been discussed by numerous
scholars, including Herskovits and Herskovits, *Dahomey*, 197, 243; Dayan, *Haiti, History, and the Gods*; and Glover, "Exploiting the Undead."

30. Manbo Maude, interview by Eziaku Nwokocha, in person, Boston, October 9,
2017.

31. Manbo Maude, interview by Eziaku Nwokocha, phone interview, Philadelphia, October 11, 2021.

32. Manbo Maude, interview by Eziaku Nwokocha, phone interview, Philadelphia, October 11, 2021.

33. Manbo Maude, interview by Eziaku Nwokocha, phone interview, Philadelphia, October 11, 2021.

34. Manbo Maude, interview by Eziaku Nwokocha, phone interview, Philadelphia, October 11, 2021.

35. Nikol is a pseudonym.

36. Because Manbo Maude's temple in Jacmel welcomes many visitors from outside Haiti, mostly from the United States, speaking English can be a valuable asset for
Haitians. They are able to offer their services as a translator and travel to places they
might not have had access to otherwise.

37. Laurel, interview by Eziaku Nwokocha, in person, Jacmel, July 23, 2018.

38. Laurel is a pseudonym.

39. Felipe is a pseudonym. Felipe, interview by Eziaku Nwokocha, in person, Jacmel, July 23, 2018.

40. Felipe, interview by Eziaku Nwokocha, in person, Jacmel, July 23, 2018.

41. Laurel, interview by Eziaku Nwokocha, in person, Jacmel, July 23, 2018.

42. Bailey, *Butch Queen Up*, 104–77.

43. Bailey, 5.

44. Bailey, 5.

45. Laurel, interview by Eziaku Nwokocha, in person, Jacmel, July 23, 2018.

46. Marica Ochoa is helpful for exploring the production of femininity through symbols and performance, as well as how femininity can become material. Ochoa, *Queen for a Day*.

47. Personal communication, July 25, 2016.

Chapter Three

1. Shori is a pseudonym.

2. Shori, interview by Eziaku Nwokocha, phone interview, Philadelphia, March 13, 2016.

3. Vante'm Pa Fyem, interview by Eziaku Nwokocha, phone interview, Philadelphia, February 27, 2020.

4. Manbo Maude, interview by Eziaku Nwokocha, phone interview, Philadelphia, August 7, 2020.

5. Manbo Maude, interview by Eziaku Nwokocha, phone interview, Philadelphia, August 7, 2020.

6. Manbo Maude, interview by Eziaku Nwokocha, phone interview, Philadelphia, August 21, 2020.

7. Manbo Maude, interview by Eziaku Nwokocha, phone interview, Philadelphia, August 7, 2020.

8. Babbas, interview by Eziaku Nwokocha, Skype interview, Philadelphia, February 26, 2018.

9. Vante'm Pa Fyem, interview by Eziaku Nwokocha, phone interview, Philadelphia, February 27, 2020.

10. Babbas, interview by Eziaku Nwokocha, Skype interview, Philadelphia, February 26, 2018.

11. Babbas, interview by Eziaku Nwokocha, Skype interview, Philadelphia, February 26, 2018.

12. Scott, *Headwraps*, 21.

13. Camp, *Closer to Freedom*, 84.

14. Shori, interview by Eziaku Nwokocha, phone interview, Philadelphia, March 12, 2018.

15. Shori, interview by Eziaku Nwokocha, phone interview, Philadelphia, March 12, 2018.

16. Brown, *Mama Lola*, 76.

17. Kaplan, "Ideology, Beliefs, and Sacred Kingship," 118.

18. Pérez, "Portable Portals," 35–62.

19. Shori, interview by Eziaku Nwokocha, phone interview, Philadelphia, March 12, 2018.

20. Vante'm Pa Fyem, interview by Eziaku Nwokocha, phone interview, Philadelphia, March 13, 2018.

21. Taylor, *Black Is Beautiful*, 2–3.

22. Manbo Maude, interview by Eziaku Nwokocha, phone interview, Philadelphia, March 13, 2018.

23. Kelley, *Race Rebels*, 47.

24. Kelley, 47; and Scott, *Domination and Arts of Resistance*, xii.

25. Kelley, *Race Rebels*, 42–43.

26. Samentha, interview by Eziaku Nwokocha, phone interview, Philadelphia, March 12, 2018.

27. Manbo Maude, interview by Eziaku Nwokocha, phone interview, Philadelphia, August 7, 2020.

28. Vante'm Pa Fyem, interview by Eziaku Nwokocha, phone interview, Philadelphia, February 27, 2021.

29. Vante'm Pa Fyem, interview by Eziaku Nwokocha, phone interview, Philadelphia, February 27, 2021.

30. Vante'm Pa Fyem, interview by Eziaku Nwokocha, phone interview, Philadelphia, February 27, 2021.

31. Natasha, interview by Eziaku Nwokocha, phone interview, Philadelphia, March 11, 2018.

32. Kelley, *Race Rebels*, 51.

33. As I explained in chapter 1, my extended conversations with Haitian women regarding the length of ritual skirts provided me with knowledge as to what would be regarded as appropriate for the ceremony.

34. Natasha, interview by Eziaku Nwokocha, phone interview, Philadelphia, March 11, 2018.

35. Taylor, *Black Is Beautiful*, 12.

36. Nadège is a pseudonym.

37. Nadège, interview by Eziaku Nwokocha, phone interview, Philadelphia, March 13, 2018.

38. Nadège, interview by Eziaku Nwokocha, phone interview, Philadelphia, March 13, 2018.

39. Babbas, interview by Eziaku Nwokocha, Skype interview, Philadelphia, March 11, 2018.

40. Babbas, interview by Eziaku Nwokocha, Skype interview, Philadelphia, March 11, 2018.

41. Samentha, interview by Eziaku Nwokocha, phone interview, Philadelphia, March 12, 2018.

42. The contention of White people's presence in Black religions is not unique to Vodou. For example, in *Three Eyes for the Journey*, 147–48, Stewart interviews Kumina practitioners who argue that White people should not be there because they cannot get spirit. "White people can't hear the drum," one Kumina priestess told Stewart in an interview. Another asked, "How can White supremacists ask the Bongo Ancestors for help?" For some Kumina practitioners, White supremacy is the main reason that people of African descent are suffering.

43. Samuel is a pseudonym.

44. I thank anthropologist Tim Landry for encouraging me to sit with audience members during Vodou ceremonies, in addition to helping practitioners with their

spiritual outfits. This suggestion was crucial because it confirmed audience members' curiosity about Manbo Maude's sartorial choices.

45. Brown, *Mama Lola*, 404.

46. Deren, *Divine Horsemen*; Brown, *Mama Lola*; McAlister, *Rara!*; Richman, *Migration and Vodou*; Rey and Stepick, *Crossing the Water*; and Landry, "Moving to Learn," are White scholars of Haitian Vodou and Vodou initiates who have made contributions to the study of Haitian Vodou.

47. Liam is a pseudonym.

48. Scholars of African Diasporic religions like Matory, *Black Atlantic Religion*, and Landes, "A Cult Matriarchate and Male Homosexuality," have discussed men who are viewed as sexually passive, such as feminine gay men, as being more receptive to spiritual possession. "Macho" heterosexual men or traditionally masculine gay men are not as receptive. This is a result of the view that passive men's "submission to sexual penetration" makes them naturally suited for possession, or penetration, by the spirits.

49. Samentha, interview by Eziaku Nwokocha, phone interview, Philadelphia, March 12, 2018.

50. Natasha, interview by Eziaku Nwokocha, phone interview, Philadelphia, March 11, 2018.

51. Natasha, interview by Eziaku Nwokocha, phone interview, Philadelphia, March 11, 2018.

52. Samuel, interview by Eziaku Nwokocha, phone interview, Philadelphia, March 8, 2018.

53. Bailey, *Butch Queen Up*, 17.

54. Matory, *Black Atlantic Religion*, 207–16.

55. Another important work on gender and sexuality in Black Atlantic religion is Tinsley, "To Transcender Transgender," 131–46.

56. Vin Pouwe, interview by Eziaku Nwokocha, phone interview, Philadelphia, February 9, 2021.

57. Vin Pouwe, interview by Eziaku Nwokocha, phone interview, Philadelphia, February 9, 2021.

58. Vin Pouwe, interview by Eziaku Nwokocha, phone interview, Philadelphia, February 9, 2021.

59. Vin Pouwe, interview by Eziaku Nwokocha, phone interview, Philadelphia, March 21, 2021.

60. Vante'm Pa Fyem, interview by Eziaku Nwokocha, phone interview, Philadelphia, February 27, 2021.

61. Manbo Maude, interview by Eziaku Nwokocha, phone interview, Philadelphia, August 7, 2020.

Chapter Four

1. Zeta, interview by Eziaku Nwokocha, video recording, Jacmel, July 24, 2015.

2. Zeta, interview by Eziaku Nwokocha, video recording, Jacmel, July 24, 2015.

3. Morgan, *The Sacred Gaze*, 3.

4. Zeta, interview by Eziaku Nwokocha, video recording, Jacmel, July 24, 2015.

5. Zeta, interview by Eziaku Nwokocha, video recording, Jacmel, July 24, 2015.

6. Zeta, interview by Eziaku Nwokocha, video recording, Jacmel, July 24, 2015.

7. Karen McCarthy Brown's definition of a pret savann: a Vodou functionary who plays the role of Catholic priest in certain types of ritualizing; literally, "bush priest." Brown, *Mama Lola*, 405.

8. Brown, 55–56.

9. Manbo Maude, interview by Eziaku Nwokocha, phone interview, Philadelphia, February 13, 2019.

10. René and Houlberg, "My Double Mystical Marriages," 287–99; McGee, "Dreaming in Haitian Vodou," 83–100.

11. Manbo Maude, interview by Eziaku Nwokocha, phone interview, Philadelphia, February 13, 2019.

12. Manbo Maude, interview by Eziaku Nwokocha, phone interview, Philadelphia, February 13, 2019.

13. Manbo Maude, interview by Eziaku Nwokocha, phone interview, Philadelphia, February 13, 2019.

14. Manbo Maude, interview by Eziaku Nwokocha, phone interview, Philadelphia, February 13, 2019.

15. Brown, *Mama Lola*, 96, 235.

16. Ochoa, *Queen for a Day*, 2.

17. Manbo Maude, interview by Eziaku Nwokocha, phone interview, Philadelphia, February 13, 2019.

18. I found in my time in Jacmel, Port-au-Prince, Boston, Miami, and Montreal that women and queer people often move to a different temple to avoid sexual abuse or misconduct by those with spiritual authority. Although there is little academic work on this issue, primarily because of the redemptive work that many scholars feel obliged to do in response to the denigration of Vodou and other African Diasporic religions, there are informal conversations about sexual abuse and misconduct occurring on blogs and social media.

19. Zeta, interview by Eziaku Nwokocha, video recording, Jacmel, July 24, 2015.

20. Matory, *Black Atlantic Religion*, 207–9.

21. Vante'm Pa Fyem, interview by Eziaku Nwokocha, phone interview, Philadelphia, December 12, 2021.

22. Brown, *Mama Lola*, 96.

23. Eddie, interview by Eziaku Nwokocha, phone interview, Philadelphia, February 4, 2019.

24. Eddie, interview by Eziaku Nwokocha, phone interview, Philadelphia, February 4, 2019.

25. Simon is a pseudonym.

26. Conversation during ceremony with Simon in Jacmel, July 2015.

27. Thompson, *Flash of the Spirit*, 180.

28. Thompson, 181.

29. Brown, *Mama Lola*, 101.

30. Eddie, interview by Eziaku Nwokocha, phone interview, Philadelphia, February 5, 2019.

31. Eddie, interview by Eziaku Nwokocha, phone interview, Philadelphia, February 5, 2019

32. Eddie, interview by Eziaku Nwokocha, phone interview, Philadelphia, February 6, 2019.

33. Eddie, interview by Eziaku Nwokocha, phone interview, Philadelphia, February 6, 2019.

34. Eddie, interview by Eziaku Nwokocha, phone interview, Philadelphia, February 7, 2019.

35. Eddie, interview by Eziaku Nwokocha, phone interview, Philadelphia, February 7, 2019.

36. Eddie, interview by Eziaku Nwokocha, phone interview, Philadelphia, February 8, 2019.

37. Eddie, interview by Eziaku Nwokocha, phone interview, Philadelphia, February 8, 2019.

38. Eddie, interview by Eziaku Nwokocha, phone interview, Philadelphia,

39. McGee, "Dreaming in Haitian Vodou," 83–100, and Bourguignon, "Dreams and Dream Interpretation," 262–68.

40. Beaubrun, *Nan dòmi*, 276.

41. Eddie, interview by Eziaku Nwokocha, phone interview, Philadelphia, February 8, 2019.

42. Eddie, interview by Eziaku Nwokocha, phone interview, Philadelphia, February 8, 2019.

43. Manbo Maude, interview by Eziaku Nwokocha, phone interview, Philadelphia, February 13, 2019.

44. Eddie, interview by Eziaku Nwokocha, phone interview, Philadelphia, February 8, 2019.

45. Joel, interview by Eziaku Nwokocha, phone interview, Philadelphia, February 24, 2019.

46. Joel, interview by Eziaku Nwokocha, phone interview, Philadelphia, February 24, 2019.

47. Joel, interview by Eziaku Nwokocha, phone interview, Philadelphia, February 24, 2019.

48. Manbo Maude, interview by Eziaku Nwokocha, phone interview, Philadelphia, February 13, 2019.

49. Manbo Maude, interview by Eziaku Nwokocha, phone interview, Philadelphia, February 13, 2019.

50. Manbo Maude, interview by Eziaku Nwokocha, phone interview, Philadelphia, February 13, 2019.

51. Casselberry, *Labor of Faith*, 6.

Dènye Panse

1. Manbo Maude, interview by Eziaku Nwokocha, phone interview, Philadelphia, February 7, 2021.

2. Vante'm Pa Fyem, interview by Eziaku Nwokocha, phone interview, Philadelphia, February 7, 2021.

3. Manbo Maude, invited lecture via Zoom for Professor Eziaku Nwokocha's "Spirit Possession in Caribbean Religion" course, Princeton University, October 27, 2021.

4. Vante'm Pa Fyem, interview by Eziaku Nwokocha, phone interview, Philadelphia, February 7, 2021.

5. Vante'm Pa Fyem, interview by Eziaku Nwokocha, phone interview, Philadelphia, February 7, 2021.

6. Vante'm Pa Fyem, interview by Eziaku Nwokocha, phone interview, Philadelphia, February 7, 2021.

7. Vante'm Pa Fyem, interview by Eziaku Nwokocha, phone interview, Philadelphia, April 10, 2021.

8. Vante'm Pa Fyem, interview by Eziaku Nwokocha, phone interview, Philadelphia, February 7, 2021.

9. Vante'm Pa Fyem, interview by Eziaku Nwokocha, phone interview, Philadelphia, February 6, 2021.

10. Vante'm Pa Fyem, interview by Eziaku Nwokocha, phone interview, Philadelphia, February 6, 2021.

11. Vante'm Pa Fyem, interview by Eziaku Nwokocha, phone interview, Philadelphia, February 6, 2021.

12. Vante'm Pa Fyem, interview by Eziaku Nwokocha, phone interview, Philadelphia, February 6, 2021.

13. Vante'm Pa Fyem, interview by Eziaku Nwokocha, phone interview, Philadelphia, February 6, 2021.

14. NPR, "George Floyd's Impact on the Fight for Racial Justice," May 25, 2021, https://www.npr.org/2021/05/25/1000273932/george-floyds-impact-on-the-fight-for-racial-justice; and History, "Sandra Bland Dies in Jail After Traffic Stop Confrontation," July 10, 2020, https://www.history.com/this-day-in-history/sandra-bland-dies-in-jail.

15. Vante'm Pa Fyem, interview by Eziaku Nwokocha, phone interview, Philadelphia, February 6, 2021.

16. BBC, "Remembering Nigeria's Biafra War that many prefer to forget," January 15, 2020, https://www.bbc.com/news/world-africa-51094093; and CNN, "I Looked for Death but I couldn't find it," January 16, 2020, https://edition.cnn.com/2020/01/15/africa/biafra-nigeria-civil-war/index.html?utm_source=fbCNNi&utm_campaign=africa&utm_medium=social&fbclid=IwAR3HdBxA-BcA6Zge2yVEqoMDz38rLR mdlgLTV-ThQM-EWQQm89yV57Skk5k.

17. Babbas, interview by Eziaku Nwokocha, phone interview, Philadelphia, January 18, 2022. Vodou song sung and translated by Babbas.

18. Babbas, interview by Eziaku Nwokocha, phone interview, Philadelphia, January 18, 2022.

19. Babbas, interview by Eziaku Nwokocha, phone interview, Philadelphia, January 18, 2022.

Bibliography

Allen, Jafari. *¡Venceremos? The Erotics of Black Self-Making in Cuba*. Durham: Duke University Press, 2011.

Asad, Talal. *Genealogies of Religion: Discipline and Reasons of Power in Christianity and Islam*. Baltimore: Johns Hopkins University Press, 1993.

Bailey, Marlon M. *Butch Queens up in Pumps: Gender, Performance, and Ballroom Culture in Detroit*. Ann Arbor: University of Michigan Press, 2013.

———. "Gender/Racial Realness: Theorizing the Gender System in Ballroom Culture." *Feminist Studies* 37, no. 2 (2011): 365–86.

Barnard, Malcolm. *Fashion Theory: A Reader*. London: Routledge, 2007.

Barro, Robert J., and Rachel M. McCleary. *The Wealth of Religions: The Political Economy of Believing and Belonging*. Princeton: Princeton University Press, 2019.

Bay, Edna G. *Asen, Ancestors, and Vodun: Tracing Change in African Art*. Urbana: University of Illinois Press, 2008.

Beaubrun, Mimerose P. *Nan dòmi: An Initiate's Journey into Haitian Vodou*. San Francisco: City Lights Books, 2013.

Bellegarde-Smith, Patrick. *Haiti: The Breached Citadel*. 2nd ed. Boulder: Westview Press, 2004.

Bellegarde-Smith, Patrick, and Claudine Michel, eds. *Haitian Vodou: Spirit Myth and Reality*. Bloomington: Indiana University Press, 2007.

Blier, Susan. "Vodun: West African Roots of Vodun." In *Sacred Arts of Haitian Vodou*, ed. Donald J. Cosentino, 61–87. Los Angeles: UCLA Fowler Museum of Cultural History, 1995.

Bolles, Augusta Lynn. *Sister Jamaica: A Study of Women, Work, and Households in Kingston*. Lanham, MD: University Press of America, 1996.

Bourguignon, Erika. "Dreams and Dream Interpretation in Haiti." *American Anthropologist* 56, no. 2 (1954): 262–68.

Brown, Karen McCarthy. *Mama Lola: A Vodou Priest in Brooklyn*. Berkeley: University of California Press, 1991.

Brown, Ras Michael. *African-Atlantic Cultures and the South Carolina Lowcountry*. New York: Cambridge University Press, 2012.

Brown, Vincent. *The Reaper's Garden: Death and Power in the World of Atlantic Slavery*. Cambridge, MA: Harvard University Press, 2010.

Bui, Tung X., and Melvin F. Shakun. "Negotiation Processes, Evolutionary Systems Design, and NEGOTIATOR." *Group Decision and Negotiation* 5 (1996): 339–53.

Byam, L. Dale. "Communal Space and Performance in Africa." In *Radical Street Performance: An International Anthology*, ed. Jan Cohen Cruz, 230–37. New York: Routledge, 1998.

Camp, Stephanie M. H. *Closer to Freedom: Enslaved Women and Everyday Resistance in the Plantation South*. Chapel Hill: University of North Carolina Press, 2004.

Cantave, Alix. "Incorporation or Symbiosis: Haitians and African Americans in Mattapan." *Trotter Review* 19 (January 2010): 107–23.

Casselberry, Judith. *The Labor of Faith: Gender and Power in Black Apostolic Pentecostalism*. Durham: Duke University Press, 2017.

Chauncey, George. *Gay New York: Gender, Urban Culture, and the Making of a Gay Male World, 1890–1940*. New York: Basic Books, 2019.

Coates, Carrol F. "Vodou in Haitian Literature." In *Vodou in Haitian Life and Culture: Invisible Powers*, ed. Claudine Michel and Patrick Bellegarde-Smith, 181–98. New York: Palgrave Macmillan, 2007.

Cohen, Cathy. "Punks, Bull Daggers, and Welfare Queens: The Real Radical Potential of 'Queer' Politics." *GLQ* 3 (1997): 437–85.

Collins, Patricia Hill. *Black Feminist Thought: Knowledge, Consciousness, and the Politics of Empowerment*. 2nd ed. New York: Routledge, 2000.

———. *Black Sexual Politics: African Americans, Gender, and the New Racism*. New York: Routledge, 2004.

Covington-Ward, Yolanda. *Gesture and Power: Religion, Nationalism, and Everyday Performance in Congo*. Durham: Duke University Press, 2015.

Cox, Aimee Meredith. *Shapeshifters: Black Girls and the Choreography of Citizenship*. Durham: Duke University Press, 2015.

Cunningham, Michael, and Craig Marberry. *Crowns: Portraits of Black Women in Church Hats*. New York: Doubleday, 2000.

Davis, Dána-Ain, and Christa Craven. *Feminist Ethnography: Thinking through Methodologies, Challenges, and Possibilities*. Lanham, MD: Rowman & Littlefield, 2016.

Dayan, Joan. *Haiti, History, and the Gods*. Berkeley: University of California Press, 1995.

Deren, Maya. *Divine Horsemen: The Living Gods of Haiti*. London: Thames and Hudson, 1953.

Desmangles, Leslie. *The Faces of the Gods*. Chapel Hill, NC: Chelsea House, 1992.

Dubois, Laurent. *Avengers of the New World: The Story of the Haitian Revolution*. Cambridge, MA: Belknap, 2005.

Dunham, Katherine. *Island Possessed*. Chicago: University of Chicago Press, 1969.

Ebron, Paulla A. *Performing Africa*. Princeton, NJ: Princeton University Press, 2002.

Edmonds, Barrington Ennis, and Michelle A. Gonzalez. *Caribbean Religious History: An Introduction*. New York: New York University Press, 2010.

Geurts, Kathryn Linn. *Culture and the Senses: Bodily Ways of Knowing in an African Community*. Berkeley: University of California Press, 2002.

Gilroy, Paul. *The Black Atlantic: Modernity and Double Consciousness*. Cambridge, MA: Harvard University Press, 1993.

Glover, Kaiama L. "Exploiting the Undead: The Usefulness of the Zombie in Haitian Literature." *Journal of Haitian Studies* 11, no. 2 (2005): 105–21.

Hall, David. *Lived Religion in America: Toward a History of Practice*. Princeton: Princeton University Press, 1997.

Hammond, Charlotte. "Decoding Dress: Vodou, Cloth and Colonial Resistance in Pre- and Post-Revolutionary Haiti." In *Vodou in the Haitian Experience: A Black Atlantic Perspective*, edited by Joseph L. Celucien and Nixon S. Cleophat, 85–96. Lanham, MD: Lexington Books, 2016.

Hansen, Karen Tranberg. "The World in Dress: Anthropological Perspectives on Clothing, Fashion, and Culture." *Annual Review of Anthropology* 33 (2004): 369–92.

Hartman, Saidiya V. *Scenes of Subjection: Terror, Slavery, and Self-Making in Nineteenth-Century America*. New York: Oxford University Press, 1997.

Heo, Angie. "The Divine Touchability of Dreams." In *Sensational Religion: Sensory Cultures in Material Practice*, ed. Sally M. Promey, 435–40. New Haven, CT: Yale University Press, 2014.

Herskovits, Melville. *Myth of Negro Past*. Boston: Beacon Press, 1958.

Herskovits, Melville, and Frances Herskovits. *Dahomey: An Ancient West African Kingdom*. New York: J. J. Augustin, 1938.

Heywood, Linda M. *Central Africans and Cultural Transformations in the American Diaspora*. Cambridge: Cambridge University Press, 2009.

Heywood, Linda M., and John K. Thornton. *Central Africans, Atlantic Creoles, and the Foundation of the Americas, 1585–1660*. Cambridge: Cambridge University Press, 2007.

Higginbotham, Evelyn. *Righteous Discontent: The Women's Movement in the Black Baptist Church, 1880–1920*. Cambridge, MA: Harvard University Press, 1993.

Hucks, Tracey E. "'Burning with a Flame in America': African American Women in African-Derived Traditions." *Journal of Feminist Studies in Religion* 17, no. 2 (Fall 2001): 89–106.

———. "Perspectives in Lived History: Religion, Ethnography, and the Study of African Diasporic Religions." *Practical Matters* 3 (2010): 1–17.

Hume, Lynne. *The Religious Life of Dress: Global Fashion and Faith*. New York: Bloomsbury Academic, 2013.

Hurbon, Laënnec. *Dieu dans le Vaudou Haïtien*. Paris: Payot, 1972.

Hurston, Zora Neale. *Tell My Horse: Voodoo and Life in Haiti and Jamaica*. New York: Harper and Row, 1938.

Jackson, Regine O. "After the Exodus: The New Catholics in Boston's Old Ethnic Neighborhoods." *Religion and American Culture* 17 (Summer 2007): 191–212.

———. "The Uses of Diaspora among Haitians in Boston." In *Geographies of the Haitian Diaspora*, ed. Regine O. Jackson, 135–62. New York: Routledge, 2011.

James, C. L. R. *The Black Jacobins*. New York: Vintage Books, 1938.

Jesús, Aisha Beliso-De. *Electric Santería: Racial and Sexual Assemblages of Transnational Religion*. New York: Columbia University Press, 2015.

Johnson, E. Patrick, and Mae G. Henderson. *Black Queer Studies: A Critical Anthology*. Durham: Duke University Press, 2005.

Johnson, Paul Christopher. *Diaspora Conversions: Black Carib Religion and the Recovery of Africa*. Berkeley: University of California Press, 2007.

Johnson, Sylvester A. *The Myth of Ham in Nineteenth-Century American Christianity: Race, Heathens, and the People of God*. New York: Palgrave Macmillian, 2004.

Kaplan, Flora Edouwaye S. "Some Thoughts on Ideology, Beliefs, and Sacred Kingship among the Edo (Benin) People of Nigeria." In *African Spirituality: Forms,*

Meanings, and Expressions, ed. Jacob Olupona, 114–51. New York: Crossroads, 2000.

Keeling, Kara. *The Witch's Flight: The Cinematic, the Black Femme, and the Image of Common Sense.* Durham: Duke University Press, 2007.

Kelley, Robin D. G. *Race Rebels: Culture, Politics, and the Black Working Class.* New York: Free Press, 1994.

Kirschenblatt-Gimblett, Barbara. *Destination Culture: Museums, Tourism, and Heritage.* Berkeley: University of California Press, 1998.

Landes, Ruth. "A Cult Matriarchate and Male Homosexuality." *Journal of Abnormal and Social Psychology* 35 (1940): 386–97.

Landry, T. R. "Moving to Learn: Performance and Learning in Haitian Vodou." *Anthropology and Humanism* 33 (2008): 53–65.

Long, Charles H. *Significations: Signs, Symbols, and Images in the Interpretation of Religion.* Philadelphia: Fortress Press, 1986.

Maldonado-Estrada, Alyssa. *Lifeblood of the Parish: Men and Catholic Devotion in Williamsburg, Brooklyn.* New York: New York University Press, 2020.

Matory, Lorand J. *Black Atlantic Religion: Tradition, Transnationalism, and Matriarchy in the Afro-Brazilian Candomblé.* Princeton: Princeton University Press, 2005.

McAlister, Elizabeth. *Rara!: Vodou, Power, and Performance in Haiti and Its Diaspora.* University of California Press, 2002.

McClaurin, Irma. *Black Feminist Anthropology: Theory, Politics, Praxis, and Poetics.* New Brunswick, NJ: Rutgers University Press, 2001.

McDannell, Colleen. *Material Christianity: Religion and Popular Culture in America.* New Haven, CT: Yale University Press, 1995.

McGee, Adam. "Dreaming in Haitian Vodou: Vouchsafe, Guide, and Source of Liturgical Novelty." *Journal of the Association for the Study of Dreams* 22, no. 2 (2012): 83–100.

Métraux, Alfred. *Voodoo in Haiti.* New York: Schocken, 1972.

Michel, Claudine, and Patrick Bellegarde-Smith. *Vodou in Haitian Life and Culture: Invisible Powers.* New York: Palgrave Macmillan, 2007.

Migraine-George, Thérèse. "From Masisi to Activist: Same-Sex Relations and the Haitian Polity." *Journal of Haitian Studies* 20, no. 1 (2014): 8–33.

Miller, Monica. *Slaves to Fashion: Black Dandyism and the Styling of Black Diasporic Identity.* Durham: Duke University Press, 2009.

Mintz, Sidney. "The Caribbean as a Socio-Cultural Area." *Cahiers d'Histoire Mondiale* 10, no. 4 (1966): 912–37.

———. *Sweetness and Power.* New York: Viking, 1985.

Mobley, Christina Frances. "The Kongolese Atlantic: Central African Slavery and Culture from Mayombe to Haiti." PhD diss., Duke University, 2015.

Morgan, David. *The Sacred Gaze: Religious Visual Culture in Theory and Practice.* Berkeley: University of California Press, 2005.

Mullings, Leith. *On Our Own Terms: Race, Class, and Gender in the Lives of African-American Women.* New York: Routledge, 1996.

Nwokocha, Eziaku. "The 'Queerness' of Ceremony." *Journal of Haitian Studies* 25, no. 2 (2019): 71–90.

Ochoa, Marcia. *Queen for a Day: Transformista, Beauty Queens, and the Performance of Venezuela Femininity*. Durham: Duke University Press, 2014.

Olupona, Jacob. *Beyond Primitivism: Indigenous Religious Traditions and Modernity*. New York: Routledge, 2003.

———. *World Spirituality: An Encyclopedic History of Religious Quests*. Vol. 3, *African Spirituality: Forms, Meanings, and Expressions*. New York: Crossroads Press, 2000.

Orsi, Robert. *History and Presence*. Cambridge, MA: Harvard University Press. 2016.

Otero, Solimar. *Archives of Conjure: Stories of the Dead in Afro Latinx Cultures*. New York: Columbia University Press, 2020.

Oyěwùmí, Oyèrónké. *The Invention of Women: Making an African Sense of Western Gender Discourses*. Minneapolis: University of Minnesota Press, 1997.

Pérez, Elizabeth. "Portable Portals: Transnational Rituals for the Head across Globalizing Orisha Traditions." *Nova Religion* 16, no. 4 (2013): 35–62.

———. *Religion in the Kitchen: Cooking, Talking, and the Making of Black Atlantic Traditions*. New York: New York University Press, 2016.

Price-Mars, Jean. *So Spoke the Uncle: Ainsi Parla L'oncle*. Washington, DC: Three Continents Press, 1983

Promey, Sally. *Sensational Religion: Sensory Cultures in Material Practice*. New Haven, CT: Yale University Press, 2014.

Raboteau, Albert J. *Slave Religion: The "Invisible Institution" in the Antebellum South*. New York: Oxford University Press, 2004.

Raj, Razaq, and Kevin A. Griffin, eds. *Religious Tourism and Pilgrimage Management: An International Perspective*. CABI, 2015.

René, Georges, and Marilyn Houlberg. "My Double Mystical Marriages to Two Goddesses of Love: An Interview." In *Sacred Arts of Haitian Vodou*, edited by Doonald J. Cosentino. 287–88. Los Angeles: UCLA Fowler Museum of Cultural History, 1995.

Renne, Elisha P. *Cloth That Does Not Die: The Meaning of Cloth in Bùnú Social Life*. Seattle: University of Washington Press, 1995

———. "Dressing in the Stuff of Dreams: Sacred Dress and Religious Authority in Southwestern Nigeria." *Dreaming* 14, nos. 2–3 (2004): 120–35.

———. *Death and the Textile Industry in Nigeria*. London: Routledge, 2020.

Rey, Terry. "Kongolese Catholic Influences on Haitian Popular Catholicism: A Sociohistorical Exploration." In *Central Africans and Cultural Transformations in the American Diaspora*, ed. Linda M. Heywood, 265–88. Cambridge: Cambridge University Press, 2009.

Rey, Terry, and Alex Stepick. *Crossing the Water and Keeping the Faith: Haitian Religion in Miami*. New York: New York University Press, 2013

Richman, Karen E. *Migration and Vodou*. Gainesville: University Press of Florida, 2005.

Rush, Dana. *Vodun in Coastal Benin: Unfinished, Open-Ended, Global*. Nashville: Vanderbilt University Press, 2013.

Sanders, Paula, and Akinwumi Ogundiran. *Materialities of Ritual in the Black Atlantic*. Bloomington: Indiana University Press, 2014.

Scott, Georgia. *Headwraps: A Global Journey*. New York: Public Affairs, 2003.

Scott, James C. *Domination and the Arts of Resistance: Hidden Transcripts.* New Haven, CT: Yale University Press, 1992.

Sharpe, Christina Elizabeth. *In the Wake: On Blackness and Being.* Durham: Duke University Press, 2016.

Sheller, Mimi. *Democracy after Slavery: Black Public and Peasant Radicalism in Haiti and Jamaica.* Gainesville: University Press of Florida, 2000.

Stewart, Dianne M. *Three Eyes for the Journey: African Dimensions of the Jamaican Religious Experience.* New York: Oxford University Press, 2005.

Strongman, Roberto. *Queering Black Atlantic Religions: Transcorporeality in Candomblé, Santería, and Vodou.* Durham: Duke University Press, 2019.

Taylor, Paul C. *Black Is Beautiful: A Philosophy of Black Aesthetics.* Hoboken, NJ: Wiley-Blackwell, 2016.

Thompson, Robert Farris. *Flash of the Spirit: African and Afro American Art and Philosophy.* New York: Random House, 1983.

Thornton, John K. *Africa and Africans in the Making of the Atlantic World, 1400–1680.* Cambridge: Cambridge University Press, 1993.

———. "The Development of an African Catholic Church in the Kingdom of Kongo, 1491–1750." *Journal of African History* 25, no. 2 (1988): 147–67.

———. *A History of West Central Africa to 1850.* Cambridge: Cambridge University Press, 2020.

———. "'I Am the Subject of the King of Congo': African Political Ideology and the Haitian Revolution." *Journal of World History* 4, no. 2 (1988): 181–214.

———. "Les racines du vaudou. Religion africaine et société haïtienne dans la Saint Domingue prérévolutionnaire." *Anthropologie et Sociétés* 22, no. 1 (2002): 85–102.

———. "Religious and Ceremonial Life in the Kongo and Mbundu Areas, 1500–1700." In *Central Africans and Cultural Transformations in the American Diaspora*, ed. Linda Heywood, 71–90. Cambridge: Cambridge University Press, 2009.

———. "Revising the Population History of the Kingdom of Kongo." *Journal of African History* 62, no. 2 (2021): 201–12.

———. "On the Trail of Voodoo: African Christianity in Africa and the Americas." *The Americas* 44, no. 3 (1988): 263–67.

Tinsley, Omise'eke Natasha. *Ezili's Mirrors: Imagining Black Queer Genders.* Durham: Duke University Press, 2018.

———. "To Transcender Transgender: Choreographies of Gender Fluidity in the Performances of Mildred Gerestant." In *No Tea, No Shade: New Writings in Black Queer Studies*, ed. E. Patrick Johnson, 131–46. Durham: Duke University Press, 2020.

Trouillot, Michel-Rolph. *Haiti State against the Nation: The Origins and Legacy of Duvalierism.* New York: Monthly Review Press, 1990.

———. *Silencing the Past: Power and the Production of History.* Boston: Beacon Press, 1995.

Tselos, Susan. "Dressing the Divine Horsemen: Clothing as Spirit Identification in Haitian Vodou." In *Undressing Religion: Commitment and Conversion from a Cross-Cultural Perspective*, ed. Linda B. Arthur, 45–64. Oxford: Berg, 2000.

Turner, Victor. *The Anthropology of Performance*. New York: Performing Arts, 1986.

Vanhee, Hein. "Central African Popular Christianity and the Making of Haitian Vodou Religion." In *Central Africans and Cultural Transformations in the American Diaspora*, ed. Linda Heywood, 243–64. Cambridge: Cambridge University Press, 2009.

Weisenfeld, Judith. *New World A-Coming: Black Religion and Racial Identity during the Great Migration*. New York: New York University Press, 2016.

White, Shane, and Graham White. *Stylin': African American Expressive Culture from Its Beginnings to the Zoot Suit*. Ithaca, NY: Cornell University Press, 1998.

Wilcken, Lois. *The Drums of Vodou: Lois Wilcken Featuring Frisner Augustin*. Tempe, AZ: White Cliffs Media, 1992.

Index

adornment: and gender, 6, 130; and marriage, 135–36, 140, 145, 148–54; and pleasing the divine, 23–24, 41, 57; in preparation, 87–88, 102; and race, 111–14; and ritual, 1–4, 7, 11–12, 38, 50–53, 70, 73, 162, 166; and sexuality, 129. *See also* fashion

aesthetic(s): assemblage, 97; and fashion, 30, 51, 112; and ritual, 1–3, 7, 9, 29, 73, 98, 162; same-gender spirit affinity (Ezili Dantò), 151–52; and spirits, 1, 166; and toned-down femininity, 120. *See also* labor, aesthetic

Africa (African): African religions, 3–9, 13–16, 24; and Catholicism, 109; Central, 1, 13–16, 27, 107, 176; fabrics, 27, 38; heritage, 160; households, 26; "looking" African, 93–100; *se gwo Blan nwa* or *se gwo Afrikenn*, 23; Southern, 9; Vodou spirits as African royalty, 54, 90; West, 1, 13–16, 27, 37, 107, 173, 176. *See also* African Diasporic religions; African religions

African Diasporic religions: Black Atlantic, 16, 29; and conversion politics, 21–22; and embodiment, 87; and fashion, 4–10, 45–46, 52, 159; and Gede, 37; *Ginen*, 108; and labor, 56, 58; and marriage, 128; material culture, 157; materially present, 1, 21–24; in Maude's communities, 88–90; ritual outfits, 102; Vodou in networks of, 13–18, 29; women's power in, 117–18; and Zeta's religious dress, 126. *See also* Candomblé; Ifa; Santería

agriculture, 17, 27–28, 65–66, 70–73, 124, 126, 131

alcohol, 49, 75, 100, 109, 111, 127, 140: bars, 75, 83; beer, 72; drinking, 23, 59–60, 83; rum, 65, 71, 82, 111, 132, 139–40, 143–44; wine, 132

altars: displays, 22; and labor, 61, 75, 78, 101; personal, 85, 151; in ritual, 1, 41–42, 109, 111; and spiritual marriage, 126–31, 139–46; and whites, 100

Anais, 155, 174–75

ancestors, 1, 37, 65, 90–92, 108, 138, 165, 167, 170–73

animals: cows, 68; chickens, 68, 75, 139–40; goats, 68, 70, 75; pigs, 139–40; ritual, 61, 132, 139

ason (sacred rattles), 33, 35, 110, 124

Astride (seamstress), 48–49

audience: and Blackness, 24; and communication, 155–58, 163, 166–68; defined, 3–4; and fashion, 1, 7–9, 30, 42–45, 160–62, 176; and food, 22; and gender, 12, 39, 120–22; and hair wraps, 87; and labor, 57–59, 69–73, 79–82; and queerness, 10, 117, 120–21; and ritual, 8; and sexuality, 37, 40; and social constructions, 88, 107–116, 122–23; and spectacle, 11, 13, 20, 34, 37, 52–53, 175; and spiritual marriage, 125–29, 133–40, 145, 150

authenticity, 2, 45, 89, 93, 96, 106, 113–15, 125

authority: and *Blan*, 89; and clothing, 120; colonial, 14; masculinity, 39; Maude's, 56, 77, 162; and queer people, 123; religious, 53; spiritual, 2; of Vante'm Pa Fyem, 159–60, 174; and women, 41, 164

Azaka. *See* Kouzen Zaka

Babbas, 92, 103–5, 173–74
Badagri (Ogou), 149–50
bad luck, 146, 152–53, 165
Bailey, Marlon M., 8, 43, 48, 88, 116. *See also* ballroom
ballroom, 8–9, 43, 48, 62, 80, 88, 158
Beaubrun, Mimerose P., 31
Beauvoir, Max, 3, 23
belief: and Africana religions, 13–16, 173; and the body, 7; and community building, 56, 80, 88–92, 175; and clothing, 3–4, 103, 105, 157, 160, 166; and labor, 56; privileged in study, 21; regarding gender, 10, 12, 158; and ritual, 52–53, 138; and spirits, 43, 114–16, 154; and Vodou, 107–8
belonging: and dreams, 151–54; and fashion, 88, 99, 101, 104; Haiti, 171; and race, 90
Benin, 13, 15, 31, 49, 93, 173: Fon, 15, 31, 65
Blackness (Black): Americans, 17–18, 23; anti-Blackness, 4–5, 16; Atlantic, 16, 19; authority, 56; Blackness, 59; ceremonial leaders, 1; creativity, 24; and fashion, 45–46, 176; of gods, 106–7; and hair wrapping, 87, 93, 96–102; Haiti as, 170; and magic, 22; marriage ceremonies, 126, 136; and possession, 109–17, 164; queer people, 8–10, 117–18, 122–23, 140–42, 164; religious legacies, 155–60; sacred space, 16, 89; solidarity, 101; and Vodou, 87–92. *See also* Africa; African Americans; Africana religions; enslavement
Blan (foreigner), 23, 88–89, 100, 106, 110–13, 168, 172
Bland, Sandra, 190n14
bodies (body): beautification of, 129; and blood memory, 173; and fashion, 4, 7, 9, 11, 42–43, 74, 149; and power, 164; and queerness, 12; and ritual, 1, 9, 49; size, 48; as temple, 149; vessel for spirits, 11, 39–40, 97, 103, 113–18,

127, 135–42, 146, 175; and women, 40. *See also* embodiment; possession
body size: average, 110; comments about, 23, 48–49
brassiere, 51
Brazil, 7, 13, 16, 95
Brijit, Gran, 37, 39
Brown, Karen McCarthy, 21, 32, 143
byen marle, 98

Candomblé, 7, 16, 58, 95, 117, 158
card readings, 1, 32
Casselberry, Judith, 23, 56–57
children (child): and Ezili Dantò, 1, 32, 155; and immigration, 171; and labor, 75; Maude's biological, 19, 159; spiritual, 43, 160, 174; support of, 61–62, 66. *See also* Pa Fyem, Vante'm; *ti feỳ*
Christianity (Christian), 13–14, 22, 40, 128, 149, 172–73
cisgender: gay men, 75; Houngans, 73; in Maude's communities, 8; and possession, 11–12, 39, 136, 140, 154, 163–64; researcher identity, 22; white women, 114, 117–18
class, 17, 20, 28, 34, 42, 119, 168, 170
cleaning, 42, 61, 63, 75, 78, 100, 105, 127, 139, 146
clothing (garment): ancestral, 168; as archive, 3; and authority, 120; and belief, 304, 103, 105, 157, 160, 166; and belonging, 19–20, 100–1; and Catholicism, 143; and connection to lwa, 30–32; costs, 38, 47, 49, 106, 133, 161; creates electricity, 103; donations, 161; and gender, 117–22; and Kouzen, 73–74; and labor, 20, 53, 57–61, 75–78; and materiality, 4; and power, 2, 103, 105, 158–60, 167; ritual, 6–8, 18, 23, 38–43, 49, 116, 124, 129–30, 175; and secrecy, 47; and spiritual energy, 102–6; and spiritual marriage, 126, 146, 148, 153–54; and status, 1, 34–35, 81–83, 133, 139. 161,

Natasha, 100–1, 110, 115–16
Nigeria, 13, 15, 22–23, 31, 48–49, 93–96, 122, 171–73. *See also* Igbo; Yoruba
Nikol, 75–77
Nimbo (Gede), 37
nonbinary, 8, 154

Ochoa, Marcia, 134
Ogou, 49, 91, 120–22, 131–32, 136–37, 149–52, 165. *See individual deities by name*
ordination, 127
Oyěwùmí, Oyèrónké, 6
oyibo, 172

Pa Fyem, Vante'm: and ancestral legacy, 168–72; chosen by Ezili Dantò, 155; double life, 165–66; explains *Blan*, 88–89; and fashion, 72–73, 154; and gender, 119–20; and head wraps, 96; and race, 100; and spiritual authority, 159–63, 174–75; as translator, 20, 33, 47, 155; and vodou legacies, 164–67; and whiteness, 92–93; written contracts, 161
pa pale, 21
Papa Loko, 28
parties, 20, 140, 171–72
patriarchy, 12, 154, 164
performance: Black, 87–88, 115; and fashion, 46, 126, 157–60; and gender, 12; and identity, 113, 117, 141; Igbo, 174; and marriage, 135–37; and possession, 32, 37–40, 175; and queerness, 154; and race, 116; and ritual, 8–13, 22, 24, 56–58, 70, 73, 159; studies, 6
Petwo, 15, 32, 49, 131, 142–43, 174
pilgrimage, 13
pleasure, 129, 148, 151
possession (pran lwa): Black women's care and, 71, 112–14; defined, 11–12; and dreams, 147; and fashion, 7, 30, 41–42; and gender, 32, 157, 163–64; and injury, 162; and labor, 57, 70–73,

77–78, 97; of Maude, 21, 41–43; and queerness, 10–12, 111–18, 123; and spiritual marriage, 135–42, 154; transcorporealty, 11; as Vodou practice, 1; of white people, 88, 98
pou mwen, 143
Pouwe, Vin, 118–19
power: and appearance, 57; and Catholicism, 14; colonial, 37; and Dantò, 138; and fashion, 2, 4, 9, 88, 103, 166–67; and gender, 32, 39–41, 117; healing, 90–91; and identity, 10; and *Petwo*, 143; and race, 107; ritual, 28; spiritual, 7, 30, 95, 162–64
pran lwa. *See* possession
prèt savann, 126–27, 143–45
privacy, 20, 47, 57, 129, 147, 150, 158
Promey, Sally, 4
protection: of children, 1; of clothing, 105; of Ezili Dantò, 17, 21, 32, 134, 144; of Gran Ezili, 142; and Ogou, 137; protectiveness, 47, 161, 168; from spirits, 3, 70–71, 95, 108, 130; of Vodou, 5
pupa, 28

queer (queerness): and Black women in ceremonies, 117–23; and clothing, 73; and ballroom culture, 8–9, 158; and Gede, 37, 39; intersex, 134; kisses, 141–42; and possession, 114–15, 141–42; and ritual practice, 134; self-identity, 22–23; and spiritual marriage, 129–30, 135–36, 164; and spiritual vogue, 157; studies, 6; and Vodou, 10–12

race (racial): in ballroom culture, 158; and *Blan*, 100, 106; and community, 88–91, 106–7; and fashion, 84; and gender, 163; and head wraps, 98–99; identities, 157; interracial, 90; intraracial, 18, 92; and material culture, 6–7, 19; mixed-race, 168; racial division, 100–1, 106–7, 112–17,

164; and ritual, 18, 21, 87, 98, 112–14; and sex, 40, 112, 117; and spiritual vogue, 157; and Vodou, 90, 116

racism (racist), 18, 89–92, 97, 170

Rada, 15, 49, 65, 131–32

reciprocity, 4, 52, 163, 167

relationships: business, 27; and dreams, 148–154; in ethnographic work, 158–59; and fashion, 2, 157, 161–62; to Maude, 133; in ritual, 69; during spirits, 42, 52, 163, 167; and spiritual marriage, 128, 147; and structural categories, 7–8, 19–20, 56, 87, 136. *See also*: labor, emotional

respect: aristocratic, 37; disrespect, 21, 105, 115, 149, 152–53, 163; and ethnography, 21, 89–90; and fashion, 82, 105; and head coverings, 87; for spirits, 34, 52, 67, 104, 113, 118, 122, 147, 164; for temples, 79–82

reverence, 2–3, 53, 57, 105, 113, 129, 141

Rey, Terry, 14

rituals: bathing, 139, 146, 148; clothes as archive, 3; clothing, 18, 23, 49, 61, 75–76, 81, 102–3, 124, 133, 167; dagger, 21, 138–44, 148; efficacy, 2, 23, 79, 83; faith labor, 56–58, 156; holy water, 70; *kanzo*, 31, 78; in the kitchen, 63; to please gods, 42, 53; preparation, 27, 30, 63, 81–82, 100–6, 116, 124, 133, 139–40, 147–48, 174; procession, 50–53, 108, 110; ritual fashion, 1, 53, 98–99, 102; speech, 39. *See also* initiation rites; labor, ritual; performance

Roman Catholicism, 13–14, 22, 26, 70, 108–9, 127, 143, 160, 165

runway, 42, 50

Sacramento, CA, 85, 95, 171

sacredness (sacred): bell, 35; Black spaces, 16–19; and clothing, 4, 103–5; dagger, 140; and diaspora, 16; destruction of, 92; herbs, 65, 139; knowledge, 22, 95; Mapou tree, 51,

139; and marriage, 127; sacred gaze, 12, 125; and secular, 14; space, 35; and ritual, 53. *See also ason; koulie;* temples, *potomitan*

Samentha, 98–100, 105–6, 112–16

Samuel, 107–11, 116

Santería, 7, 58, 95, 158

seamstresses, 29, 47–49, 68–69, 133, 175: Astride, 48–49

secrets/secrecy, 14, 21–22, 47, 150, 155, 158, 166

self-presentation, 56–57, 80, 83, 118–19

Senegal, 93

sensation, 6–7, 103–4, 157–58

sensory (sensorial), 4, 7, 12, 30, 52, 88, 103–4, 129, 137, 148–49

sewing, 48, 61, 68, 132. *See also* seamstresses

sexuality (sex): contact before ceremonies, 78; and fashion, 18–21; and Gede, 17, 36–40; identities, 84, 157; and labor, 56, 75, 123; and material culture, 6–7; prostitutes, 40; and ritual, 112–18, 157–58; and sacred space, 87–89; sexism, 18, 97; sexual abuse, 40, 77, 188n18. *See also* ballroom culture; *nan dòmi*; queerness; spiritual marriages

Shori, 59–60, 69, 85, 87, 93–97, 101, 107, 144

Simbi, 132, 152

Simon, 140–42

skin color: and *Blan*, 89; Brown, 25, 168; dark, 32–33, 122, 151; of gods, 107; light, 32–33, 101, 148, 151. *See also* race

skirt, 1, 29, 31, 50–51, 71, 73, 81–82, 101, 108, 117, 120–21, 126, 132

slavery. *See* enslavement

smell, 4, 25, 46, 50–52, 85, 111, 127, 129, 151

song (singing): and ceremonies, 32–33, 43, 49–52, 108–11, 126–27, 140, 162; and clothing, 32, 41; in dreams, 150; and expertise, 166; and Igbo, 95, 173–74